The growth of t[he]
tanker, 1886–1980

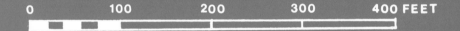

0   100   200   300   400 FEET

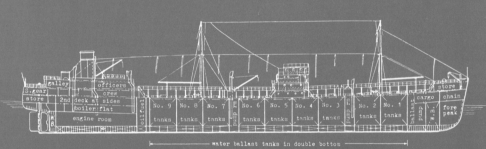

COMANCHEE, 1936

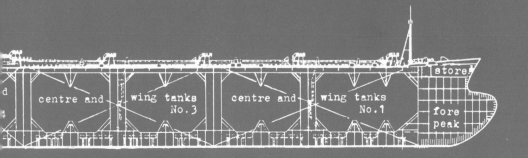

SAILING SHIP TO SUPERTANKER

Overleaf:
An early oil well at Titusville, Pennsylvania, in 1861. The man in the top hat is Edwin L. Drake, who two years earlier had inaugurated the North American petroleum industry with his discovery of oil at Titusville.

SAILING SHIP TO SUPERTANKER

The hundred-year story of British Esso and its ships

by

W. H. Mitchell
and
L. A. Sawyer

TERENCE DALTON LIMITED
LAVENHAM . SUFFOLK

1987

Published by
TERENCE DALTON LIMITED

ISBN 0 86138 055 X

Text photoset in 11/12pt Garamond

Printed in Great Britain at
The Lavenham Press Limited, Lavenham, Suffolk

Contents

By the same authors

BRITISH STANDARD SHIP SERIES
Empire Ships of World War II
The Oceans, the Forts and the Parks
British Standard Ships of World War I

AMERICAN STANDARD SHIP SERIES
The Liberty Ships (2nd edition 1985)
Victory Ships and Tankers
From America to United States
(in four parts)

MERCHANT SHIPS OF THE WORLD SERIES
Cruising Ships
Tankers

The Cunard Line—A Post-War History
The Cape Run (Revised edition 1987)

Introduction

A PECULIAR thing about oil is that comparatively few people actually see it. The great power source has lain just below the earth's crust for at least ten million years—a time span of countless millions of decomposing sea creatures, of benthos and other rotting substances, sealed in mud deposits.

Now, in its crude form, it is searched for, drilled for, pumped into pipeline or container and sent to the refinery where it is turned into fuels, greases and other by-products. Then it is sold to the consumer and mostly burned to nothing. Yet, during the twentieth century, its application so greatly helped to make the world go round. But few see it . . .

The ancient civilisations knew of it. They found it useful for heating and for lighting and the thick crude oil which seeped into small pools of glutinous tack they used as a preservative on wood; and in a form of pitch it was mixed with reed and caulked into seams between the timbers of ships.

But the world had been well shaken into the industrial revolution and the great steam age before oil was "rediscovered" in the late 1850s. This discovery was different. Some oils, readily available in small quantities on the earth's surface, were being used for lighting and heating, but this find was below the earth's surface. It was in a tremendous but unknown quantity. And it had to be brought to the surface.

Edwin L. Drake, a one-time railway employee known as the "Colonel", was the driller, working for the Seneca Oil Company. Titusville was the site, a small town in Pennsylvania, a mile or so east of Meadville and a mile or so west of the Allegheny River. His drilling contraption was merely a tower of wood and from its top beams the drill—a heavy punch—was lifted into and out of the well. The drill movement was from an adjacent walking-beam—a see-saw device, worked up and down at one end by a steam engine which thumped the drill into the ground at the other. On 17th August, 1859, the bit, at sixty-nine and a half feet, struck oil, and those who had smirked at Drake's efforts now looked in wonder as the ambitious, the enterprising and the fortune-hunter jostled for places in the area of new wealth.

The true oil age had begun . . .

The discovery of oil in Pennsylvania in 1859 had been preceded by a discovery in Western Ontario, Canada, in 1857; it was immediately followed by a find in Romania, in the frontal ranges of the Carpathian Mountains, in 1860. Shortly after the find in the United States production began in Russia, using American drilling techniques, and by the end of the century an area near Baku was producing half of the world production. These were the main areas of petroleum in the nineteenth century; the finds of the twentieth century began in May, 1908, in Khuzistan; in Iraq in 1927 when the Kirkup field was found; Bahrain in 1932, the Dammam field in Saudi Arabia and the Burgan field in Kuwait both in the later 1930s.

The American oil yield in the first two or three years quickly increased, although the amount actually produced was difficult to estimate because the various forms of transport tended to confuse an overall picture. However, in late 1860 it was recorded that so much oil was being produced that thousands of barrels were going to waste. The River Allegheny was covered with oil for much of the way below Franklin and fears were entertained that the supply would soon be exhausted. By 1862 the price was ten cents a barrel; there was little export trade and the home trade, in its infancy, was awaiting a suitable lamp.

Oil was introduced into Britain as an illuminant. Oil for the lamps . . . Then there were oils for lubrication, for heating and later for the internal combustion engines. In America in 1895 a trade name was registered—it was "Petrol". The speed in the growth of the industry was astounding; so was the evolution of the ships that brought the oils and spirits to Britain.

The continuing story of expansion is traced through the Anglo-American Oil Company Ltd., a British company, registered in London in 1888 but affiliated with the Standard Oil Company of New Jersey. Its aims were to import oils and form a distributing network. This is the story of the ships used to transport the oil and it continues through the wars, with the tankers growing larger and larger and the fleet of the smaller distributing ships increasing in number. There are many additional notes and asides to the main story as it unfolds; all, however, are related, even if in some cases distantly. But the theme, the transport of Anglo-American oil and the story of British Esso, continues throughout the book. At times it has been found necessary to bring in connecting detail regarding the parent Standard Oil Company (New Jersey) and its other affiliates, and activities of the subsidiaries of Anglo-American are also recorded.

Statistics are restricted and only given in limited form, for amounts of one million tons of oil or one million gallons of petrol are hard to visualise. However, where considered necessary, they have been recorded.

Details of the ships include length (oa = overall, otherwise the length is between perpendiculars); BB = Bulbous bow. Gross tonnage (gt), which often fluctuates with structural alterations, is also shown and the deadweight (tdw) capacity of the ship is included in many instances. This latter tonnage is the amount of oil in long tons, plus stores and bunkers, to bring a ship from her light to load waterline, that is, the carrying capacity of the ship. Propulsion is shown as: T3cyl = Triple expansion engines; Quad = Quadruple

The modern oil industry was just six years old when this photograph was taken at Pioneer Run, Oil Creek, Pennsylvania, in 1865. All ground was by then sold or leased, and production was over 6,000 barrels a day. The office in the foreground houses the Shoe and Leather Petroleum Company and the Foster Farm Oil Company.

expansion engines; or Oil. An asterisk (*) against a ship's name indicates the movement of that vessel from Anglo-American or Esso ownership.

Southampton
and London
November, 1986

W. H. Mitchell and
L. A. Sawyer

CHAPTER ONE

The Oil Begins to Flow

JOHN Davison Rockefeller was born on a small farm in New York State in 1839. At the age of sixteen he moved to an office in Cleveland and was soon a partner in a firm of commission brokers, Clark & Rockefeller. In 1862, only three years after the discovery of oil in Pennsylvania, he began showing much interest in the new industry and set out to tour and see for himself the booming oil producing regions in Pennsylvania.

After the discovery of oil in 1859 independent owners began producing oil from shallow wells. From the wells it was moved in barrels by horse-drawn vehicles over rough tracks to the refineries. There, some rough form of kerosene was distilled from the crude oil. Kerosene, used for lighting and heating, was the only marketable product in those early days.

At the end of his tour Rockefeller concluded that the industry was full of romantic gamblers and unproven facts and was no place for a man who always based his calculations on hard reality and not on hunches. The new industry was dangerously uncertain, with the unpredictable price of crude oil fluctuating wildly, due to the drilling activities of oil-dizzy prospectors, many of whom were there merely on the chance of making a quick profit. The price of crude oil in 1862, for instance, was as low as ten cents a barrel; in 1864 it was as high as twelve dollars. Production would far exceed refinery capacity in one month, only to fall behind the next, and these wild swings forced producers and refiners alike out of business.

Rockefeller and his associates could clearly see what was wrong in the industry, concluding that the oil trade must be stabilised and, astute enough to see a great future in the oil refining business, they decided to do something about it.

In 1863, after an approach by an Englishman, a mechanical genius named Samuel Andrews, Rockefeller, then twenty-three years of age, and his partner entered the oil business, investing four thousand dollars to have a refinery built at Cleveland, Ohio. The plant consisted of a few shacks and a cluster of chimneys, but John D. Rockefeller had taken his first step towards becoming one of the richest men in the world.

Andrews had, indeed, developed a process which produced a larger

The 125,331 gross ton tanker *Esso Dalriada* discharging her cargo at Fawley. Built in 1973 in Sweden, she served in the Esso fleet for eleven years.

Skyfotos

percentage of better quality oil than any previously used. Within two years Rockefeller bought out Clark's share in the refinery and the firm had become Rockefeller & Andrews.

Rockefeller hated waste. He accounted for every cent. Oil residue left after all refinery processes had been carried out, which in other refineries was usually returned to the ground, he sold. Old iron plates, broken and defunct machinery, unwanted timber—all was sold to scrap merchants, and oil was purchased direct from the wells, brought in barrels which he had made for his own use.

By 1870 the partners were operating the most prominent business in Cleveland, and in New York premises were established to sell oil. In the June of that year all their interests were incorporated as the Standard Oil Company (Ohio), the "Standard" title being taken from one of their refineries, the Standard Works, its name reflecting the principle of maintaining high, uniform quality so that customers, once gained, would be kept. Offices were established in Broadway, New York, and across the harbour in New Jersey stood the company's physical assets, a refinery, a kerosene plant and barrel factory at Bayonne; another refinery, the Eagle Works under construction at Jersey City; and some docks at Weehawken.

Within two years all remaining independent oil interests in Cleveland had collapsed, twenty-one of the twenty-six refineries selling out under pressure. From a production capacity of 1,500 barrels per day the Standard output rose to 10,000 per day after three months, which gave it over 20% of the refinery capacity of the whole of the United States. But by now an oil war between various oil regions had begun, with cut-throat contracts being made with railways, lake and river services as a market for oil was found in western states. The outcome of this was the formation of associations of the small producers and refiners, but they were unable to present a strong front and broke up. Rockefeller absorbed his rivals.

It was then quite evident to Rockefeller and his associates that the small local firms, faced with transportation problems between regions, could simply not survive in the highly competitive trade and they concluded that a combination of firms over a large area was the logical formula for the oil business. Between 1873 and 1875 they formed a loose alliance with other successful oil men in and around Cleveland, New York, Pittsburgh and Philadelphia and soon the Standard Oil Company had developed a complex of refineries, pipeline companies and marketing organisations in almost nationwide activities.

The combination became known as the Standard Oil Trust in 1882, the result of state laws which forbade the original Ohio company to own property in other states. The trustees held the shares of the various companies involved, including those of the Standard Oil Company of New Jersey, established as an operating company to take over the New Jersey properties of the Standard Oil Company (Ohio). The Trust, with no legal name or charter, envisaged the eventual formation of a Standard Oil Company in each state, although only seven were actually organised.

A new head office of the Standard Oil Company of New Jersey was set up in New York in 1882 and through it the company was charged to develop and administer a thoroughly integrated system for extracting liquid raw material from the earth; for transporting it by new and economical means; for refining it into a variety of useful products, and for finding new and wider markets for them.

The entire system of Standard Oil was based on production in quantity, and at first kerosene was the dominant product. From its refinery at Bayonne nearly two and a half million barrels was produced in 1883, making it the foremost in the country. However, this production was far in excess of what the American customer alone could consume and the company built up a large export trade in kerosene, the principal petroleum product of the nineteenth century. The refineries were also producing lesser by-products including various grades of gasolene (thrown away in the early days), naphtha and benzine, not only for use in stoves but for removing lanolin grease from wool, for the manufacture of various lacquers, paints and varnishes and for oil cloth and patent leathers.

Illuminating oils were produced for locomotive headlamps, paraffin went to candlemakers; it was used for matches, sweets and chewing gum. Their oils and greases lubricated everything from textile mills to horsedrawn vehicles. They also made petroleum jelly.

For years the company carried on their export trade entirely through representatives of foreign distributors in the United States. Thus, the company responsibility ended at the quayside.

But the company was far from free of foreign competition. In the 1880s the impact of competition from Russia's Baku oilfields, where, it was said, "a barrel of oil cost less than a barrel of water", began to be felt. Marketing of the Baku oil was done with vigour, especially in the Near East and Far East. In some areas of the Far East trade dropped from near-monopoly to a mere 10% share in only five years.

To meet this competition Standard Oil began to acquire a direct interest in European marketing companies and in 1888 their first foreign affiliate, Anglo-American Oil Company, was set up to market United States oil exports to the British Isles.

In 1892 the Trust was obliged to liquidate and remained "in liquidation" for more than five years before its dissolution, the company name becoming Standard Oil Company (New Jersey), the bracketed name (New Jersey) commonly added to distinguish it from other Standard companies.

Fourteen years later, in 1906, the United States Federal Government sued to compel "Jersey Standard" to give up its stock holdings in all thirty-three affiliated Standard companies, charging in effect that the company by virtue of its ownership in stock was able to exert unduly large influence on the domestic petroleum industry. The outcome of a protracted legal battle was that in 1911 the Supreme Court ordered a further dissolution. However, the Standard Oil name had become a valuable asset and those companies which had used the name in their respective marketing areas decided to retain it.

Several of these companies, even today, still have "Standard Oil" in their corporate titles, although they are completely separate organisations. The Standard Oil Company (New Jersey) is entirely separate from, for example, Standard Oil Company of California, Standard Oil Company (Indiana) or Standard Oil Company (Ohio).

Oil for the lamps

Not so many years before the Pennsylvania oil strike, paraffin had gradually been developed as an illuminant and for use in cooking. The spirit, a mixture of hydrocarbons, had first been produced about 1830 by distillation of coal, but nearly twenty years were to pass before a Glasgow chemist, James Young, in 1848 obtained the hydrocarbons by the destructive distillation of bituminous shale. This led to the founding of a mineral oil industry in Scotland, producing paraffin in gaseous, liquid and solid wax forms. The industry became fair-sized, the oils being used in lamps and the solid paraffin, when purified as paraffin wax, being used for waterproofing, candles and in the modelling of fruit, etc.

In America, the supply of lubricants and lighting oils had for years come from animal fats and oils and the tall glass-chimney whale-oil lamp was a feature of many drawing-rooms and much superior to the flickering tallow candle, if indeed, any lights were used at all, for much of the population retired at sun-down and arose at sun-up.

However, the exploitation of the whale over centuries was beginning to have an effect. The rate of killing had been such that whaling ships had to hunt in more distant waters and the scarcity of oil was pushing up its price. And worse was to come, for in the ensuing Civil War of 1861–65, Confederate ships decimated the Yankee whaling fleet.

Meanwhile, in the 1850s, James Young had patented his method of obtaining liquid hydrocarbons from smokeless cannel coal and shale and by 1861, when the Civil War commenced, more than thirty plants in America were making "coal oil" to burn in lamps. But, with whale oil running out, a rich reward awaited anyone who could find a ready and inexpensive source for the production of an illuminant. Indeed, there were some who feared the possibility of an industrial crisis unless another source could be found. It came in 1859 at Titusville. The distillate of the rock-oil (petroleum), found hitherto in oily ground seepages, would fuel the lamps of America. Slowly kerosene, the new source of lubricant and illuminant, supplanted whale oil.

The "new look" kerosene lamp was to travel worldwide and petroleum to oust whale oil in the industrial field. Life in countless families changed. No longer was daily routine regimented by dawn and dusk. Now, with adequate light radiating from the table lamp, children could play games, sewing and darning could be done and books read and studied. By the early 1880s treadle sewing-machines were available, washing-machines worked by a handle

An advertisement for an early washing machine, 1880.

PRICE - THIRTY-FIVE SHILLINGS.

THE "SWIFT WASHER"
WILDING'S PATENT.

THE BEST WASHING MACHINE
FOR FAMILY USE.

It effectually washes every Woven Material, from the heaviest blanket to the finest Lace, without any injury whatever to the fabric to work, requires no hand-rubbing, can be fixed instantly washing-tub, and is an essential requisite household, for itself in

helped tired arms, as did the revolving brushes of carpet sweepers. Then came the magic lantern—pictures projected on a hung bedsheet or wall and illuminated with a kerosene lamp.

It was the time of invention. In 1882 New York opened its first electricity generating station. Ten years later the electric kitchen was featured in the Chicago World Fair. It was the time of the aeroplane, moving pictures, typewriters and fountain pens. And the world moved on—to fans and irons, to cookers and vacuum cleaners. Wonder followed wonder in those early, transitional years of the oil age.

The early tankships

There is no doubt that liquids, including oils, have been carried in odd quantities in many ships over many years, but it is generally recognised that the first true deep sea cargo of oil was carried in 1861.

At first, a trial shipment of five barrels of oil was transported as general cargo quite successfully and later in the year Peter Wright and Sons of

Oil scouts, the forerunners of today's petroleum geologists, photographed in Pennsylvania in 1884. Their methods were necessarily crude, the indications they sought being mainly seepages of crude oil from the ground.   *Esso*

Philadelphia chartered the brig *Elizabeth Watts*, 110 feet in length and with a deadweight capacity of 224 tons, to load a cargo of oil, in barrels, for London. At Philadelphia she loaded 901 barrels of rock oil and 428 barrels of coal oil—about 200 tons—and with an extremely fire-nervous crew, part "crimp", she left the Delaware River on 19th November. Fifty-two turbulent days later, on 9th January, 1862, the *Elizabeth Watts* arrived in Victoria Dock, London, where the cargo, which had taken ten days to load, took twelve to discharge. The freight rate for the voyage was eight shillings per barrel.

This success caused an enormous surge of expansion in the export of oil in barrels and many of the smaller types of sailing ships, which were then being ousted from the dry cargo trades by high running expenses, were turned to carrying barrel cargoes at reduced freight rates. But the barrel trade was really uneconomic, for about one-fifth of the deadweight was of the barrel itself; there was also the problem of leakage, not only resulting in the loss of oil but causing a fire hazard; the barrels depreciated rapidly; and with the wasted space, a ship sometimes lifted only half of her true capacity.

So it was that shippers began looking for alternatives. The case oil trade came and with it there was a reduction in leakage. But the packaging was very expensive, ten one-gallon, or two five-gallon cans being the standard quantities to be cased. And few cans were returned to be used again.

However, the demand for oil became insatiable and experiments began to find a suitable way of carrying oil in bulk. Soon, tanks were being installed in the hulls but there were many difficulties, one being the expansion of the oil as temperature rose in the tanks that were full. As early as 1863 two iron, barque-rigged sailing ships were built for the Petroleum Trading Company, newly formed with Rogers and Sons of Newcastle who were the builders. They were named *Atlantic* and *Great Western* and measured 416 gross tons on a length of 139 feet and breadth of 28 feet. Each had four pairs of tanks amidships, transverse and longitudinal bulkheads, and the idea was for the expansion of the oil to enter the fore and main masts which had been built hollow. Each ship could carry 700 tons, but both were later converted to dry cargo carrying.

Then there was the *Ramsey*, a 690-ton iron sailing ship, built in the Isle of Man in 1863 for Wakefield and Company. She had sealed tanks from which there were siphons which dipped into adjacent water-filled tanks. When the oil expanded it forced water up the siphon, but neither oil nor vapours could escape and the oil returned on contraction. The idea was patented and the ship given good insurance rates, but within a short time she too was carrying dry cargoes.

Passenger tankships

Ideas and modifications continued into the 1870s and early in the decade the Red Star Line came out with a startling plan to carry emigrants and general cargo from Belgium to Philadelphia and passengers and oil on the return run. Three ships were envisaged in the service and orders were given to Palmers Shipbuilding and Iron Company on the Tyne. The first ship of the Red Star fleet was the *Vaderland*, 320 feet in length and 2,748 gt and with engines aft. Between the machinery and the oil tanks was a cofferdam providing deep trunks for expansion. There was space of two feet between the tanks and the side of the ship forming a double skin and the lower part of the ship was entirely for the carrying of oil up to the lower deck, with an expansion trunk extending to the upper deck and the passenger accommodation on either side of it. But the American port authorities, objecting to the unquestionable hazard, would not give a passenger licence and after a good deal of wrangling, dry cargo was substituted for oil and carried, very inconveniently, in the tanks.

In the two slightly longer ships that followed—*Nederland* (1873) and *Switzerland* (1874)—the layout was the same, except that the two-cylinder compound engines were placed amidships. About this time the Norwegian barque *Lindesnaes*, built in 1869, was converted from dry cargo by fitting planking and felt over her lower holds to make an oil-sealed tankspace. Her tank space was transversely divided and washboards were fitted to break the flow of the liquid cargo, which caused dangerous movements to the ship.

Caucasian oil

Baku, a district of Azerbaijan, is on the west coast of the inland Caspian Sea and it was the remoteness of the Baku oilfields from foreign and even home markets that prompted the movement of its oil in bulk. Baku not then being connected by rail to the Black Sea, the only outlet for oil was northwards, up the Caspian Sea, to Astrakhan, at the mouth of the River Volga, and then up that great waterway for distribution. Barrels were used to carry the oil, but timber brought from Russia for their manufacture cost half the price of the petroleum. This was extremely expensive and between 1873 and 1875 oil prices fell from three shillings per centner[1] to one penny.

Ludwig Nobel, related to Alfred B. Nobel, the Swedish engineer who had developed the oil trade of the area, experimented in carrying worthless petroleum residuum in a wooden barge and was surprised that only a small leakage occurred. The advantage was enormous and the oil easily pumped in and out of the barge. A fleet was soon constructed for the Caspian Sea, later spreading to the Volga.

The *Zoroaster* of 1878 at first carried oil in iron tanks, but then loaded straight to the hull. So successful was this that more steamers appeared in the Caspian Sea, moving oil to the Volga and transshipping to the river craft which fed the railway network of Europe. The *Zoroaster*, of 400 tons carrying capacity, was far in advance of anything yet built. Her engines however, were amidships, although this arrangement was altered in the *Spasatel* of 1882 whose engines were placed aft, with a cofferdam between them and the carrying tanks.

Nobel formed the Black Sea Navigation Company in 1885 and ordered some steamships with tanks. It was intended that oil would be shipped from Libau, a Latvian seaport, where it arrived by trans-European railways from Caucasia, to London where it would compete with American oil. Much oil was already being shipped from Libau into Germany. Caucasian oil was also soon to be shipped from Batum, in the Black Sea, through the 560-mile Trans-Caucasian railway and a pipeline from Baku.

Also in this important oil year of 1885 a cargo steamer, *Fergusons* (1,504gt), built by Bertram Haswell and Company, Sunderland, was converted to a tank steamer by Craggs and Sons, Middlesbrough. The significance of this was that it was specially done in order that John M. Lennard and Sons could fulfil conditions for a long timecharter to lift oil from Batum for Nobel Brothers of Antwerp. The ship duly loaded oil at Batum into tanks which had been closely shaped to fit into her hull shape, and discharged at Antwerp. Three years later she was blown to pieces in an explosion at Rouen. The storage tanks at Antwerp were later acquired by Standard Oil.

The first oil cargo of 1,000 tons from Libau arrived in the *Petrolea* in Regent's Canal Dock, London, in 1886 and permission was obtained to sink a pipe below ground from the dockside to Bow Common, where the oil was pumped into lead-lined tanks. The bulk oil trade into Britain had begun.

In this same year of 1886 came the first British-built tank steamer for Alfred Suart and Company, London. The *Bakuin* was built by Wm Gray and Company, West Hartlepool. The hull bottom was cellular; from there to the height of the 'tween decks, oil storage extended to the side. More oil compartments were fitted in the 'tween decks, though not to the side. Additional transverse bulkheads gave facilities for the carrying of different grade oils. In September, 1902, the *Bakuin* was lost by fire while in drydock at Callao Bay, Peru.

A charge of nitroglycerine is detonated in an oil well at Tidi-out Road in the United States to break through a tight rock form-ation.   *Esso*

9

It was Lane and MacAndrew, oil merchants and brokers, who arranged the first bulk shipment of Caucasian oil from Libau to the Thames in 1886.

In 1887 they went on to form the Kerosene Company and had a small coaster, *Valeria*, originally built 1881 (Yard No. 1, Hill's Albion Dockyard, Bristol), converted at Wallsend Slipway to an oil carrier, her bulkheads modified to give her three tanks. The ship then loaded at Thames Haven for Portsmouth, Exeter and Gloucester, the first British ship to sail in the coastal oil distribution trade. This developed into the Trans-Caucasian Oil Company, then became the Consolidated Oil Company, Antwerp, and later, part of the British Petroleum Company (not the Anglo-Persian founder). Lane and MacAndrew did much business in arranging ship construction, charters and brokerage in the Caucasian oil business. The three ships *Darial*, *Elbruz* and *Kasbek*—named after Caucasian mountain areas—were delivered in 1888–89, moved to Galbraith, Pembroke & Company in 1895 and then, in 1899, joined the Anglo-American fleet.

By 1884 the amount of oil being exported from America each year was well on the way to two million tons, much of it still being carried in wooden sailing ships.

The Glückauf

Then into the picture came Wilhelm Anton Riedemann,[2] a shipowner of Geestemunde, who had the sailing ship *Andromeda*. She had been built at Liverpool in 1865, was 1,876 gross tons on measurements of 270 feet in length and 37 feet in breadth and was converted to an oil carrier by installing seventy-two steel tanks in the hold, to fit in with the hull structure. This ship was considered to be the first true tankship and could carry 3,000 tons of oil. The ship was a success and Riedemann's next step was a steamship, to be

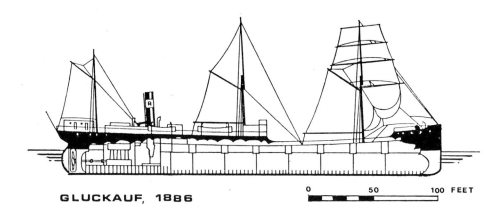

GLUCKAUF, 1886   0   50   100 FEET

Glückauf, the first ocean-going steamship specifically designed to carry oil in bulk.   *Esso*

designed from the hull up as a tanker. But he could not find a German shipyard that would build a new coal-burning tanker and eventually placed an order with Armstrong, Mitchell and Company, of Newcastle on Tyne.

Her hull was 300 feet in length, 37 feet in breadth and her draught was 24.5 feet. All positive findings from the many experimental ships were embodied in her design and a new feature was the positioning of fore and aft expansion tanks which became a standard inclusion of tanker design. The hull was part steel, part iron. The hold was longitudinally divided by a centreline bulkhead and many compartments extended to the hull itself, but there was no double bottom to avoid the collection of dangerous gases. An elaborate pumproom was below deck and discharge of her cargo took twelve hours.

Launched as *Glückauf* ("Good luck"), she was of 2,307 gross tons and had a lifting capacity of 3,020 tons of oil, which equated to some 22,000 barrels. She was electrically lighted.

In July, 1886, the *Glückauf* arrived at New York but there met opposition from shore labour, the longshoremen, oilmen and coopers all claiming that her construction speeded up the loading and discharge of cargo. They were quite right, for her three-day loading system would have taken ten times as long in sailing ships. So the shore labour refused to allow her coal and she actually had to go to St John's to replenish her bunkers for the return eastbound Atlantic crossing.

The *Glückauf* has gone down in history as the prototype of the tanker, while Riedemann went on to play his part in the early years of the Deutsch-Amerikanische Petroleum-Gesellschaft, Hamburg. The *Glückauf* sailed until 1893 when she went ashore on Fire Island, in the approaches to New York and was wrecked.

❊   ❊   ❊

In the United States oil was flowing in great quantities and Philadelphia was establishing itself as a major oil port. The related refining industry was growing and more refineries were being constructed. There were big refineries at Hunters Point and Newtown Creek on Long Island. Standard Oil had extensive works and jetties at Bayonne, New Jersey, and at Point Breeze on the Schuylkill River, near to its junction with the then sprawling outskirts of Philadelphia. Ships loaded here; kerosene spilling from pipeline to ships' tanks; case oil in its thousands loading from the wharves for China and Japan. There were also refineries near the oil town of Pittsburgh, on the banks of the Allegheny. Sites for early refineries were chosen near a railway or as high as practical on sloping ground to take advantage of gravity flow.

Kerosene was also flowing into Europe and great competition was developing from the oilfields of Caucasia. Standard Oil saw this as the time to extend their interests and an executive team crossed the Atlantic to tour Europe, its aim being to regularise tanker sailings and to increase imports of American oil into Europe. In the event the team succeeded in arranging for an amalgamation of some of the largest and most important companies in Europe. Also included were their fleets of tank steamers and the sailing ship *Hainaut*. Under the German flag of the Deutsch-Amerikanische Petroleum-Gesellschaft, Hamburg, were listed:

	Built	Gross tons		Built	Gross tons
Glückauf	1886	2,307	*Bürgermeister Petersen*	1889	2,794
Energie	1888	2,765	*Elise Marie*	1889	3,194
Minister Maybach	1887	2,486	*Helgoland*	1890	2,397
Willkommen	1887	2,893	*Geestemunde*	1890	2,750
Paula	1888	2,703	*Brilliant*	1890	3,189
Gut Heil	1888	2,736	*Standard*	1890	2,764

Dutch-flag ships of American Petroleum Company, Rotterdam, were:

	Built	Gross tons		Built	Gross tons
La Flandre	1888	2,018	*La Hasbaye*	1888	2,568
Charlois	1888	2,677	*La Campine*	1890	2,595
Chester	1888	2,568	*Bremerhaven*	1890	3,393
Ocean	1888	2,560			

The sailing tanker *Hainaut* of 1887 (1,783 gt) belonged to F. Speth and Company, Antwerp.

Two more significant happenings took place in the year 1888. The tanker *Standard*, built by Delaware Iron Shipbuilding and Engineering Works (J. Roach and Sons), Chester, Pennsylvania, was the first tanker built in the United States. Her gross tonnage was 832, she was just 162 feet in length and 30 feet in breadth, iron-built and fitted with triple expansion engines. As a tanker she was regarded as not being very successful and became a barge, *S. O. Co of New York No. 56* (589 gt), then *S. T. and Co No. 56* and, finally, *Socony No. 56*, all over a period of forty-eight years.

The second happening was undoubtedly the more important. In the United States Standard Oil was growing and while thousands of eager European emigrants were looking westwards to a new life, Standard Oil looked east towards a potentially huge European market. In 1888 the first of Standard Oil's foreign affiliates was formed and registered in London. Its title was Anglo-American Oil Company and its immediate aim was to supply kerosene and paraffin wax to a growing market. It was destined to become one of the largest companies in Britain.

✳   ✳   ✳

In 1907 the Isherwood bracket system of longitudinal framing was patented and the first ship to be built in this manner was the 4,196 gt British flag steam tanker *Paul Paix*, completed at the Tees Dockyard, Middlesbrough, by R. Craggs and Sons in 1908 for J. M. Lennard and Sons. Craggs also turned out the 3,100 gt *Gascony* for D. McIver Sons and Company on the same lines and overseas shipbuilders began building some in the same way.

Joseph Isherwood realised that although general cargo ships were built with transverse vertical ribs, or frames as they were called, there was no fore and aft support between them. In the case of tankers, as the cargo rested directly on the ship's bottom skin, the main need was for longitudinal strength.

Between the tank bulkheads the Isherwood design called for widely spaced deep transverse frames, riveted to the hull and decks and slotted for longitudinal stiffeners to be placed at the decks, sides, bottom and tank top. These were stopped and bracketed at the transverse bulkheads. With this design the vessel was able to withstand enormous vertical stress.

However, the brackets were found to cause oil leakage and Isherwood later modified the system by eliminating all brackets to the longitudinals.

Up to 1925, 1,502 ships were built with the Isherwood system, including several hundred tankers, and in July, 1926, the first ship with the Isherwood bracketless system, the 7,100 gt *British Inventor*, was delivered by Palmers, Newcastle, to the British Tanker Company; she was found to be a great success.

Isherwood later took an interest in the outward hull form and from experiments in the early 1930s developed an "Arcform" rounded form design, the sides of the ship arched or curved, instead of being straight. Three cargo ships were constructed by Sir Joseph W. Isherwood and Company to this special design, which included longitudinal framing at the bottom, *Arcwear* from Short Brothers, Sunderland, *Arctees* from Furness Shipbuilding Company and *Arcgow* from Lithgows, Port Glasgow, all in 1934.

CHAPTER TWO

Anglo-American

THERE is no doubt that the agreement formed in Europe laid the foundations of a huge European-American bulk oil import organisation. However, it did not include Britain, for there Standard Oil was ready to launch its first overseas affiliate.

Anglo-American Oil Company came into existence on 27th April, 1888, was duly noted in the national press, but aroused more interest in those who were marketing the oils of the day. An office was opened at 16 Great St Helens,* in London's business quarter, and on 6th June, 1888, the Board had its inaugural meeting. The prime decision made was that a national distributing network for imported oils should be working in two years.

The announcement read:

American Refined Products

The long established superiority of "Tea Rose", "Royal Daylight", "White Rose" and "Westminster" American Petroleum oils is well known to the Trade and to Consumers. In order to meet the increasing demand for these Oils, we have arranged to import them in bulk as well as in barrels. We shall fill the Oil which we import in bulk into barrels at our own wharves, and buyers will receive the Oil in tight and clean packages.

Our Tank steamers, *Manhattan* and *Bayonne*, are in advance of any tank steamers afloat, and each has a carrying capacity of 4,000 tons, equivalent to 28,000 barrels of Oil by each steamer.

To cover the special requirements of London buyers, we have completed the construction of a large storage wharf at Purfleet, which will be worked in connection with our Depots at Ailsa Street, Bow Creek; Canal Wharf, Chalk Farm Road; and Albany Wharf, Camberwell.

Anglo-American were justifiably proud of their two new ships. The *Bayonne* was the first, launched sideways by the brothers A. and J. Inglis from their yard at Pointhouse into the River Kelvin, which runs into the Clyde. There were nine pairs of tanks in the ship, and using the two pumps fitted the oil cargo could be discharged in ten hours. The sistership,

*The company moved twice more before 1903: to Dock House, Billiter Street, and to 22 Billiter Street.

Manhattan, was also Clyde-built. On negotiating their construction the Anglo-American representatives arrived with well-defined ideas and made it clear to the shipbuilders that in these they could not be swayed.

In 1891 the Anglo-American Company took delivery of the slightly smaller *Weehauken*, built on the Tyne, but returned to the Clyde for their

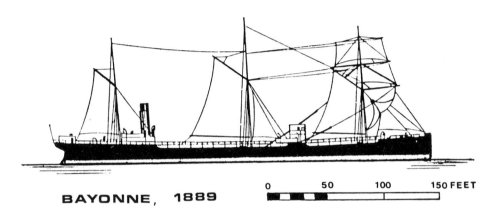

BAYONNE, 1889

0   50   100   150 FEET

next group of three sisterships. The first two, *Delaware* and *Lackawanna*, were built by D. J. Dunlop and Company, Port Glasgow, the *Potomac* by the Inglis brothers again. All three were capable of lifting 4,700 tons of oil. It was the *Potomac* that discharged the first bulk cargo of oil at Dublin on 2nd February, 1899, 1,206,200 gallons of illuminating oil. Her arrival inaugurated the new trade with Dublin and a new oil installation with pumping plant and storage tanks was opened on the north side of Alexandra Dock. Anglo-American's seventh ship in the first seven years, *Chesapeake*, was delivered from Dunlop in 1895. She could carry 5,200 tons of oil.

The petroleum industry was at that time involved in gas for lighting, in fuel for generating steam and in metallurgical operations. Along Britain's roads and lanes rumbled Anglo-American horse-drawn tank wagons in an ever-expanding distributing organisation, their trade names of "Tea Rose", "Royal Daylight" and others emblazoned on the tank sides.

Selling of illuminating oils had been introduced by the local merchant and shopkeeper, practically every ironmonger owning a tank of some sort in which to store paraffin. Then, as demand increased, Anglo-American began organising distributing centres where oil could be stored in bigger quantities and distributed to local retailers. And demand increased again.

The age of the motor car really started as the century changed and there began an increase in demand at the beginning of the twentieth century for types of oils other than lamp oil.

15

The *Delaware* of 1893, one of a group of three sisterships built on the Clyde.

Motor spirit, the power base of the motor car, was required in growing quantities. And Anglo-American arranged for the sole importation of Pratt's Motor Spirit. It was sold in two-gallon green cans, could be seen everywhere and possessed a trade name that was to last for three decades.

The main receiving point was at Purfleet, where Anglo-American ships discharged cargoes into storage tanks. From there a coastal distribution service to other area centres began, the first Anglo-American coaster, *Osceola*, participating in 1897. By the turn of the century there were storage tank farms at Hull, Norwich and Newcastle on the East Coast; Manchester, Glasgow, Bristol and Plymouth in the West, and at Dublin. But this was only a beginning . . .

At the turn of the century the Sunderland Shipbuilding Company completed the *Hudson* and the next three years saw the completion of *Seneca*, *Kennebec* and *Schuylkill* by Russell and Company, Port Glasgow. They were not sisterships, indeed, the deadweight tonnage varied from 6,000 tons in the *Hudson* to 8,400 in the *Schuylkill*. However, they were similar in that they were all constructed as dry cargo ships, specially for carrying case oil, at that time a trade greatly expanding in the East.

In 1903, Anglo-American took delivery of their largest ship; a vessel of

9,196 gross tons and a cargo capacity of just under 12,000 tons. In fact, she was the largest tanker in the world, 531 feet length overall and 63 feet 3 inches in breadth. She was also the largest ship ever built on the lower reaches of the Clyde. Unlike the usual style of naming ships after North American rivers, she was named *Narragansett*, after an inlet on the south-east coast of Rhode Island. The ship had three decks and her hull construction included eighteen transverse bulkheads, subdivided by longitudinal bulkheads to give twenty-seven compartments. Her triple expansion engines, which gave 13 knots, were amidships and a circular tunnel passed through eight separate oil compartments from the engine room for the shaft. Expansion tanks were placed between the main and upper decks and there were two pumprooms—one each side of the engines—the four pumps being capable of discharging at 900 tons per hour and taking about twelve hours for the complete cargo, although she usually stayed in port some forty-eight hours.

The *Narragansett* could be transformed to take dry cargo, if necessary. Steam connections were fitted for tank cleaning or fire extinguishing and a fan in each pumproom was connected by piping to each tank for suction and renewal of foul air. She had sixteen derricks and nine steam winches. Extra

An advertisement postcard for Anglo-American oils.

cargo space was available in the 'tween decks and lighting by side lights through the ship's side was arranged so that troops, or cattle, could be carried. Her best round voyage from the Tyne in ballast, returning to the Thames with a full cargo of oil from New York, was made in twenty-seven days. The prototype of the *Narragansett* was the smaller *Tuscarora*, built in 1898.

Distribution ashore was steadily improving and a motor tank wagon for distributing oil was built in 1905, capable of carrying 800 gallons. Its speed on British roads was about eight miles an hour, but the replacement of the horse-drawn wagons was still more than a decade away. Over one thousand horses were in Anglo-American stables in those years just before the Great War, with teams drawing heavy wagons on which was carried a cylindrical tank holding 500 gallons.

Two other interesting tankers were built in that first decade of the new century. As early as 1892 the Standard Oil Company began carrying oil in barges across the Atlantic and even round Cape Horn to San Francisco and to Japan. On the Atlantic in 1908 Anglo-American introduced a different horse and cart partnership that was to last for twenty-three years. This was the tanker *Iroquois* with its dumb-barge companion, *Navahoe*, which it towed back and forth, the two ships between them carrying 18,000 tons of oil and earning the soubriquet "Horse and Cart". The *Iroquois* was the first large tanker to be given twin screws. She had quadruple expansion engines, with steam from four boilers. Her average speed, with or without tow, was 10 knots.

The other interesting ship was the *Cheyenne*, one of the very few tankers to be given two centreline funnels.

From the early experiments of 1897, when Italian naval ships succeeded in sending messages over a twelve-mile range in the Gulf of Genoa, wireless telegraphy had been steadily developed yet, in 1907, only 139 merchant ships carried wireless and practically all of those were passenger ships.

Two Anglo-American tankers had wireless installations fitted in 1908 and evidence of the importance of the equipment was to be shown a few years later. On 9th October, 1913, the *Volturno*, 3,581 gt, owned by the Canadian Northern SS Company, was in mid-Atlantic in heavy seas, with over 600 emigrants on board from Rotterdam for New York, when fire broke out. The *Volturno* made urgent distress calls and ten ships answered, including the Cunard Line's *Carmania*. After standing by helplessly in the heavy seas the *Carmania* made another appeal which prompted a reply from the *Narragansett*—"Yes, will come with the milk in the morning". She duly arrived and pumped out oil to calm the sea, enabling 521 survivors of the 657 persons on board the *Volturno* to be rescued by lifeboats from the ships standing by.

Just prior to the outbreak of war in 1914 the Anglo-American fleet numbered twenty-six steam tankers, and with eight sailing ships was the largest single oil-carrying fleet in the world.

The three major areas of oil production at that time were the United States, Russia and Mexico. In the war year of 1914 no less than 400,483,000 (42-gallon) barrels of oil were produced, of which 266,000,000—or some 63%—were contributed by the United States. The Russian figure was sixty-seven million and Mexico twenty-one million. When hostilities ceased Mexico became the second largest producer, with Persia producing ever larger quantities.

Anglo-American steam tankers 1889–1914

	Completed	Gross tons
Bayonne	8.1889	3,294

Built by A. & J. Inglis Ltd., Glasgow.
Measurements: 330 feet length × 42 feet breadth.
Engines: T3cyl.
*1895: (Akt. Ges. Atlantic).
1905: (Soc. Italo Americanes del Petrolis (A.G. Atlantic)).
1917: (La Columbia Soc. Mar. Trasporto del Petrolio e
 Derivanti, Genoa).
1924: Sold for breaking up.

	Completed	Gross tons
Manhattan	9.1889	3,284

Built by D. J. Dunlop & Co., Port Glasgow.
Measurements: 330 feet length × 42 feet breadth.
Engines: T3cyl.
*1899: (Akt. Ges. Atlantic).
23.9.1910: Sailed from New York for Algiers with a cargo
 of petroleum. Missing, not heard of since.

	Completed	Gross tons
Weehauken	1891	2,784

Built by Armstrong, Mitchell & Co. Ltd., Newcastle.
Measurements: 310 feet length × 40 feet breadth.
Engines: T3cyl.
*6.4.1911: (J. I. Jacobs & Co. Ltd. (Oil & Molasses
 Tankers Ltd.)).
1927: *Vioca* (Soc. di Nav. Cameli, Italy).
1928: (Soc. Anon Cameli, Italy).
4.1937: Scrapped Italy.

The *Narragansett* at Purfleet jetty in 1915. She had been converted to oil-burning in 1909.   *Esso*

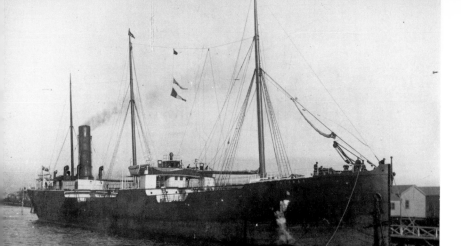

Potomac, built 1893.

Chesapeake, built 1895. *Tom Rayner*

Tuscarora, built 1898 and renamed *Powhatan* in 1912.

Delaware	6.1893	3,855	Built by D. J. Dunlop & Co., Port Glasgow. Measurements: 345 feet length × 44 feet breadth. Engines: T3cyl. 1.1929: Sold to Hughes, Bolckow for breaking up at Blyth.
Potomac	1893	3,868	Built by A. & J. Inglis Ltd., Glasgow. Measurements: 345 feet length × 44 feet breadth. Engines: T3cyl. 26.9.1929: Wrecked on Mastic Point, NE coast of Andros Island, Bahamas (voyage: Baytown/London).
Lackawanna	2.1894	3,855	Built by D. J. Dunlop & Co., Port Glasgow. Measurements: 345 feet length × 44 feet breadth. Engines: T3cyl. *1910: Exchanged for a larger ship from Deutsch- Amerikanische Petroleum-Gesellschaft. 1910: *Sirius* (Deutsch-Amerikanische Petroleum- Gesellschaft). 1919: (Soc. Anon Andora, Genoa). 1922: *Fiamma* (Soc. Anon Andora, Genoa). 1924: (Samengo & Mussinelli, Genoa). 1925: *Maya* (G. Massabo, Italy). 1927: (Soc. Anon Petroliera, Genoa). 1928: (Soc. Anon Cisterne Italiane). 5.9.1941: Sunk by submarine (HMS *Perseus*) torpedo, 6 miles south of Tenedo, off Dardanelles, 39.43N 25.57E.
Chesapeake	8.1895	4,521	Built by D. J. Dunlop & Co., Port Glasgow. Measurements: 370 feet length × 47 feet breadth. Engines: T3cyl. 6.12.1911: Explosion of naphtha vapour, 40.20N 48.40W, in North Atlantic. On fire, abandoned (voyage: New York/Algiers).
Tuscarora	1898	6,117	Built by Sir James Laing, Sunderland. Measurements: 420 feet length × 53 feet breadth. 8,000 tdw. Engines: T3cyl (amidships). 1912: *Powhatan* (Tank Storage & Carriage Co. Ltd). *1916: (Standard Transportation Co. Ltd. (Hong Kong)). 6.4.1917: Sunk by submarine (*U.66*) torpedo 25 miles N by W of North Rona, 59.32N 6.03W (voyage: Sabine/ Kirkwall) whilst serving as an Admiralty oiler.
Genesee	1889	2,767	Built by Armstrong, Mitchell & Co. Ltd., Newcastle as *Darial* (Lane & MacAndrew). Measurements: 310 feet length × 40 feet breadth. Engines: T3cyl. 1895: (Galbraith, Pembroke & Co.). 6.1899: *Genesee* (Anglo-American Oil Co. Ltd.). 1924: Scrapped.

The *Genesee* was attacked several times by U-boats. Two attacks were made in the North Sea on 23rd March, 1917, and six months later, on 27th September. In both attacks the torpedoes missed. Then, on 1st January, 1918, again in the North Sea, the *Genesee* was hit. She listed heavily to port and the Master sent most of the crew to an escorting patrol boat. Then the ship righted herself and with the four remaining crew was brought to Hartlepool. She suffered further damage, again in the North Sea, on 21st July, 1918, but still managed to reach port.

Suwanee	1888	2,736	Built by Armstrong, Mitchell & Co. Ltd., Newcastle, as *Kasbek* (Lane & MacAndrew). Measurements: 310 feet length × 40 feet breadth. Engines: T3cyl. 1895: (Galbraith, Pembroke & Co.). 6.1899: *Suwanee* (Anglo-American Oil Co. Ltd.). *1901: (Galbraith, Pembroke & Co.). 20.4.1917: Attacked by submarine gunfire, North Atlantic. 1925: Scrapped Holland.
Hudson	5.1900	3,679	Built by Sunderland Shipbuilding Co. Ltd. Measurements: 356 feet length × 45 feet breadth. Engines: T3cyl. *1911: *Hudson Maru* (Tatsuma Kisen KK). 1931: *Nagato Maru* (Nippon Godo KK). 1934: *Toten Maru* (Nippon Suisan KK). 11.6.1944: Sunk by torpedo from U.S.S. *Barb* in Pacific Ocean, 46.58N 143.50E.
Seneca	1901	4,848	Built by Russell & Co., Port Glasgow. Measurements: 390 feet length × 52 feet breadth. Engines: T3cyl. 1912: *Aspinet* (Tank Storage & Carriage Co. Ltd.). *1916: (Standard Transportation Co. Ltd., Hong Kong). 1923: *Hakkai Maru* (Kita Shina KK). 1931: (Mitsuwa Shokai KK). 7.1934: Scrapped Japan.

The case oil trade was generally regarded as being the near-monopoly of the sailing ship fleet, but there were some steamships built for it.

One steamer was the *Seneca* which Anglo American obtained from Russell and Company in

The *Genesee*, acquired by Anglo-American in 1899.

1901. After transfer to the Tank Storage and Carriage Company as *Aspinet* she was requisitioned for the carriage of petroleum and then transferred again to Hong Kong registry.

In 1923 she became *Hakkai Maru* of Kita Shina KK (North China S.S. Co.) and was registered at Dairen for the purpose of obtaining certain Japanese flag privileges. In 1931 she was sold to another owner in the same port.

Appalachee	1.1894	3,767	Built by Tyne Iron Shipbuilding Co. Ltd., Newcastle, as *Duffield* for Northern Petroleum Tank S.S. Co. (Hunting & Son). Measurements: 340 feet length × 44 feet breadth. Engines: T3cyl. 6.1901: *Appalachee* (Anglo-American Oil Co. Ltd.). 25.2.1918: Damaged by submarine torpedo off N. Ireland. Towed in. *1926: *Clizia* (G. Masabo, Italy). 1927: (Ape Anon Petroliere, Italy). 1942: (German Navy). 25–26.8.1944: Scuttled in River Gironde. Broken up *in situ*.
Tonawanda	1893	3,416	Built by Armstrong, Mitchell & Co. Ltd., Newcastle, as *Lucigen* (H. E. Moss & Co., Liverpool). Measurements: 330 feet length × 43 feet breadth. Engines: T3cyl. 4.1901: *Tonawanda* (Anglo-American Oil Co. Ltd.). 2.6.1917: Torpedoed by submarine in English Channel, but reached port. 1923: Scrapped.
Ottawa	1888	2,742	Built by Armstrong, Mitchell & Co. Ltd., Newcastle as *Elbruz* (Lane & MacAndrew). Measurements: 309 feet length × 40 feet breadth. Engines: T3cyl. 1895: (Galbraith, Pembroke & Co.). 4.1900: *Ottawa* (Anglo-American Oil Co. Ltd.). 6.2.1921: In wireless communication, but then went missing (voyage: Port Lobos/Manchester—fuel oil).

The *Ottawa* was in Admiralty service between August 1914 and December 1918. On 21st January, 1921, she sailed from Mexico for Manchester with a bulk cargo of 3,600 tons of fuel oil, routed via Norfolk, Virginia, from where she left on 2nd February.

Subsequently, the tanker was in wireless telegraphy communication with other vessels, the last one, the British steamer *Dorington Court*, on 6th February. Shortly after, there was a hurricane in the area, in which the French steamer *Victorieux* (1911, 5,692 gt) and the Belgian-owned *Bombardier* (1920, 3,162 gt) were abandoned.

There is little doubt that the *Ottawa* was also a victim of the storm, for the British-flag steamer *Esperanza de Larrinaga* (1907, 4,981 gt) and the Italian vessel *Monte San Michelle* (1920, 6,547 gt), which, respectively, sailed on the same day from Norfolk and New York, also went missing.

Housatonic	2.1893	3,893	Built by Naval Construction & Armaments Co. Ltd., Barrow, as *Northern Light* (G. Crosham, Lane & Co., London). Measurements: 347 feet length × 45 feet 6 inches breadth. Engines: T3cyl. 1896: (Lennards Petroleum Carrying Co., London). 4.1901: *Housatonic* (Anglo-American Oil Co. Ltd.). 1.1908: Wrecked on Maiden Rocks, near Larne (voyage: Barrow/New York—ballast).

Tioga	1890	2,292	Built by Burmeister & Wain, Copenhagen, as *Christine* (Danske Petroleums Akt). Measurements: 281 feet length × 37 feet breadth. Engines: T3cyl. 1902: *Tioga* (Anglo-American Oil Co. Ltd.). *1910: (Cia Bellerine (Christensen)). 4.2.1913: Stranded, South Orkney Island, South Atlantic, whilst on whaling service.
Kennebec	6.1902	5,077	Built by Russell & Co., Port Glasgow. Measurements: 405 feet length × 52 feet breadth. 1912: *Ponus* (Tank Storage & Carriage Co. Ltd.). *1916: (Standard Transportation Co. Ltd., Hong Kong). 3.11.1916: Wrecked on Byllyngwase Beach, Falmouth, whilst serving as an Admiralty oiler.
Narragansett	1903	9,196	Built by Scott & Co., Greenock. Measurements: 531 feet (oa) 512 feet length × 63 feet breadth. Engines: T3cyl (amidships). 16.3.1917: Torpedoed and sunk off Scilly Isles, 50.12N 17.34W (voyage: New York/London—lubricating oil).

The *Narragansett* had a cargo of nearly 10,000 tons of lubricating oil, destined for Purfleet, when she was lost with all hands. The only word received from the ship was a message through the Admiralty wireless, "Arriving Purfleet Saturday" and another, later "*Narragansett* sinking". There was no further trace of the ship and no wreckage found.

The *Housatonic*, built at Barrow in 1893 as the *Northern Light* and acquired by Anglo-American in 1901.

The *Tioga*, built in Denmark in 1890 and acquired by Anglo-American twelve years later.

She was one of several ships which helped in rescuing 521 passengers and crew from the *Volturno* (1910/3581gt) which caught fire and sank 9th October, 1913, on a voyage from Rotterdam to New York.

Schuylkill	6.1903	5,176	Built by Russell & Co., Port Glasgow. Measurements: 412 feet length × 52 feet breadth. Engines: T3cyl. 1912: *Oneka* (Tank Storage & Carriage Co. Ltd.). *1916: (Standard Transportation Co., Hong Kong). 1924: *Ryoka Maru* (Saka Kisen KK). 1939: (Tokai Unso KK). 15.2.1944: Sunk by U.S. mine in Okinawa Sea, 31.16N 121.45E.
Dakotah	7.1902	4,006	Built by Armstrong, Whitworth & Co. Ltd., Newcastle as *Tuscany* (Lane & McAndrew). Measurements: 350 feet length × 47 feet breadth. Engines: T3cyl. 1904: *Dakotah* (Anglo-American Oil Co. Ltd.). 1913: *Kanakuk* (Tank Storage & Carriage Co. Ltd.). 3.10.1915: On fire, sank in position 2.37S 116.43E (voyage: Balik Papan/Europe—benzine).

The barge *Navahoe* in tow of the tanker *Iroquois* at New Orleans in 1930.

Seminole	6.1903	5,864	Built by Furness Withy & Co. Ltd., West Hartlepool. Intended to be named *Gloriana*, for British Maritime Trust, but retained by the builders until 1904. Measurements: 414 feet (oa)/400 feet length × 52 feet breadth. Engines: T3cyl. 1904: *Seminole* (Anglo-American Oil Co. Ltd.). 1912: *Wabasha* (Tank Storage & Carriage Co. Ltd.). *1916: (Standard Transportation Co. Ltd., Hong Kong). 6.7.1917: Damaged by submarine torpedo in English Channel. Reached port. 1924: (Oil & Molasses Tankers Ltd. (J. I. Jacobs & Co.)). 1926: (Öl Transport GmbH, Hamburg). 1929: *Nordsee* (Öl Transport GmbH, Hamburg). 1932: Broken up.
Winnebago	11.1901	4,534	Built by Armstrong, Whitworth & Co. Ltd., Newcastle, as *Kinsman* (C. T. Bowring & Co.). Measurements: 359 feet length × 50 feet breadth. Engines: T3cyl. 1905: *Winnebago* (Anglo-American Oil Co. Ltd.). 1912: *Masconomo* (Tank Storage & Carriage Co. Ltd.). *1916: Standard Transportation Co. Ltd., Hong Kong). 1931: *Irma Schindler* (Leth & Co., Hamburg). 1936: *Burano* (Cia Italiana Maritima, Genoa). 9.1943: Taken over by German Navy. 26.8.1944: Scuttled at Pauillac, 29 miles NW of Bordeaux on south bank of River Gironde, as an obstruction to the port. 1946: Raised and cut up for scrap.

On 25th–26th August, 1944 at Bordeaux and in the River Gironde, the *Burano* was one of twenty-one merchant ships, a German destroyer and eight German minesweepers which were sunk or scuttled just prior to the liberation of Bordeaux on 31st August, 1944.

Ashtabula	8.1903	7,025	Built by Palmers Shipbuilding & Iron Co. Ltd., Jarrow, as *Graf Stroganoff* (Northern S.S. Co., St Petersburg).

> Measurements: 442 feet (oa)/428 feet length × 54 feet breadth.
> Engines: T3cyl. 10½ knots.
> 1906: *Ashtabula* (Anglo-American Oil Co. Ltd.).
> 22.2.1917: Damaged by mine, North Sea. Arrived London.
> *1930: *Alabama* (6,725 gt) (Soc. Anon. Petroleum Genoa).

On 30th December, 1941, Venezuela severed relations with Italy, and the Italian-flag *Alabama*, then under repair in the Gulf of Maracaibo, was seized by Venezuela and later acquired by the United States. She was then renamed *Osmond* and placed under the flag of Panama.

Then, on 23rd March, 1944, she was taken over by the United States Navy, renamed *Quiros* (IX 140) and sent to the Western Pacific as a mobile storage tanker. After the Pacific duties and plagued by constant machinery trouble, she was taken under tow from Kwajalein, Marshall Islands, to San Francisco, arriving on 24th October, 1945. On 7th December, 1945, she was decommissioned and reverted to the United States War Shipping Administration and to her previous name of *Osmond*. As such, she was delivered on 10th July, 1947, to the American Iron and Metal Company for breaking up.

Cuyahoga	8.1902	4,507	Built by Armstrong, Whitworth & Co. Ltd., Newcastle, as *Lucigen* (H. E. Moss & Co.).

> Measurements: 369 feet length × 48 feet 6 inches breadth.
> Engines: T3cyl.
> 4.1907: *Cuyahoga* (Anglo-American Oil Co. Ltd.).
> 1912: *Massasoit* (Tank Storage & Carriage Co. Ltd.).
> *1916: (Standard Transportation Co. Ltd., Hong Kong).
> 1928: *Tageha* (Deutsche Petroleum A.G., Hamburg).
> 1932: *Delia* (Industrie Nav. S.A., Genoa).
> 1933: Scrapped Italy.

Iroquois	10.1907	9,202	Built by Harland & Wolff Ltd., Belfast.

> Measurements: 467 feet length × 60 feet breadth.
> 11,800 tdw.
> Engines: Quad.
> 12.1946: Scrapped by Arnott, Young & Co., Dalmuir. The first large tanker with twin screws.

Navahoe	1908	7,718	Built by Harland & Wolff Ltd., Belfast.

> Measurements: 450 feet length × 58 feet breadth. A six-masted barge.
> *9.1930: (Creole Petroleum Co.).
> 28.6.1936: Scuttled, 50 miles north of Dragons Mouth, Trinidad.

The tanker *Iroquois*, with propelling machinery aft, had a housing on the poop in which there was a towing winch with a drum capacity of 500 fathoms of seven-inch wire. A steam valve controlled the winch, easing a taut wire and then picking up the slack again. With engines of 5,000 ihp she could travel at 11–12 knots.

The *Navahoe* was rigged as a six-masted "bald-headed" schooner. She had quite powerful engines powered by a large single-ended boiler, the uptake from the furnaces being through the foremast. The engines were not for propelling, but for pumping and heating. As with the *Iroquois*, steam was also supplied to a towing winch and there was also a steam winch at each mast for hoisting sails. The six masts—fore, main, mizzen, jigger, spanker and driver—each carried a fore and aft sail. The boom length was sixty-five feet, the gaffs sixty feet.

The first voyage of the pair began on 1st March, 1908, from Belfast to the United States and, with but one exception—that of a voyage to Colon and Sabine—the partnership continued in the North Atlantic until 30th May, 1917—nine and three-quarter years. Up to that time 148 crossings were made, averaging sixteen each year at a speed of just under 9 knots.

But the long period of nine and three-quarter years had to be broken, for the First World War was then at its peak, with stringent convoy organisation, hardly suitable for a big-ship tow such as the *Iroquois* and *Navahoe*. So the ships were withdrawn and placed on a Texas–Halifax, Nova Scotia, run, averaging just over 10 knots in the sixteen voyages made between June 1917 and November 1918. By the end of the war some 290,000 tons of oil had been moved for the Admiralty in just under eighteen months.

With the end of the war came release from Admiralty service and the two vessels left Baton Rouge on 24th December, 1918, bound for London. With other tankers they continued working in the Baton Rouge–London River service, although at the end of 1925 there were the beginnings of the great world depression, with all types of shipping laid up in countless rivers and backwaters and including many tankers. However, the *Iroquois* and *Navahoe* were able to continue their work, mainly between Baton Rouge and Thames Haven, until their last arrival on 17th September, 1930.

Then, after nearly twenty-three years, the *Navahoe* went off to act as a floating oil store at the mouth of the San Juan River in Eastern Venezuela. The oil terminal was at Caripito, some sixty miles up river where the ever-larger tankers were too deep to load down to their marks. So they topped off from her 90,000 barrels storage before sailing on to deep seas. But this was only a temporary measure. Loading conditions improved and after completing the cargoes of hundreds of tankers, she was towed out by one of the tankers in the summer of 1936 and scuttled in 400 fathoms.

Tamarac	1908	5,169	Built by Napier & Miller Ltd., Glasgow.

Measurements: 395 feet length × 52 feet breadth.
Engines: T3cyl.
1912: *Sequoya* (Tank Storage & Carriage Co. Ltd.).
*1916: (Standard Transportation Co. Ltd., Hong Kong).
23.3.1918: Damaged by submarine torpedo in English Channel. Reached port.
1925: *Jole Fassio* (Villain & Fassio, Italy).
31.3.1941: Set on fire by crew at Puerto Cabello. Taken over by Venezuela.
1942: Transferred to U.S. authorities, renamed *Alcibiades* (Panama flag).
8.1944: Taken over by U.S. Navy as fuel storage tanker for Pacific war zone. Renamed *Andrew Doria* (IX 132).
2.1946: *Alcibiades* (U.S. Maritime Commission).
1947: Sold for scrapping and
1948: Returned to Italian authorities.
12.1949: Scrapped Philadelphia.

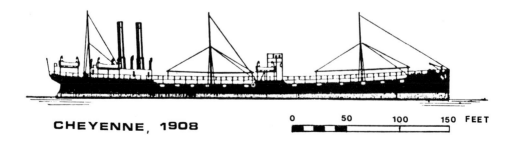

CHEYENNE, 1908

0   50   100   150 FEET

The stern of the *Iroquois*, showing the towing fairlead fitted for her "horse and cart" role with the *Navahoe*.

Tom Rayner

Saranac	9.1908	5,316	Built by Wm Gray & Co. Ltd., West Hartlepool. Measurements: 386 feet length × 52 feet breadth. Engines: T3cyl. 1912: *Satanta* (Tank Storage & Carriage Co. Ltd.). *1916: (Standard Transportation Co. Ltd., Hong Kong). 1931: Sold to Japanese buyers and 1932: Scrapped Japan.
Cheyenne	1908	4,987	Built by Swan, Hunter & Wigham Richardson Ltd., Wallsend. Measurements: 389 feet length × 51 feet breadth. 29.6.1917: Attacked by submarine torpedo in English Channel which missed. 11.11.1924: Stranded at St. Monans, Fifeshire (voyage: Grangemouth/USA—ballast). Refloated, broken up at Bo'ness. Had two funnels on centreline, each serving two boilers.

From the outbreak of war in 1914 until the armistice in 1918 the *Cheyenne* made thirty-five Atlantic crossings and never sighted an enemy submarine.

Only once was a torpedo fired at the ship. That was when she was heading down channel, west of Portland Bill, with three 7-knot drifters as an escort. The drifters were bunched astern of the *Cheyenne*, which could have made better speed without them, and the torpedo came from astern. Its track was seen and the ship altered course, the torpedo missing by twenty feet. The U-boat was not sighted.

Cadillac	1.1909	5,251	Built by Napier & Miller Ltd., Glasgow. Measurements: 385 feet length × 51 feet breadth. Engines: T3cyl. 1912: *Samoset* (Tank Storage & Carriage Co. Ltd.). *1916: (Standard Transportation Co. Ltd., Hong Kong). 20.3.1918: Sunk by submarine (*U.33*) torpedo, 50 miles N by E of Port Said while serving as an Admiralty oiler (voyage: Port Said/Brindisi—fuel oil).

Impoco	5.1910	1,683	Built by Greenock & Grangemouth Dockyard Co. Ltd., Greenock. Measurements: 242 feet length × 40 feet breadth. Engines: T3cyl. 1912: *Waneta* (Tank Storage & Carriage Co. Ltd.). *1916: (Standard Transportation Co. Ltd., Hong Kong). 30.5.1918: Sunk by submarine (*U.101*) torpedo, 42 miles SSE of Kinsale Head while serving as an Admiralty oiler (voyage: Halifax/Queenstown—oil fuel).
Lackawanna	1894	4,125	Built by J. C. Tecklenborg A.G., Wesermunde as *August Korff* for Deutsch-Amerikanische Petroleum-Gesellschaft. Measurements: 353 feet length × 45 feet breadth. Engines: T3cyl. 1910: *Lackawanna* (Anglo-American Oil Co. Ltd.). 4.1931: Broken up.
Comanchee	1912	5,601	Built by Armstrong, Whitworth & Co. Ltd., Newcastle. Measurements: 395 feet length × 52 feet breadth. 8,080 tdw. Engines: Quad. 28.7.1917: Torpedoed off North West Ireland. Repaired. *1933: *Francunion V* (Cie Venture-Weir S.A. Algiers) (Andrew Weir & Co.). A depot ship at Algiers. 1949: Sold to shipbreakers at Spezia.
Tacoma	3.1909	6,838	Built by Flensburger Schiffsbau Ges. as *Buffalo* for Deutsch-Amerikanische Petroleum-Gesellschaft. Measurements: 440 feet length × 58 feet breadth. Engines: Quad. 1913: *Tacoma* (Anglo-American Oil Co. Ltd.) (Tank Storage & Carriage Co. Ltd.). *1916: (Standard Transportation Co. Ltd., Hong Kong). 1933: Scrapped.
Tuscarora	7.1908	6,828	Built by Flensburger Schiffsbau Ges. as *Niagara* for Deutsch-Amerikanische Petroleum-Gesellschaft. Measurements: 440 feet length × 58 feet breadth. Engines: Quad. 1913: *Tuscarora* (Anglo-American Oil Co. Ltd.). 1913: *Tecumseh* (Tank Storage & Carriage Co. Ltd.). *1916: (Standard Transportation Co. Ltd., Hong Kong). 23.11.1932: Wrecked near Inhaca Point, Inyack Island, Lourenco Marques (voyage: Tandjong Oeban/Lourenco Marques—petroleum).
Wapello	4.1912	5,576	Built by Armstrong, Whitworth & Co. Ltd., Newcastle, as *Clio* for Deutsch-Amerikanische Petroleum-Gesellschaft. Measurements: 395 feet 6 inches length × 51 feet 6 inches breadth. Engines: Quad. 1913: *Wapello* (Anglo-American Oil Co. Ltd.). *1916: (Standard Transportation Co. Ltd., Hong Kong). 21.4.1917: Attacked by submarine gunfire off south-west Ireland. Returned fire. 15.6.1917: Sunk by submarine (*U.71*) gunfire, 14 miles WSW of Owers Lightvessel, 50.30N 0.57W (voyage: Philadelphia/Thames Haven—benzine), whilst serving as an Admiralty oiler.

Uncas	6.1913	4,722	Built by Greenock & Grangemouth Dockyard Co. Ltd., Greenock, for Anglo-American Oil Co. Ltd., but delivered direct to Tank Storage & Carriage Co. Ltd. Measurements: 375 feet length × 51 feet breadth. Engines: T3cyl. *1916: (Standard Transportation Co. Ltd., Hong Kong). 1924: *Nord Atlantic* (Atlantic Tank Rhederei GmbH, Hamburg). 1934: *Iossifoglu* (S. Iossifoglu, Greece). 1937: *Ilford* (Cia Primera de Nav., Panama). 1937: *Yolanda* (Cia Primera de Nav., Panama). 1939: *Santa Helena* (Cia Primera de Nav., Panama). 1941: *Campechano* (Cia Arrendataria del Monopolio de Petroleos S.A. Spain). 8.1962: Scrapped Valencia, Spain.
Winamac	8.1913	5,767	Built by Craig, Taylor & Co. Ltd., Stockton, for Anglo-American Oil Co. Ltd., but delivered direct to Tank Storage & Carriage Co. Ltd. Measurements: 412 feet length × 53 feet breadth. Engines: Quad. *1916: (Standard Transportation Co. Ltd., Hong Kong). 1934: Broken up.
Shabonee	10.1913	5,167	Built by Sir James Laing & Sons Ltd., Sunderland, for Anglo-American Oil Co. Ltd. Delivered direct to Tank Storage & Carriage Co. Ltd. Measurements: 380 feet length × 50 feet 8 inches breadth. Engines: T3cyl. *1916: (Standard Transportation Co. Ltd., Hong Kong). 1932: Sold to Chinese buyers for scrapping.

The *Comanchee*, which had a life span of thirty-seven years.   *Esso*

Tascalusa

| *Tascalusa* | 12.1913 | 6,499 | Built by Sir R. Dixon & Co. Ltd., Middlesbrough, for Anglo-American Oil Co. Ltd. Delivered direct to Tank Storage & Carriage Co. Ltd. Measurements: 420 feet 6 inches length × 54 feet 4 inches breadth. Engines: Quad. *1916: (Standard Transportation Co. Ltd., Hong Kong). |

On 10th July, 1940, being fitted with guns in preparation for Admiralty service and berthed alongside the Northern Arm at Falmouth, the ship was struck aft by bombs during an enemy air attack. Both ship and wharf caught fire and the *Tascalusa* sank by the stern, partly submerged, resting on the bottom in twenty-five feet of water, with the forward tanks keeping her bows buoyant and afloat.

Left to burn itself out, the fire was finally extinguished three days later. Remaining oil cargo on board was discharged and divers commenced patching and plugging the damaged shell plating and bulkheads.

Refloated on 29th August, the *Tascalusa* was beached on the Mylor mud flats. Declared a constructive total loss, she was sold for scrapping in November, 1940, to T. W. Ward & Company.

| *Tamaha* | 6.1914 | 6,496 | Built by Sir R. Dixon & Co. Ltd., Middlesbrough, for Anglo-American Oil Co. Ltd. Delivered direct to Tank Storage & Carriage Co. Ltd. Measurements: 420 feet 6 inches length × 54 feet 4 inches breadth. Engines: Quad. *1916: (Standard Transportation Co. Ltd., Hong Kong). 1940: (Socony-Vacuum Transportation Co., Montreal (British flag)). 1949: (Soc. Mazout Transports, Paris (Cie de Nav. Mixte, Marseilles)). 1953: Scrapped Spain. |

| *Tahchee* | 9.1914 | 6,508 | Built by Sir R. Dixon & Co. Ltd., Middlesbrough, for Anglo-American Oil Co. Ltd. Delivered direct to Tank Storage & Carriage Co. Ltd., |

Measurements: 420 feet 6 inches length × 54 feet 4 inches breadth.
Engines: Quad.
*1916: (Standard Transportation Co. Ltd., Hong Kong).
1940: (Socony Vacuum Transportation Co., Montreal (British flag)).
10.9.1941: Damaged by torpedo from *U.652* in position 61.15N 41.05W while in convoy SC 42 (Sydney NS/ United Kingdom—oil).
11.1950: Scrapped Milford Haven.

After the torpedo hit, the crew of the *Tahchee* saw in the moonlight what appeared to be the attacking submarine on the surface, some four miles away, and opened fire with their four-inch gun. Six rounds were fired and the object smashed to pieces, but when the Canadian corvette *Orillia* dashed to the scene she found only small pieces of ice; the submarine had been a small "growler".

By then the *Tahchee* was on fire and the crew took to the boats. Later, she was re-boarded, the captain and two officers extinguishing the fire. The captain then called the *Orillia* for a volunteer crew. Thirty men volunteered, three engine room ratings from the corvette and the remainder being the *Tahchee*'s crew.

Steam was raised on one boiler, and using hand steering gear, she was taken in tow by the *Orillia*, which used her own wire and the tanker's cable. Seven knots was achieved.

It was then decided to transfer oil from the tanker to the corvette, for towing a laden ship makes heavy demands on fuel. The *Orillia* slipped her tow rope but the tanker's windlass broke, the cable ran right out and all towing gear was lost. Attempts were made to bunker the *Orillia* alongside through an ordinary canvas fire hose, but as the steam heating had broken down, the heavy oil could not be made to flow. Next day, after a night of repair work on the heating, some oil was thinned and transferred, despite the continual breaking of the hoses. Then the other boiler was brought into use and the *Tahchee*, under her own steam, reached Reykjavik, 592 miles and five and a half days from the point of attack.
Note: Tahchee was a chief of the Cherokee tribe of Red Indians.

| *Tatarrax* | 1.1914 | 6,216 | Built by Scotts Shipbuilding & Engineering Co. Ltd., Greenock, for Anglo-American Oil Co. Ltd. Delivered direct to Tank Storage & Carriage Co.Ltd. |

Measurements: 420 feet length × 55 feet breadth.
Engines: Quad.
*1916: (Standard Transportation Co. Ltd., Hong Kong).
11.8.1918: Sunk by submarine (*UC.34*) torpedo and internal explosion, 32N 30.45E, while serving as an Admiralty oiler (voyage: Port Said/Alexandria—benzole).

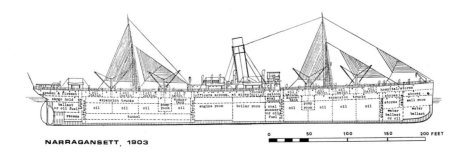

NARRAGANSETT, 1903

0   50   100   150   200 FEET

London River . . . and the Purfleet story

Within two years of the first oil cargo being brought in by the brig *Elizabeth Watts* in 1862, the annual import of oil into the River Thames reached 140,000 tons and during the next ten years the amount imported into London's river increased considerably.

But these years were not without their tragedies, for the increase in trade also brought a corresponding increase in the number of already common-place explosions involving oil-laden vessels. Clearly, safety measures had become necessary to protect the port. In 1871 an Act of Parliament gave powers to the Thames Conservancy to restrict the handling of low flashpoint oil (petroleum) to the lower reaches of the estuary and to prohibit its transportation further upriver than Thames Haven. Here, ships arriving with oil for upriver delivery had to moor at fixed buoys and discharge the cargo into barges, the Act stipulating that the oil be carried "in covered barges built of iron".

In 1875 a wharf, known as the Haven Petroleum Wharf, was constructed on the north (Essex) bank of the river, just upstream of the limit, and at the same time the bye-laws were amended to allow oil-carrying vessels to discharge there without special permission. Soon afterwards, a storage depot was added and by the turn of the century this had become a fifteen-tank "farm", capable of holding stocks of over 8,000 tons belonging to a number of importers. By the start of the First World War its storage capacity had mushroomed to some 300,000 tons in seventy-five tanks, the installation being served through three jetties.

In the Thames Estuary the Shell Company was the first in the refinery business, beginning operations in 1916 on the adjoining Shell Haven site with a single distillation unit. Acquisition of the site was a well-planned move which immediately linked the trading name and the location of the plant. The site was not given its name by the Shell Company; Shell Haven had been known by that name for centuries, appearing on sixteenth-century maps and also receiving mentions in both the famous "Diary" of Samuel Pepys and in the Domesday Book. In 1922 yet another refinery with storage depot was opened by Cory Brothers and appropriately named Coryton. Today the present refinery there is owned by the Mobil Oil Company. Its construction commenced in 1950 and the official opening ceremony was carried out by the Queen Mother in May, 1954.

A month or so after registration in 1888, the Anglo-American Company opened a storage unit at Purfleet. Despite the claims of the new company in many of its early advertisements that Purfleet was "at the mouth of the River Thames" it is very much more than halfway up the river, situated only sixteen miles from London.

Purfleet, once a small hamlet on the north (Essex) bank of the River Thames, has a history stretching back for centuries. Purfleet, or Purteflyete, or Pourtflet, or Purteflete, or almost any variation thereof, was one of King Harold's manors before the Norman Conquest and afterwards was presented by William to one of his barons as a share of the spoils of war. Thus, much of its known history begins with a most familiar date in English history, 1066.

It was not an attractive area. Most of it was marshland, and a mediaeval "sea-wall", built of reeds, had vanished. Purfleet slumbered on in rural peace, surviving plagues and fevers, continuing its quiet riverside and country existence and maintaining an ancient ferry service across the river to the opposite misty shores of North Kent. And pilgrims, on their way to Canterbury, could offer up a prayer in the nearby church of St Clement for a sober ferryman and a safe crossing. In the seventeenth century chalk diggings were begun on the surrounding land and these and the river between them quickly sealed Purfleet's destiny, isolated as it was by reason of its geographical position and its geology.

In the mid-eighteenth century the military arrived. The large powder magazines near the Royal Palace at Greenwich were moved to Purfleet and a garrison installed. Suddenly the sleepy village awoke. Five large powder stores, a quay at the waterside for the landing of the powder and barracks for the garrison were built. Men-of-war tied up alongside Magazine Wharf to

The Purfleet terminal at the turn of the century. *Esso*

take on powder before sailing, and after the Crimean War surplus powder was stored in two hulks, *Conquestador* and *Mermaid*, anchored in Purfleet Creek.

By 1812 Purfleet was described as a "small, dirty, garrison town", but what it could boast was the first railway in Essex and certainly one of the first in England. "Chalk", it was written, "was got into vessels much more easily than before, by having laid parallel strips of iron, called railroads, along which one horse can draw a wagon with three times as much as it could without the rails".

The twenty-five horses employed, it is recorded, were reduced to four when the "rail way" was laid. Redundancy, it seems, was associated with productivity some 180 years ago, if only for horses. But it was to be some years before a main line of the nation's expanding railway network was laid to Tilbury and later on to the fashionable resort of Southend-on-Sea. By 1854 the route from London was established, thousands of day trippers and excursionists mingling with passengers of the ships at Tilbury and at Gravesend on the south bank of the river.

In the 1880s there was more invasion of the tranquillity of the Purfleet riverside as the oil industry arrived. Anglo-American completed a depot there in 1888 but were not the first to come to the area, for the depot actually adjoined the premises of the already established Anglo-Russian Oil Company. The site of the new depot was on land reclaimed from the river which Anglo-American had bought, and here they erected five bulk oil

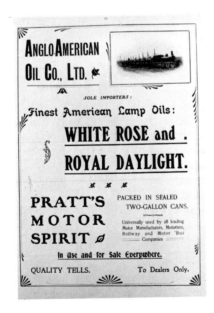

An old advertisement for Anglo-American oils.

Girls fastening and sealing the Green Cans at Purfleet.   *Esso*

storage reservoirs. A wooden jetty was built and there was also a small boiler house with a tall chimney to serve ancillary plant.

But river restrictions prevented the movement of low-flash petroleum upstream and for many years the company was forced to store its volatile commodity at the Thames Haven Oil Wharves. High flashpoint kerosene, in the five grades of "White Rose", "Crown Diamond", "Tea Rose", "Westminster" and "Royal Daylight", was handled at Purfleet. In the early days it arrived in barrels, but was soon being shipped in bulk, not only to reduce handling costs but to meet the growing demand for the product for heating and lighting purposes.

Bulk supplies were brought in by Anglo-American tankers, two of which, *Manhattan* and *Bayonne*, completed in 1889, had a more advanced design than any tanker then afloat. They wore the Anglo-American houseflag which portrayed a black eagle astride a white ball, with navy blue and deep red diagonal sections as its background colours. On arrival at Purfleet, barrels were decanted and bulk kerosene transferred to the storage tanks, these being nominally owned by the Purfleet Tank Storage Company, but situated within the confines of the Anglo-American premises. Later, the storage

37

company lost its separate identity and was absorbed into the parent group. Following kerosene, gas oils and other types of fuels were imported and with the general expansion of industry and the coming of the motor car, so were lubricating oils. For these additional products more storage facilities were installed and extra plant constructed for the complicated process of lubricating oil blending. At this stage Anglo-American acquired the adjacent oil plant owned by the Anglo-Russian Oil Company.

During the 1914–18 war, work at Purfleet continued day and night to keep to War Office and Admiralty requirements and by the end of the war there were fifty-eight large storage tanks. Purfleet was then the largest unloading and storage depot in Britain. Many of the Company's bulk-carrying tankers were taken over by the Government for war purposes, and much of the imported oil arrived in barrels again. These were immediately emptied and re-shipped on the same vessel back to the United States. But dumping the oil in the old way of cutting out the bungs and letting the contents run into a trough was not quick enough to keep the discharge going at the rate required. To eliminate this problem a device was made which made it possible to pump the oil out of 3,000 to 4,000 barrels each day, helping in quicker turnround of ships. During the Great War years the Purfleet installations were raided by German Gotha bombers and by Zeppelins, although there was no serious damage.

Twenty years later, in 1938, cautious preparations for war were again under way. One was a combined agreement between the Home Office, the Port of London Authority, created in 1908 as successor to the Thames Conservancy to administer the tidal reaches of the river, and various local authorities for the removal of the restrictions which still confined the waterborne handling of petroleum spirit to the estuary. A new limit was fixed at Crayfordness, the upstream end of Long Reach, and as Purfleet was now within this new limit it rapidly became a multi-company centre for all kinds of oil handling and bunkering, vessels no longer having to obtain special permission to discharge this far upriver. The amended limits enabled laden tankers to discharge directly overside at Anglo-American's Nos 1 and 2 jetties. To handle the increased throughput the company purchased farmland and more storage tanks were erected. Underground spirit tanks and pump rooms, each enveloped and separated by walls of chalk not less than fifty feet thick, were built into the hill behind the depot—now known as the Terminal—and these were completed just before the outbreak of war in 1939. And not a moment too soon.

Purfleet Terminal, lying on "bomber's highway"—the River Thames—was always an attactive target. During 1940, twenty direct hits were recorded and in 1941 further German air raids on the Terminal caused much devastation and destruction. Ships berthed alongside were hit and caught fire and ashore there were many fires and explosions, some of the fires burning for more than a week. There was also some loss of life. Fortunately, however, a holocaust was avoided.

Bombs on Purfleet—a photograph taken by the Luftwaffe in 1940. *Esso*

Early Anglo-American steam coasters

Coastal shipping has long been an important factor of Britain's merchant fleet. Over the centuries, long before oil became the principal source of energy, colliers were transporting the heavy and bulky cargoes of coal from the ports of the coalfields to other coastal ports and upriver wharves and depots to feed the growing industries of Britain. Along Britain's East Coast a constant stream of loaded ships moved southwards from the North-east ports to London with coal for domestic users. At first there were the sailing ships, the collier brigs, each carrying 300 or more tons. And as sail began to yield to steam there evolved the steam-driven collier, at first with engines amidships but later changing to engines aft design.

These were the ships that fed the huge gas and electricity undertakings and the great and growing industries with vast quantities of the solid fuel, so much so that the inevitable pollution, when it came, was a major problem.

The railways, canals and the roads that existed were also feeder routes in the country's internal communications system but for bulk cargoes the coaster was the cheapest form of transport, particularly in the carrying of fuels. Movements of kerosene by Anglo-American coastal ships began in British waters just before the turn of the century, much being loaded at the company's main import depot at Purfleet for transport to lesser depots around the coast.

The first coaster, *Osceola*, came in 1897 and was capable of carrying 380 tons in bulk. Her engines were amidships, there was a well deck and right aft a towing bar was fitted. She worked for many years to the South Coast of England and to Dublin and must have been one of the first ships to have been bombed by aircraft. This was in the North Sea on 22nd March, 1915. Fortunately, she was not hit. In the 1930s she moved to the Tyne area.

In the early days the coastal fleet grew but slowly. By 1904 it comprised two steamers, the *Osceola* and the recently-acquired *Imperial*, as well as the small sailing vessel *Queen of the Avon*.

The *Osceola* remained in the fleet until the 1930s and was thirty-seven years old when scrapped. The others were replaced by two specially designed steamers. The first of these was *Oneida*, built in 1908, longer and with a greater breadth than the earlier ship. Another feature was that her triple expansion engine was placed aft. She also had a well deck. The *Oneida* worked through both wars and was broken up in 1947. Another coaster, *Tioga*, was delivered in 1912. Slightly larger than both *Osceola* and *Oneida*, she was lost in 1943.

For many years the *Oneida* and *Tioga* were Britain's best coastal tankers. Both had very large tank hatches as well as special internal fittings to permit the carriage of barrels, although this was never done.

40

Anglo-American's first coaster, the *Osceola*.   *Tom Rayner*

	Completed	Gross tons
Osceola	12.1897	393

Built by D. J. Dunlop & Co., Port Glasgow.
Measurements: 141 feet length × 26 feet breadth.
Engines: T3cyl. 9 knots.
12.1934: Scrapped by South Stockton Shipbreaking Co.

Imperial	5.1898	796

Built by Tyne Iron Shipbuilding Co., Newcastle, as *Minoco*
   for the Mineral Oil Corporation (Hunting & Son).
Measurements: 200 feet length × 32 feet breadth. Built of
   iron and steel.
Engines: T3cyl.
1901: *Imperial* (Anglo-American Oil Co.).
1902: First tanker on lakes of Canada.
2.1912: (Imperial Oil Co. Ltd., Sarnia, Ontario).
7.1922: Towed to Vancouver for service in British
   Columbian waters.
1938: *Impoco* (renamed to make way for a new building of
   the same name.).
1939: Broken up by Capital Iron & Steel Co., Victoria,
   British Columbia.

Oneida	10.1908	698

Built by Greenock & Grangemouth Dockyard Co.,
   Grangemouth.
Measurements: 165 feet length × 32 feet breadth.
741 tdw.
Engines: T3cyl (aft).
7.1947: Scrapped Troon.

Oneida under way in November, 1931. *T. Rayner*

Tioga	2.1912	742	Built by Greenock & Grangemouth Dockyard Co., Grangemouth.

Measurements: 180 feet length × 31 feet breadth.
Engines: T3cyl (aft).
1.11.1943: In collision near Hartlepool, 55.40N 1.30W with British Steamer *Pundit* (19/5,305 gt) while on voyage from Middlesbrough to Grangemouth in ballast. Taken in tow but sank in vertical position, with bows above water, 5 miles from Longstone Lighthouse.
3.11.1943: Sunk by naval gunfire.
The engine of the *Tioga* was fitted for the burning of oil fuel, although she used coal throughout her career.

Apart from the steam coasters, there were two sailing ships in the coastal business:

Queen of the Avon	1856	162	Built by J. Vernon, Newcastle, as *Gudrun* for Erichson, Copenhagen.

Iron-hulled sailing vessel, rigged as a snow (two-masted, brig-rigged, with square sails on both masts).
Measurements: 101 feet length × 20 feet breadth.
1900: (Anglo-American). Used in coastwise trade, carrying oil in barrels.

Morning Star	1872	65	Built by R. M. Shrubsall, Milton, near Sittingbourne, Kent, for A. Dickinson, London.

Coasting ketch-barge, rigged as a dandy.
Measurements: 85 feet length × 18 feet breadth.
120 tdw.
1902: (B. Hill, Southsea, Hants).
1907: (Anglo-American).
1921: Disposed of.

River craft

Four small, early Anglo-American river craft shared only two names between them, the regulations concerning the duplication of names of vessels in service at the same time not coming into force until around 1911.

	Completed	Gross tons	
White Rose (tug)	1893	49	Built by D. J. Dunlop & Co., Port Glasgow. Measurements: 63 feet length × 15 feet breadth. 1895: (Anglo-American). 1954: Scrapped.
Royal Daylight (tug)	1902	83	Built by J. Stewart & Sons, Blackwall, London, as Tea Rose. Measurements: 75 feet length × 17 feet breadth. 1955: Scrapped.
Royal Daylight	1902	53	Built by Gordon Alison & Co., Birkenhead. Measurements: 72 feet length × 15 feet breadth. 1903: (Anglo-American). A tank barge for service on the River Mersey. 1947: Converted to a stationary barge.

On 14th November, 1940, the *Royal Daylight*, in tow of the tug *White Rose* (1906) in the River Mersey, was struck by the motorship *Moray Coast* (687 gt, 1940) of Coast Lines Ltd. She was towed to Salisbury Dock where she capsized and sank. The *Royal Daylight* was later raised, repaired and re-entered service. The *Moray Coast* had only been delivered a few days from Ardrossan Dockyard Ltd.

White Rose	1906	44	Built by Gordon Alison & Co., Birkenhead, as a sailing vessel. Measurements: 69 feet length × 14 feet breadth. 1926: Petrol engine fitted. 70 bhp. For River Mersey service. *1955: (A. Hutchinson & Sons).

The Esso tug *Royal Daylight* on the Thames.

Oil barges for London's rivers

On 31st March, 1910, the Anglo-American Oil Company registered a fleet of thirty-two non-propelled (dumb) barges with the recently formed Port of London Authority for the carrying of petroleum in the area of the River Thames.

There were four distinct types. Two types for use in the general waters of the river were of varied capacities, ranging from 50 to 229 tons and subdivided into either tank barges for the carriage of petroleum spirit in bulk or open barges to carry barrels and drums. The other two types were for specific use in particular tributaries or creeks of the river, such as Barking Creek/River Roding; Bow Creek/River Lea; Dartford Creek/River Darent; and in the Regent's Canal Dock area. All these waterways were described as "London canals" in port registration.

In comparison with those for general use, the canal barges were "narrow" craft of uniform size, their breadth (and depth) reduced to permit navigation in the confined waters.

All but one of these barges survived both world wars, until they were disposed of or replaced in the early 1950s. The *Lancashire*, *Suffolk* and *York* were requisitioned for war service in 1941–42 and the *Nottingham* was lost (destroyed) on 22nd August, 1940.

For river work

Open barges:	Measured from 59 feet length × 15 feet breadth to 93 feet × 23 feet. Tonnages ranged from 30 gt/50 tdw to 137 gt/229 tdw.				
	Bucks	*Brecknock*	*Cardigan*	*Denbigh*	*Durham*
	Flint	*Hants*	*Lancashire*	*Pembroke*	*York*
Tank barges:	Measured from 80 feet length × 21 feet breadth to 89 feet × 17½ feet. Tonnages ranged from 54 gt/91 tdw to 97 gt/173 tdw.				
	Cornwall	*Cheshire*	*Devon*	*Dorset*	*Surrey*
	Sussex	*Somerset*	*Stafford*	*Warwick*	

For canal work

	Measurements: 79 feet length × 14 feet breadth × 5 feet depth. Tonnage: 44 gt 75 tdw.				
Open barges:	*Bedford*	*Gloucester*	*Oxford*		
Tank barges:	*Cambridge*	*Derby*	*Essex*	*Hertford*	*Lincoln*
	Middlesex	*Norfolk*	*Nottingham*	*Rutland*	*Suffolk*

Moving the petroleum

In 1908, at the time of the formation of the Port of London Authority as successors to the Thames Conservancy, the Petroleum Acts in force regulated imports of spirit, although the export trade was free of control.

By 1911 the representatives of the petroleum trade were complaining bitterly that the import regulations stating that no oil-carrying vessels were allowed upstream of Thames Haven, in the estuary, were unduly onerous. The grounds were that a serious and unnecessary burden of charges was being placed on . . . "an article of daily increasing importance; an agent for locomotion and traction" . . . that Thames Haven was too distant and that Purfleet, nearer London, be substituted.

In the same year a Special Committee, empowered to take evidence and make recommendations, was set up to consider the problem. Its verdict was that the risks of allowing tankers to proceed further upriver could be serious for other ships and bankside industries, and it recommended that Thames Haven be maintained as the upstream limit.

However, at the same time, representations had been made for the extension of facilities for licensed craft carrying petroleum spirit above Thames Haven, which was then restricted to 45,000 gallons (150 tons) per craft, with no more than four of the craft being towed together. On this point the committee recommended that the limit, per craft, be raised to 75,000 gallons (250 tons) and suggested the granting of licences for self-propelled, specially-constructed craft with divided tank space, a total capacity not to exceed 150,000 gallons (500 tons), and the motive power to be an internal

The *Imperial*, completed in 1898 as the *Minoco*. *Esso*

combustion engine of a type in which ignition was effected otherwise than by any form of spark, flame or hot tube. These particular recommendations were accepted.

During 1912–13 the P.L.A. considered applications from the Anglo-American Oil Company for relief from certain conditions imposed by the Thames Conservancy for jetty installations at Purfleet. This restricted discharging or loading of petroleum spirit at the jetty from or into licensed barges and relief was granted, subject to certain conditions. Also, in March, 1913, the P.L.A. agreed to provide moorings at Rainham for petroleum barges unable to reach their destination in daylight, as required by the bye-laws.

Another petroleum company, Anglo-Saxon, applied in January, 1916, for permission to discharge petroleum from tank steamers at their Shell Haven jetty by means of a ship's own steam. The application was declined by the port authority in view of the bye-law which prohibited any fire or artificial light on board a petroleum ship during discharge, but at the end of war, in November, 1918, an Order was made by the Shipping Controller under the Defence of the Realm Regulations permitting discharge of petroleum in the port by a ship's own steam. The port authority protested to no avail, but the Order was revoked on 9th May, 1919.

On 15th August, 1920, an explosion occurred on the sailing barge *Dorcas*, which was in Woolwich Reach, outward bound with 450 barrels of petroleum. The vessel and cargo caught fire, drifted into barge roads and set other vessels and premises on fire. At the subsequent Court of Inquiry it was found that the standing bye-laws did not apply, the vessel carrying petroleum for export, and that no regulations controlled the suitability of a vessel for carrying such cargo.

Only five weeks later an explosion occurred on Anglo-American's empty tank barge *Warwick*, lying alongside at Millwall for repairs, due to the use of an oxy-acetylene torch to repair tanks containing a mixture of petroleum vapour and air. To prevent further casualties of a similar nature, the bye-laws were again amended.

Anglo-American applied to the P.L.A. in February, 1924, for permission to discharge low-test petroleum from sea-going vessels at their premises in Purfleet. The P.L.A.'s response was that in view of improvements to modern vessels some relaxation of the restrictions should be allowed. and it decided to allow petroleum spirit and low-test petroleum upriver to a point "seaward of Barking Creek" and proceeded to re-draft the bye-laws, revising the limit to include the storage installations at Purfleet. But Shell-Mex Ltd., the Anglo-Saxon Petroleum Company and Eagle Oil Transport Company strongly opposed the proposals, as did the London County Council, and the P.L.A. abandoned its intention to alter the limit to a point at Crayfordness.

Two years later, in 1926, it was admitted that modern electricity was not the killer it was thought to be, when both the Ministry of Transport and the P.L.A. allowed the use of electric light on a petroleum ship during discharge.

Application was again made in 1927 by Anglo-American, British Petroleum Company Ltd., Glico Petroleum Ltd., Harrisons (London) Ltd., and the Thames Land Company for a revision of the bye-laws, to permit the navigation of petroleum ships further upstream, to Crayfordness. A public

Dawn at Purfleet, 5th March, 1958: loaded lighters await their tow on the flood tide.   *Esso*

inquiry was set up to look into the matter and following its report, the Minister of Transport gave his decision:

1) That alteration in the existing limit of navigation for petroleum ships was undesirable,
2) that ships carrying not more than 1,000 tons of petroleum spirit in barrels or drums should be allowed to navigate as far upstream as Bow Creek,
3) that ships carrying not more than 2,000 gallons in barrels or drums should be allowed to navigate throughout the Port of London.

During the 1930s a variety of minor regulations came into force, and in 1937 it was permitted that tank ships and tank barges could, subject to certain safeguards, commence discharging or loading of cargo during hours of darkness. In 1938 restrictions were relaxed, allowing petroleum-laden ships upriver to the Purfleet installations and as far as Crayfordness, two miles further upstream. The additional two-mile limit, to a somewhat wider and less industrialised stretch of the river, gave tankers a better turning circle or area in which to swing without the manoeuvre having to be performed in the confined waters immediately adjacent to the oil installations.

On 4th September, 1939, the Ministry of Transport, under wartime legislation, made an Order superseding the port bye-laws although, in the main, it preserved most of the previous features. In fact, it was not until 1953 that the port bye-laws again became effective after revocation of the wartime orders.

Filling Green Cans at Purfleet in 1920. *Esso*

CHAPTER THREE

Barrels, Tins and the Sailing Oil Ships

IN THE middle years of the nineteenth century oil was used mostly for lighting and heating, but lubricating oils for the new machine age were becoming increasingly required. More and more sailing ships were being transferred from dry cargo to the expanding oil carrying trade, which resulted in some undercutting of freight rates. There were also numerous fires which caused consternation in the insurance market.

The oil barrel in which oil was first transported on the high seas was a costly freight item to carry, by reason of its shape. Too great a cubic capacity was occupied for each ton of cargo carried to make transport economical; and too many barrels leaked and had to be discarded. Yet the wooden barrel—or cask—once described as the universal package was used worldwide, its popularity in the main being due to the ease with which it could be handled. It could be rolled, up-ended, hoisted in a sling with only a pair of hooks, and instantly released. In its prime years as an undisputed universal container, one man, without mechanical aid, could handle a loaded barrel of over 400 lb in weight, a feat which could not be performed in any other way. The barrel itself was a most economical package, for in its heyday no other container would last so long or cost so little in repair.

The heavier kinds of barrels, such as those used by brewers, were made to last twenty years, while many of them lasted thirty or even forty years. The oil barrel belonged to the lighter class of cooperage, being made of only three-quarter-inch-thick oak. Its initial cost was much about the same as for a packing case of similar capacity. When empty, there was always a ready market for the barrel, frequently at a higher figure than it had cost when bought with the oil. And it would be filled again and again. Then, with time, or too damaged to hold oil, many of the remaining fine timbers could still be used by cabinet makers and other craftsmen.

In the early frenzied days of the oil business in the United States, customers bought oil in barrels which they often provided themselves. Prices were set by the barrel and just about any size and any kind qualified, so long as it suited the buyer and was not too commodious in the eyes of the seller. But such an arrangement caused a great deal of confusion, much friction and was certainly unbusinesslike. Tempers frayed, prices rose and fell and it became evident that a realistic measure had to be established. It was in June, 1866, that a group of producers in West Virginia issued an agreed declaration of their new trading terms. In part, it said ". . . we agree to sell oil not by the barrel or package, but by the gallon only. An allowance of two gallons will be made on the gauge for each and every forty gallons, in favour of the buyer." But while the gallon was specified as the measure, it was a forty-two-gallon barrel that gradually emerged as a common unit, through years of common usage. It still continues as the unit of measure in which records and statistics are kept for every drop of oil drawn from the earth. But it exists only in statistics. An actual barrel—or drum—of oil today generally contains fifty gallons.

The size of a barrel was thirty-three inches in length and twenty-five inches in diameter, with a full weight of about 400 lb. Standards were drawn up by the New York Produce Exchange that they should be made of oak, with differentiating widths to the number of hoops. They were classified: First class = refined petroleum or naphtha, Second class = crude oil, and Third class = residuum.

The next step—the tin can

In 1881 Standard Oil in the United States manufactured more than four and a half million barrels for the transport of oil and although this method of transportation was beginning to be replaced by the bulk carriage of oil, the company still produced more than three million new barrels in 1901.

However, rising in importance was the tin can. It has been first used for oil in the 1850s when it was the usual package in which coal oil was sold. In 1865 Charles Pratt, an early refiner who became an associate of John D. Rockefeller, hired a German inventor, Herman Miller, to improve the package, at a time when one man and a boy were soldering 850 cans in a day. This he did, and Miller became known as the "Father of the five-gallon can". As early as 1868 one firm, Rockefeller, Flagler and Andrews, contracted for the manufacture of 300,000 five-gallon oil cans, to be used in shipping refined products overseas. Enormous quantities were being made, their manufacture being one of the earliest mass production operations. By the late 1880s one single plant was turning out and filling 60,000 tins a day in a continuous process. This was Standard Oil's own plant, Devoe, the largest can-making factory in the world, on the East River, Long Island City. But though the Standard Oil Company still shipped much of its exports in wooden barrels, tins were preferred, in fact they were essential when they were destined for a tropical or Far East country with limited transportation facilities. Tin containers better withstood tropical heat, which sometimes cause glued barrels to develop leaks. The tin also prevented deterioriation of the oil, which often occurred with other forms of container.

At Devoe tinplate was brought in from Wales because it was cheaper than that produced in America, and in 1901 Standard Oil imported over 60,000 tons. It arrived in sheet form, packed in flat wooden boxes. These were opened by simply throwing or dropping them, the impact being usually sufficient to "spring" the lid off. A refinery was situated close to the cannery. Oil was piped from one to the other and as newly-made cans came down a chute they were filled, twelve at a time. Lined up on a sector of a turntable which revolved, the cans came under twelve measures, each of five gallons. One valve was turned—and the cans filled. A quarter-turn of the turntable and twelve more were filled . . . and so on.

Empties replaced the filled cans, whose caps were soldered on by a line of four men. Pairs of five-gallon cans were placed in wooden boxes and became case-oil. After standing for twenty-four hours to show any leakage, the boxes were nailed down and loaded through doors opening on to the East River where a ship, immediately alongside, awaited its cargo.

Case-oil

The oil container had certainly changed, but it was still expensive packaging. Damaged and leaking tins caused seepage into the timbered holds of the ships, which hindered the finding of return cargoes. Once opened and unpacked ashore, the wooden cases were useless and the wood had to be discarded for local use. So were the tins. Yet the era of the tin was an important phase in the petroleum industry and the tin can was used long after the shipment of oil in bulk had been introduced. It became an important and sometimes essential part of community life, especially in the East where there was a continual and increasing demand for kerosene. The tin was easy to handle on unmade paths, tracks and foreshores; two cases could conveniently be slung across the back of a pack animal. Tins also became invaluable in remote parts of the world as household utensils and even as building material, hammered flat to become roofing and walls of village huts. The case which contained the tins measured twenty and three-quarter inches long, ten and a half inches wide and fifteen inches in depth and the weight of tins and case was 80 lb gross. The tins were hermetically sealed with a screw cap for later use.

In the closing years of the century the power-driven tankship was in its ascendancy, the sailing ship slowly on its way out, yet there was still trade for low cost cargo. The long-haul voyages to India and Japan were much more economical under sail and in countries where houses often lacked light of any kind, kerosene was welcomed. Bulk oil storage installations had not yet reached the East in any great number, neither were there many lines of distribution for oil in bulk.

Anglo-American carefully studied the market potential of China and the Far East and at the end of the century began acquiring ships for a case-oil trade. By then, case-oil was considered a "clean" cargo when handled and carried; quite suitable for stowage in a general cargo hold. A marketing name for the kerosene was chosen. It was "White Camelia".

Case-oil was not quite new. Some had been sent from Russia to China a few years previously and some came from Sumatra in the 1890s, first in cases, then in bulk.

The sailing ships left the North-east ports of the United States and returned with coal from Australia, ore from Vizagapatam and tea from Hong Kong. Between 1899 and 1901 twelve sailing ships were acquired by Anglo-American to begin the Far East case-oil trade, eight more being ordered from British shipyards. By 1903 all were in service and such was the trade that in 1907 there were still seventeen sailing vessels in the Anglo-American fleet, mostly four-masted and very economical steel barques, all flying the Red Ensign.

Building up a market in China proved particularly difficult. The people were accustomed to using vegetable oils for lighting, extracted from the peanut and the bean; kerosene was new and considered dangerous; and the producers of local vegetable illuminants informed the peasant masses in anti-kerosene propaganda that it was "a product of human bones" and should not be used. Moreover, there was no suitable receptacle in which to burn kerosene until the agents of the parent Standard Oil Company imported for their own trade, to sell for a nominal sum, a simple, sturdy little lamp with a tin bowl and a small glass chimney that became known in China as "Mei Foo" or "beautiful companion". It very soon became a familiar household object.

The sailing ships used Hong Kong and Shanghai, the chief ports for the markets of China. In the harbour of Hong Kong, crown colony of Britain since 1841 and at the mouth of the Chu Kiang (Pearl) River, the barques discharged their thousands of cases of tinned kerosene. Each case with two tins, the two full tins weighing sixty-five pounds; each tin containing five gallons of illuminant . . . oil for the lamps of China.

The oil companies were big importers, some operating through agencies. There were also many local importers, all part of the huge distributing network. By river craft the cases were carried up the Canton River; to Nan-Ning on the Si Kiang (West) River, which was to become a treaty port in 1907; by junk along the south China Sea coast, by ageing steamers across the straits to Formosa, and 200 miles south west, to Hainan. The distribution area from Hong Kong was regarded to be south of the 25° parallel. Hundreds

Unloading case-oil from a riverboat in Ceylon, 1910.   *Brown Brothers*

of ships of many types carried the cases in hazardous conditions. There were old wooden sailers, vintage tramp steamers, and junks of all sizes, complete with family. Some regulations were applied to the vessels; electrical wiring was forbidden to the hold; a cofferdam between hold and stokehold was essential; vents had to be screened with wire mesh and an oil-tight bulkhead between the forward hold and fo'c'stle or chain locker was required.

Shanghai, 900 miles north-west from Hong Kong, is on the Yellow Sea coast. Greatest of Chinese ports, it stands twelve miles up the Hwangpu tidal stream which flows into the estuary of the mighty Yangtse-Kiang, its source 3,200 miles distant in the high plateau of Tibet. There, in Shanghai's huge, bustling harbour, the barques would discharge their case-oil, many cases for transshipment to river craft and junks; some for storage. Some cases would be carried to the very heart of China; then on by road, path or track to the remotest of villages, there to be sold by the case, by the tin or even by the wine bottle. Stone-built stores, with iron roof and wooden supports, were erected at the port, each to hold 200,000 cases; so much did trade grow that there was soon a total storage capacity for two million cases.

Some kerosene in bulk was imported in small quantities by several oil companies at Amoy, Swatow and Hankow from Russia and Sumatra for local consumption, but importations at Hong Kong and Shanghai were treated

53

The barque *Lawhill* leaving Falmouth for le Havre, 29th May, 1929.

differently. At these ports there was great competition between importers and local merchants. The two-tin pack from the United States weighed 65 lb, but by using locally produced tins, a weight of 68 lb could be obtained, a useful bartering margin. Some bulk oil was re-shipped coastwise in bulk in small quantities. At Shanghai imports of oil were regularly checked by Customs officials to determine the specific gravity and so assess the gallonage liable to duty. However, no flashpoint test was made, the term flashpoint apparently then being quite unknown to both Customs and local oil merchants.

And the trade grew, two million cases each year being imported in the sailing ships as the century began.

Many technological improvements in the carriage of oil by sea can be attributed to the oil sailers in which new ideas were tested, abandoned or adopted. Among the latter were the fitting of expansion tanks, the trials and monitoring of pressure control of expansion and the introduction of bulkhead tanks. Other modifications and improvements were tried in these ships, then later added to the steam tankers being constructed in ever-increasing size for the carriage of oil in bulk.

Disposal of the sailing ship fleet began about 1909. There were eight left in 1911; four, *Brilliant*, *Daylight*, *Calcutta* and *Drumeltan*, still sailed for Anglo-American in 1914 but only one, *Calcutta*, was left after the war ended.

The acquired ships

	Completed	Gross tons	
Alcides	10.1892	2,704	Built by Greenock & Grangemouth Dockyard Co. for John R. Haws & Co., Liverpool. Measurements: 312 feet length × 43 feet breadth. Four-masted steel barque. 1901: (Anglo-American). *1911: Sold (Norwegian). 8.1917: Torpedoed and sunk off Tory Island.

The *Alcides* had double topgallant yards and royals and carried a main spencer (trysail), very useful in light winds. She had splendid accommodation, large rooms and was well furnished. Her best passage under the Haws' flag was in 1895 when she sailed from Hong Kong to New York in 83 days.

Calcutta	1892	1,694	Built by the Naval Construction & Armaments Co., Barrow, as *Unionen*, for Vestlandske Petroleum Co., Bergen. Measurements: 240 feet length × 40 feet breadth. Three masted steel barque. 1900: *Calcutta* (Anglo-American). 1912: (Tank Storage & Carriage Co. Ltd.). 1916: (Anglo-American).

A centreline bulkhead and six transverse bulkheads divided her hull, except at the ends, into ten oil tanks and her load displacement, reckoning on 2,540 tons of oil cargo, crew and stores, was 3,570 tons. The oil could be offloaded in twenty-four hours, the pumps driven by a donkey engine. Her masts were stepped on the main deck over the oil tanks and there was still room for 'tween deck storage of dry cargo between the upper and main decks. She was given electric lighting in the accommodation, but this was considered too risky for the navigation lights.

The first voyage of the *Calcutta* for Anglo-American was in April, 1900, from Queenstown for Philadelphia to load batching oil for Calcutta. She made several similar voyages and the usual programme, after discharging in Calcutta, was to proceed to another port in the East to load general cargo for the United States or Europe. The homeward cargoes generally consisted of sugar, rice, sago and other products of the East. A round voyage usually took about a year.

In December, 1904, on a voyage from Leith to Philadelphia, the *Calcutta* encountered heavy weather in the Atlantic. This partly dismasted the ship and disabled her steering, but she was able to make temporary repairs and reached port after sixty-five days. In 1906 it was decided to send her to take up trade across the Pacific and she sailed to San Francisco by way of Australia, loading a cargo of wool at Newcastle, New South Wales, before taking up the run between San Francisco and Shanghai. Her record passage was in 1907 when she arrived in Shanghai forty-seven days out from San Francisco and after five days in port, made the return passage in only thirty-four days. On this passage she made a run of 302 miles in one day. The next year she lost her topmasts in a typhoon off Japan, but completed the passage to San Francisco in fifty-two days. A year later she again lost her topmasts, but reached Woosung only fifty-four days out from California. The *Calcutta* returned to home waters in 1915 to become a destroyer fuelling depot ship at Falmouth, this work being done by two pumps worked by a large tank boiler abaft the foremast. When war ended the ship was released from this service, refitted by her owners to carry cadets and placed in the transatlantic oil trade again. She carried eleven apprentices on her first voyage from Liverpool to Philadelphia, but this arrangement did not last long and in 1921 she was withdrawn and moored in Southampton Water, opposite Hamble, serving as a fuel barge. In 1923 she was sold for breaking up. The *Calcutta* was the last of the oil sailers owned by the Anglo-American Oil Company.

Colonial Empire	3.1902	2,436	Built by John Reid & Co. Ltd., Port Glasgow, for George Duncan & Co.'s "Empire" Line.

Measurements: 302 feet length × 43 feet breadth.
Four-masted steel barque.
1908: (Cook & Dundas, London).
13.11.1915: Ashore on Cardinaux Rocks, near Belle Island
  (voyage: St Nazaire/Port Talbot—ballast). Refloated, but
1916: Registration closed.
1917: Re-registered, (H. & C. Grayson Ltd., Liverpool),
  then sold to Anglo-American.
17.9.1917: Foundered on a submerged rock on Thunder
  Bolt Reef, Delagoa Bay (cargo of kerosene and oil).

The *Colonial Empire* was "baldheaded", with two topsails and two topgallants but no royals, making five sails on each of the three forward masts. She was one of the first sailing ships to be given bilge keels in an endeavour to keep her steady and minimise rolling in calm weather or long swells.

The iron four-masted barque *Drumeltan* was built in 1883 and was bought by Anglo-American in 1899 after she had been twice salvaged in the Far East. She became a barge in 1931.   *Esso*

Drumeltan	11.1883	1,908	Built by Russell & Co., Greenock, for James Gillison and Joseph Chadwick, Liverpool, who built up the "Drum" Line of sailing ships.
			Measurements: 267 feet length × 40 feet breadth.
			Four-masted iron barque.
			1894: (F. C. Farnham & Co., Shanghai).
			4.1894: Stranded on coast of Japan.
			1899: (Anglo-American).
			1912: (Tank Storage & Carriage Co. Ltd.).
			*1916: (Standard Transportation Co., Hong Kong).
			1921: *Margaret Overman* (Browne & Willis, Puntarenas, Costa Rica).
			1931: Converted to barge, renamed *Brooklyn* (A. & S. Transport Company of Newark, N.J.).

After stranding on the island of Tanagasima, off the coast of Japan, the *Drumeltan* was pulled off by a ship of the British China Squadron, towed to Nagasaki and anchored. There she was abandoned as a constructive total loss by the underwriters and was sold to a London company. She then stranded again, this time on Saddle Island, some eighty miles south-east of Shanghai. Salved by the Shanghai Dock Company, she was towed back to Shanghai. Here she was repaired and re-rigged by them and then loaded for New York under the Chinese flag. In New York she was sold to Anglo-American.

Falls of Ettrick	3.1894	2,264	Built by Russell & Co., Port Glasgow, for Wright, Graham & Co.'s "Falls Line".
			Measurements: 278 feet length × 42 feet breadth.
			Four-masted steel barque.
			25.7.1894: Stranded, 15 miles N by E of the Eastern Channel Lightship, Bay of Bengal. Abandoned, refloated, towed to Calcutta (voyage: Liverpool/Calcutta—salt).
			1899: (Anglo-American).
			24.7.1903: Stranded on Windsor Reef, Sunda Straits (voyage: Sourabaya/Delaware—sugar).
			*6.11.1903: Sold by auction.

The Falls Line of Glasgow

This firm was begun in 1874 from a partnership of Wm. Wright and a Captain Michael Breakenridge. At first, Wright and Breakenridge worked in the timber trade, but, with the influence of ex-seaman Breakenridge, turned their attention to shipowning.

The yard chosen for the building of their first ship, *Clyde Falls* (later *Falls of Clyde*), was Russell and Company, Port Glasgow, who had only established their shipyard in 1874. However, Russell and Company were to go on to build all nine of the sailing ship fleet of the Falls Line, six four-masted full-rigged ships and three four-masted barques. The ninth, and last, sailing ship built for Wright and Breakenridge was *Falls of Ettrick*, a steel four-masted barque. She was, indeed, the only steel sailing vessel in the fleet; all others had iron hulls.

The Falls Line was re-styled The Falls Line S.S. Company Ltd. in 1902 and owned eight steamships before ceasing operations in 1917.

Glendoon	1894	1,981	Built by A. Rodger & Co., Port Glasgow.
			Measurements: 266 feet length × 40 feet breadth.
			Steel full rigged ship.
			1901: (Anglo American).
			*1911: (O. Gotaas, Christiania, Norway).
			1916: (A. S. Bruusgaard, Dammen, Norway).
			17.4.1917: Torpedoed in South West Approaches on voyage from Iquique with nitrate.

One of seven stump topgallant yarders built by Rodgers between 1893–97 for Sterling and Company's "Glen" Line of Glasgow.

Hainaut	1887	1,783	Built by Barrow Shipbuilding Co. for F. Speth & Co., Antwerp. Measurements: 249 feet length × 40 feet breadth. Three-masted full rigged ship. Carrying petroleum (2,525 tons) in bulk. Named after a province of Belgium. 1891: (American Petroleum Co., Rotterdam). 1910: (Anglo-American). 1912: (Tank Storage & Carriage Co. Ltd.). *1914: *Marti* (Cia Cubana de Transporte de Miels of Havana). 1950: Still afloat as a molasses barge.

The Barrow Shipbuilding Company

Started in February, 1871, the Barrow Shipbuilding Company was founded by the Duke of Devonshire, and with him was Robert Duncan, already an eminent Clydeside shipbuilder. In close proximity to the yard were deposits of rich haematite iron ore from which high grade iron was produced.

First buildings included three steamers for the Ducal Line, trading from Calcutta, and another enterprise was the Barrow Ocean S.S. Company. But this was not a success and the Anchor Line took over the three ships, *Anchoria*, *Devonia* and *Circassia*. In 1881 the Inman Line had the beautifully-lined, part-steel and part-iron *City of Rome* built, but her North Atlantic performances were not good and she was no great competitor to the White Star ships of the day.

In February, 1888, the Naval Construction & Armaments Company Ltd. was incorporated and took over the yard on 1st March. In 1892, another sailing tankship was completed, the *Unionen*, which later became Anglo-American's *Calcutta*. As well as merchant ship building the new company began building war vessels of many types. A contract was awarded to them in 1894 for the construction of H.M.S. *Powerful* from which many warship orders followed and led to a merger in 1896. The new title of the 57-acre shipyard was Vickers, Son & Company, but in the next year the name was changed again to Vickers, Sons and Maxims Ltd. In 1911 the title became Vickers Ltd., by then one of the largest yards in the country. When Armstrong, Whitworth & Company were in difficulties in 1927, a merger took place and Vickers-Armstrongs Ltd. was formed which went on to construct aircraft carriers, cruisers, destroyers and submarines and, in the merchant shipbuilding sector, large passenger liners for P & O, Canadian Pacific, Orient S.N. Company and Furness Withy, while its Tyne yard construction later included tankers for Esso.

Johanna	1891	1,756	Built by J. Smit, Alblasserdam, for own account. Measurements: 240 feet length × 37 feet breadth. Steel full rigged ship. 1899: (Anglo-American). 11.1909: Foundered off Delaware Breakwater (voyage: New York/Manila).
Juteopolis	12.1891	2,842	Built by W. B. Thompson & Co. Ltd., Dundee, for C. Barrie's Calcutta–Dundee jute trade. Capable of carrying 20,000 bales of jute. Measurements: 310 feet length × 45 feet breadth. Four-masted steel barque. 1899: (Anglo-American). *1911: (George Windram & Son, Liverpool). 1917: (Marine Navigation Co. of Canada Ltd. (Sir W. Garthwaite)). 1920: Renamed *Garthpool*. 11.11.1929: Wrecked, Fast Sand Head, Boa Vista Island, in the Cape Verde Group (voyage: Hull/Adelaide—ballast).

The steel full-rigged ship *Glendoon* in the River Avon near Bristol after having passed to the Norwegian flag. *Esso*

Kentmere	6.1883	2,520	Built by W. H. Potter & Son, Liverpool, for Fisher & Sprott, London. Measurements: 300 feet length × 42 feet breadth. Four-masted iron full rigged ship. 1896: (G. Croshaw & Co., London). 1897: (Anglo-American). Converted to a four-masted barque. *1909: (Pacific S.N. Co.). Hulked at Punta Arenas, Chile. 1909: (Lamport & Holt Ltd). Hulk. 3.1924: Sold.
King George	1894	2,242	Built by Russell & Co., Port Glasgow, for J. A. Walker & Co., Glasgow. Measurements: 278 feet length × 42 feet breadth. Full rigged ship. 1903: (Anglo-American). 24.11.1909: Stranded, Third Point, Straits of Sunda, Java (voyage: New York/Hong Kong). Total loss.

Lawhill	9.1892	2,942	Built by W. B. Thompson & Co. Ltd., Dundee, for C. Barrie, Dundee.

Measurements: 333 feet (oa)/317 feet length × 45 feet breadth.

Four-masted barque.

1899: (Anglo-American).

1904: Dismasted and re-rigged as a baldheaded barque. Topgallant masts stepped abaft topmasts.

*1911: (G. Windram & Co., Liverpool).

1914: (A. Troberg, Mariehamn, Finland).

1917: (Captain Gustaf Erikson, Mariehamn—in group ownership).

1918: (Captain Gustaf Erikson). Became sole owner while ship was held by Allies at Brest.

Employed in the South Australian grain trade and was in the grain fleet in 1927. Last pre-war voyage was Port Victoria to Falmouth. Laid up in Rothesay Bay in 1939. Sailed for Port Victoria and left there in May, 1941, arriving East London (South Africa) July, 1941, where she was held as a prize as Finland had joined with Germany in war.

4.1942: (Government of South Africa).

Application for ownership granted by the Prize Court at Cape Town.

9.1942: Sailed for Bunbury, Western Australia, and continued in the grain trade to South Africa until 1946.

1946: (Lawhill (Prop) Ltd., Cape Town). One voyage.

1947–48: (C. V. Webb, Cape Town).

1948: (Mario da Silva Jr., Lourenco Marques).

1949: Laid up Delagoa Bay.

1957: Beached near mouth of Matola River.

1959: Cut up for scrap.

Charles Barrie and Sons

The *Lawhill* and *Juteopolis* were ships originally owned by Charles Barrie and Sons of Dundee, the largest of eleven sailing ships which the company owned between 1881 and the early years of the new century.

The firm was founded in 1881 by Charles Barrie, born in 1840, who had been a seaman since the age of fifteen. As Master in Smith's City Line, with an immense knowledge of the Bay of Bengal Calcutta jute trade, he bought ships and it was to the jute trade that he looked for freight.

Dundee had been gaining importance as a jute cloth manufacturing centre since the early 1830s, the first shipment direct from Calcutta arriving in April, 1840, in the barque *Salma*, and by the 1880s

the city enjoyed a virtual world monopoly in the production of jute cloth and flax products, with increasing exports reaching a peak in the mid-1880s.

The first ship acquired by Barrie in 1881 was the American-built *Adelaide Baker*; his second in that year was Smith's *City of Calcutta* which was quickly renamed *Calcutta*. The third ship, *Dundee*, was a barque of 2,060 gross tons, built to Barrie's order by W. B. Thompson, Dundee.

Then five ships were acquired from Donald Currie's "Castle" Line. These were iron barques, *Arundel Castle*, *Tantallon Castle*, *Pembroke Castle*, *Roslin Castle* and *Carisbrooke Castle*, which became *Chittagong*, *Dacca*, *Glasgow*, *London* and *Errol* respectively. They were followed by the steel barques *Juteopolis* and *Lawhill*, both from W. B. Thompson's yard at Dundee in 1891–92. *Lawhill* was named from Dundee Law, the conspicuous hill at the back of the city.

As the last decade of the century came, the trade altered, with more and more Indian spinning mills, and manufactured gunnies taking the place of the raw jute. A more regular service was deemed necessary. So, in 1895, was born the "Den" Line of steamers and eighteen were to wear the Barrie flag. Then came the 1914–18 war, a shortage of jute and the submarine. One "Den" steamer was sunk in 1916, the remaining ships sold, mainly to Furness, Withy and Cunard.

Finally, in 1923, then with a one-ship fleet, it was decided to change the policy of shipowning and the 5,485 gt *Den of Airlie* was sold to the German flag.

Lyndhurst	9.1886	2,311	Built by A. McMillan & Son, Dumbarton, for W. R. Price & Co. Measurements: 295 feet length × 42 feet breadth. Four-masted barque. 1899: (Anglo-American). 21.8.1911: On fire, burnt out.

The *Lyndhurst* had discharged part of her cargo of 70,000 cases of naphtha and twenty-five cases of kerosene in Delagoa Bay, Durban and Algoa Bay and had sailed for Cape Town when, on 21st August, sixty-seven miles from Mossel Bay, she suffered a terrific explosion forward which caused some hatch covers to be blown through the topsail. Her crew members were rescued by a nearby Clan Line steamer. The *Lyndhurst* was later sunk by gunfire from H.M.S. *Pandora*.

Sindia	12.1887	3,068	Built by Harland & Wolff Ltd., Belfast, for T. & J. Brocklebank Ltd. Measurements: 329 feet length × 45 feet breadth. Four-masted barque. 1.2.1888: Maiden voyage from Liverpool to Calcutta. 1900: (Anglo-American). 15.12.1901: Aground at Ocean City, New Jersey, about ninety-five miles south of Sandy Hook (voyage: Kobe/New York). Attempts to refloat the ship were unsuccessful and she became a landmark.

Opposite: The four-masted barque *Juteopolis*, built in 1891 for the Calcutta–Dundee jute trade.

Right: The *Lawhill* at Gravesend, 30th September, 1934. She, too, had been built for Charles Barrie and Sons of Dundee for the jute trade.

The British-built ships

	Completed	Gross tons	
Nonpareil	1900	3,414	Built by Wm Hamilton & Co., Port Glasgow. Measurements: 323 feet length × 46 feet breadth. Four-masted barque. The *Nonpareil* left New York in the autumn of 1900 and a few days later was in hurricane conditions. The cargo shifted, the ship capsized and went on her beam ends. The crew was taken off by the steamship *Glengoil.* After being abandoned the *Nonpareil* drifted thousands of miles before sinking.
Comet	2.1901	3,414	Built by Wm Hamilton & Co., Port Glasgow. Measurements: 323 feet length × 46 feet breadth. Four-masted barque. 3.1901: Partially dismasted. 1912: (Tank Storage & Carriage Co. Ltd.). *1913: *Orotava* (Rhederei Akt. Ges. von 1896, Hamburg). During 1914–18 war was interned at Santa Rosalia, Mexico. 1918: Allocated to France when war ended. 1921: *James Dollar* (Robert Dollar, San Francisco). 1928: *Ororava* (Canadian Robert Dollar Co., Vancouver, B.C.). A barge.

The *Comet*, like the *Nonpareil*, was also in trouble after leaving New York, being dismasted and then returning to the port of departure. In the case of *Nonpareil* the shifting of her cargo had been caused by bad stowage, but after the second casualty it was decided the ships had been too heavily rigged. The size of the *Comet's* yards was reduced and she continued in the case-oil trade to the Far East, returning with bulk cargoes or in ballast.

Brilliant	5.1901	3,765	Built by Russell & Co., Port Glasgow. Measurements: 352 feet length × 49 feet breadth. Four-masted steel barque. 1912: (Tank Storage & Carriage Co. Ltd.) *1914: *Perkeo* (Deutsch-Amerikanische Petroleum-Gesellschaft). 1915: *Bell* (A. Monsen, Tonsberg). Sold as a prize of war. 30.3.1916: Torpedoed by submarine, sank off Ushant.

When launched, *Brilliant* and her sistership *Daylight* were the largest windjammers under the British flag and the largest four-masters in the world. They could carry 150,000 cases of oil. Because the water ballast tanks of 2,000 tons were converted to carry cargo, the ships survived the transition to bulk oil carrying, which started in 1910. The conversion was, indeed, made in that year at New York. The ships were the only Anglo-American conversions from case oil.

Daylight	1.1902	3,756	Built by Russell & Co., Port Glasgow. Measurements: 353 feet length × 49 feet breadth. Four-masted steel barque. 1906: Caught fire at Yokkaichi, Japan. Scuttled, then raised and continued trading.

On dissolution of the Standard Oil Company in 1911 the *Daylight* was sold in 1912 to the Tank Storage and Carriage Company Ltd. Three years later *Daylight* and other ships of that fleet were transferred to the Standard Transportation Company of Hong Kong, a subsidiary of the Standard Oil Company of New York. She continued in the kerosene trade from San Francisco to the Orient until she made her last round voyage to Manila in October, 1920, with 150,235 cases, arriving back at San Francisco in June, 1921, with 1,428 tons of copra. This was her last voyage as a four-masted barque.

The four-masted barque *Brilliant* could carry 148,000 cases, the equivalent of 30,000 barrels of oil.   *Exxon*

The *Daylight* was sold to Charles Nelson and Company, of San Francisco, in the summer of 1921, for the timber trade, but her deep tanks made long timber difficult to stow and she lay in Oakland Creek until May, 1924, when she was sold to James Griffiths and Sons of Long Beach, California, who quickly stripped her to her lower masts to become a barge for the movement of gypsum rock from San Marco on the Gulf of California to Long Beach.

About 1934 the *Daylight* was laid up at Winslow, Washington, and remained there until 1942–43, when she was acquired by Murray, Simonsen and Company Limited, of Rio de Janeiro, and renamed *Tangara* (3,811 gt). A twenty-year-old engine was installed to work twin screws and a squat funnel was placed aft. Officially, she was of barquentine rig. The *Tangara* continued to carry 2,000-ton oil cargoes in her deep tanks under the Brazilian flag until 1953 when she was broken up.

Rigging Notes: When barque-rigged the *Daylight's* bowsprit was 61 feet. Fore, main and mizzen masts were 173 feet deck to truck; jigger 153 feet. Her course yards were 100 feet between the plugs; royals 52 feet and her spanker boom 56 feet. Topgallant masts and royal yards were of Oregon pine.

Eclipse	6.1902	3,090	Built by A. Rodger & Co., Port Glasgow.

Measurements: 327 feet length × 46 feet breadth.
Four-masted steel barque.
1910: Run down off Pernambuco by French sailing ship *Dupleix*. Some 15,000 cases of oil were jettisoned and she eventually made port for temporary repairs.
*1912: *Egon* (G. J. H. Siemens & Co., Hamburg). Interned in Mexico during the 1914–18 war.
1918: Acquired by A. M. Dollar & Co., San Francisco, through the British Shipping Controller. Renamed *Janet Dollar*.
1924: Last voyage, timber for Tsingtao. Laid up there.
1927: Purchased by Chinese cement company and:
1928: Towed to Morrison Point, Chin Kiang. Hulked in Yangtse River.

Arrow	4.1902	3,090	Built by by A. Rodger & Co., Port Glasgow. Measurements: 327 feet length × 46 feet breadth. Four-masted steel barque. *1911: *Parma* (F. Laeisz, Hamburg, Flying "P" Line). During 1914–18 war was interned in Chile; later allotted to Britain. 1922: Repurchased by F. Laeisz and resumed work in the South American nitrate trade. 1930: (R. de Cloux, Mariehamn). 31.7.1936: Being moved into Princes Dock, Glasgow, by two tugs pulling against the wind, the *Parma* suddenly veered and struck an observation tower on the pierhead. Coping stones on the quay wall were dislodged and sprung open the steel bow of the *Parma*, loosening large plates and almost wrecking the bow. She was on a voyage from Australia to Glasgow via Falmouth with 5,000 tons of wheat. Sold as a hulk and 1936: (Red. A/B Parma (J. V. Wennstrom, Mariehamn)). 1937: (Barnett Bros., London). 1938: Broken up.
Radiant	1.1903	1,974	Built by A. Rodger & Co., Port Glasgow. 265 feet length × 40 feet breadth. Four-masted steel barque. *1912: *Perim* (Sterne & Somaberne Oelwerke). 1918: Seized while at Antwerp and returned to United Kingdom. 1921: Registered with the Italian Government. 1921: (Soc. Anon. Commerciale & Industriale Ligure Apuana, Genoa). 1923: Scrapped Italy.
Alacrita	7.1903	1,974	Built by A. Rodger & Co., Port Glasgow. Measurements: 265 feet length × 40 feet breadth. Four-masted steel barque. 4.8.1907: Left Delagoa Bay for Philippines to load; no further trace, presumed foundered.

Russell and Company

The founder of this company was Joseph Russell, son of a Baptist minister in London, who was one of the outstanding figures in Clydeside shipbuilding during the second half of the nineteenth century. He began his career with Hoby and Company, Renfrew (later Simons and Company), moving to Hill and Company, Port Glasgow, before returning to London when that company finished in 1869.

By that time his heart was in Clydeside and the opportunity to return there came in 1874 when he joined in partnership with Anderson Rodger to form Russell and Company at the small Bay Yard at the east end of Glasgow where they began constructing hulls. In 1879 the company moved to larger facilities at Port Glasgow Graving Dock in which ships were constructed, and a yard in Main Street, Greenock. The company flourished and, in 1880, turned out seven sailing ships and four steamship hulls.

Then came a change of policy as cargo sailing ships began to be ousted by the evolving tramp

The four-masted barque *Daylight* preparing to anchor at Philadelphia. Her crew consisted of three mates, bo'sun, sailmaker, six apprentices, twenty-eight able seamen, carpenter, donkeyman, two cooks and two stewards. *Esso* steamer. The company turned to the construction of standardised sailing ships and also acquired the Kingston Yard of Henry Murray and Company, Port Glasgow, in 1881, the four building berths there quickly being increased to twelve and then to fourteen. A bonus with this acquisition was the chief draughtsman of the yard, William Lithgow, who had such organising ability that Russell and Rodger took him as a partner. The new yard was used for the building of sailing ships, steamers being constructed at Greenock.

The firm flourished, heading the shipbuilding tables year after year, building cheap but fine quality standard hulls and participating in funding shipowners for new construction. Indeed, in the 1880s a complete fleet for Crawford and Roat's "Port Line" was built with other ships for James Nourse and the German Rickmers Company. In 1890 there were no fewer than twenty-six sailing ships and eight steamship hulls constructed, which put the company at the top of the world's building lists. Included in these buildings was R. W. Leyland and Company's four-masted ship *Liverpool*, 3,400 tons and the largest sailing ship under the Red Ensign.

One year later Joseph Russell retired and the partnership was dissolved, the remaining partners sharing the yards between them.

William Lithgow carried on the name of Russell and Company, working the yards at Greenock and Kingston. The latter was sold in the later 1890s to Carmichael, Maclean and Company, but they built only just over twenty steamers before collapsing and the yard was re-acquired by Lithgow who completed outstanding contracts. When William Lithgow died in 1908 his sons James and Henry took over and Lithgows Ltd. was formed in 1918.

Meanwhile, Anderson Rodger took over the Bay Yard at Port Glasgow as A. Rodger and Company, and went on to build many steamers. One of the last to be built under his name was Hogarth Shipping Company's *Baron Jedburgh*, 4,418 gt, in 1912, and in that year the yard returned to Russell and Company after Rodger's death.

Anglo-American had two ships built by Russell and Company, *Brilliant* and *Daylight*, and four more by Rodger, *Eclipse*, *Alacrita*, *Radiant* and *Arrow*. Of the sailing ships acquired by Anglo-American, three, *Drumeltan*, *Falls of Ettrick* and *King George*, were from the Russell yard, one ship, *Glendoon*, coming from Rodger and Company.

American sailers

About the same time as the eight British sailing ships were ordered, Standard Oil Company of New Jersey contracted for three from A. Sewall and Company, Bath, Maine. Built of steel, they were four-masted with dimensions of 332 feet length and 45 feet breadth. They worked from the United States and flew the American flag. All were sold to the Alaska Packers' Association whose salmon fleet was based at San Francisco. The fleet sailed each year to the canneries of Alaska with supplies and brought back tinned salmon.

	Completed	Gross tons	
Acme	1901	3,288	4.1913: *Star of Poland* (Alaska Packers' Association). 15.9.1919: Stranded at Katsumra, Japan.
Astral	1900	3,292	11.1910: *Star of Zealand* (Alaska Packers' Association). Proved to be a rather slow sailer and: 1927: Laid up Alameda. 1936: Left for shipbreakers in Japan and arrived Yawata after a voyage of eighty-two days.
Atlas	1902	3,381	11.1910: *Star of Lapland* (Alaska Packers' Association). 1935: Sold to Japanese shipbreakers. 1936: Left Alameda for Osaka.

The *Thomas W. Lawson*, the only seven-masted schooner, was carrying a cargo of lubricating oil for Anglo-American on her last voyage in 1907.

Thomas W. Lawson	1902	5,218	Built by the Fore River Ship & Engineering Co., Quincy, Mass., for the Coastwise Transportation Company of Boston. Measurements: 395 feet (oa)/375 feet 6 inches length × 50 feet breadth. Seven-masted steel schooner.

Constructed of steel, this multi-masted schooner, the world's largest fore-and-aft sailing ship, was built to recover coastwise trade which was being lost to the railways through the increasing running costs of American ships. This giant, the only seven-masted schooner, was certainly built with economy in mind and was worked with a crew of only eighteen. One design principle was that all halyards and topping lifts were led to two steam winches, one forward, one on the aft deckhouse.

There was 40,617 square feet of canvas. The seven lower masts were 135 feet and to each was fitted a 58 feet Oregon pine topmast to give a mast weight of 20 tons. The first three were foremast, main and mizzen; the remainder were termed jigger, driver, pusher and spanker—often quoted in confused order.

The *Thomas W. Lawson* was built to carry coal from Hampton Roads to the New England ports, usually Boston or Portland, and was designed to carry 7,500 tons of coal on a draught of 26 feet and 11,000 tons on 28 feet, although the choice of port was limited with such a draught. In 1904 she was sent to Newport News for conversion to an oil carrier, being fitted with fourteen tanks, and worked from Texas ports to Philadelphia. Then, on 27th November, 1907, after loading a cargo of lubricating oil for Anglo-American at Marcus Hook, she left for London on her one and only crossing of the Atlantic; to her end on Heleweather Reef, off Annet Island in the Scillies.

The crossing was rough at the start, working up to storm force in the early days of December. The ship lost most of her canvas; the deck was continuously swept by high seas; hatches were stove in and all lifeboats swept overboard. She became stern heavy and some of the oil cargo was pumped overboard from the stern tank. The days went by and on the fifth successive day of the storm the Bishop Rock light was seen, but was mistaken for a passing ship. Realisation came too late; the schooner was then very close inshore, trapped among rocks and reefs. It was 11 p.m., Friday, 13th December. There was no room to manoeuvre and not enough sail to tack. The ship, in bad water and in a serious plight, put out two anchors to await an abating of the wind. But as the day changed, so did the ever-violent wind, veering to NNW. It was not long before both anchor cables gave in the tremendous running seas and the *Thomas W. Lawson* touched on the Heleweather Reef, near Stag Rock. Rigging sagged; the masts swayed in the storm's ferocity. Then they crashed down. The ship broke in two; sixteen of the crew were swept overboard and a flood of oil poured from ruptured tanks in the boiling sea. A dim, wild dawn revealed only broken wreckage on the outer reef as the St Agnes lifeboat made her second approach to the broken vessel. There were no survivors to be taken from the wreckage—the only two had been washed ashore.

The four-masted barque *Arrow*, one of eight British-built sailing ships constructed for Anglo-American at the turn of the century. *Esso*

CHAPTER FOUR

The Turn of the Century

THE development of the motor car was to produce an almost insatiable demand for motor fuel and for lubricating oils, and that demand was reflected quite naturally in the growth of Anglo-American.

The first practical gas engine was made in 1860, and two years later a Belgian engineer named Lenoir, working in France, fitted a gas engine to a cart. In Britain, which already had steam-driven vehicles, the "new-fangled contraption" was greeted with scepticism. Perhaps caution was justified at the time, but the work of Nicolas August Otto in producing the first successful internal combustion engine, of Karl Benz, who in 1885 made a two-seater motor tricycle using a scaled down four-stroke engine and electrical ignition, and of Gottlieb Daimler, who in partnership with Wilhelm Maybach brought out a high-speed petrol engine in 1883, proved that the internal combustion engine and the motor car would together be a force to be reckoned with.

For a time the motor car was the toy of the rich, but then in 1901 Ransom Eli Olds introduced a scheme that was to change the world; the assembly line. It was a principle that was taken up with enthusiasm by Henry Ford, the recognised pioneer of the cheap mass-produced car, who formed the Ford Motor Company in 1901.

At the start of the new century Anglo-American Oil Company were already showing great confidence in the future. In 1900 they issued a booklet for the "Motor Carist" in which it was announced that as the motor car had come to stay the company was arranging for the sole importation of Pratt's Motor Car Spirit into Britain. Charles Pratt, who gave his name to the product, was an early associate of Standard Oil's founder and was himself a director of that company.

Almost overnight the spirit was being sold everywhere—in shops, at Post Offices, in chemists, town emporiums and village stores alike. And always in Anglo-American's green two-gallon can, the can in which it was to be marketed for over twenty years. The company quickly found themselves responsible for the importing, distribution and sale of three-quarters of all petrol being used in Britain. At the same time there came a tremendous increase in the demand for other products; fuel oil for the generating of steam; oil for the production of illuminating gas used in the lighting of towns and cities; the need for lubricating oils grew and grew. Anglo-American brand names at the Motor Show of 1909 included Pratt's Perfection Motor Spirit, Royal Daylight, White Rose and Crown Diamond paraffin, a vaporising oil called Gladiator and Anglo Liquid Fuel. There was also Aero Naphtha, a motor spirit for the aeroplane, then very much in its infancy.

Meanwhile, in America Henry Ford had brought out his Model T, a low-priced automobile which reached the market in October, 1908. By 1912

Echoes of wartime alarms in an advertisement for Pratt's motor spirit issued in the post-war years. *Esso*

the Ford was being assembled in factories from coast to coast at a rate of 20,000 each month, and shortly before war broke out in Europe the assembly line was superseded by the moving conveyor belt. The millionth Model T (nicknamed "Tin Lizzie") came in 1915. Between 1908 and 1927, when production ceased, over 16,500,000 Model T Fords were produced.

By 1914 car showrooms and garages were opening everywhere. The demand for the motor car had created its own supply, and in that year the number of cars on British roads had risen to 132,000; there were also some 120,000 motor cycles.

After the war, mass production of the motor car spread. Tracks and lanes became tarmac roads, new highways were laid and the necessity for new traffic laws emerged. The pattern of living was changing.

The Royal Navy turns to fuel oil

In 1889 the British Government was under pressure from both the Board of Admiralty and the exponents of a "might is right" naval strategy to authorise a big increase in naval expenditure, but it remained unconvinced by their arguments and four years later was actually contemplating a reduction in expenditure, not only as a moral virtue but as a national necessity. Further pressure and some drastic action was required before its opinion was changed.

In November of the same year another Admiralty proposal demanded huge expenditure on new construction over the following five years in order to counter a situation which was likely to develop in 1896–97 when a French naval building programme was due to be completed. The years of 1894–95 would see Britain with nineteen first class battleships; France would have ten, Russia three. But in the following year France and Russia were due to complete six more, bringing them, jointly, to equal the battleship strength of the Royal Navy, as well as possessing many powerful ships in their "second line" fleets. It was therefore regarded as imperative that Britain should lay down many first class ships during 1894–96 for completion by 1898 in order to keep abreast of the foreign fleets.

However, in Parliament, a resolution put forward for the additional tonnage was countered by Prime Minister Gladstone, who stated that under the existing circumstances the Government did not entertain any apprehension regarding the supremacy of Great Britain, but made no reference to the critical years ahead. There followed a furious Parliamentary row and the Navy Board threatened to resign *en bloc* if their advice was rejected. On 8th December, 1893, a draft shipbuilding programme for 1983–98 was presented and the Government accepted it, although the increase in its estimated cost led to the Prime Minister's retirement.

The newbuilding programme was impressive and included nine battleships, twenty-two first, second and third class cruisers, six ram cruisers, eighty-two destroyers and forty gunboats, sloops and torpedo boats.

The battleships

The nine battleships constructed were each of 14,900 tons displacement on measurements of 390 feet × 75 feet and were fitted with a main armament of 4 × 12-inch and 12 × 6-inch guns. Propelling machinery was triple expansion steam, developing 10,000 s.h.p. for a speed of 17 knots. Coal bunker capacity was for a maximum of 1,900 tons, plus a subsequent provision for 400 tons of oil. The ships were known as the "Majestic"-class, the lead ship, *Majestic*, being completed in December, 1895, at Portsmouth Naval Dockyard. The sixth completion, *Mars*, from Cammell Laird,

Birkenhead, in June, 1897, was the first large ship to be fitted for oil burning in 1904 and 400 tons of oil fuel was added to her capacity, the maximum bunker capacity being reduced by 200 tons. All except *Jupiter* and *Illustrious* were later fitted for oil burning, although earlier they were "mixed-fuel" ships, the oil being sprayed on the coal and not burned separately.

A few years later, in 1905, there began the era of the "Dreadnoughts", a name that was to displace the term "battleship" for a decade. The *Dreadnought*, laid down in Portsmouth Dockyard on 2nd October, 1905, and completed on 3rd October, 1906, was the first large warship to be given steam turbine propulsion, which gave her three knots over the old battle fleet, with bunkerage for both coal and oil, for it was now realised that the days of the coal-fired capital ships were coming to an end.

By the time the 1912 naval shipbuilding programme was proposed a minimum speed of 25 knots had become necessary in order to contain the anticipated German High Seas Fleet of 1914–15. But such a speed as this could only be attained by the use of oil fuel. Already some British destroyers depended on it, although most of the Navy's big ships still used oil as an auxiliary by spraying it on the coal. The proposal to replace British coal with

A battleship of the "Majestic"-class, some of which were fitted for oil burning.

foreign oil rocked the very foundations of naval policy and raised a whole series of vital problems embracing supply, transport and storage, as well as of financial outlay. The decision was taken by Winston Churchill, then First Lord of the Admiralty, and the Royal Navy was turned over to oil burning. No more coal-burning battleships, cruisers or destroyers were ordered. An agreement in May, 1914, with the Anglo-Persian Oil Company[3] secured the Navy's future oil and this led to the nation's acquisition of a controlling share in that company's interests.

One result of this change in naval strategy was the "Queen Elizabeth"-class of battleships of the 1912 building programme, the first really big ships to be oil-fired.

The destroyers

In October, 1898, the 280-ton "A"-class torpedo boat destroyer *Surly* was converted to burn oil as fuel; she emitted clouds of evil-smelling, choking, black smoke from her three funnels every time her sprayers were turned on. Six years later the "B"-class *Spiteful*, 365 tons, joined in the experiment, also being fitted to burn liquid fuel. Then in November, 1904, the Admiralty decided that ocean-going destroyers were to burn oil fuel and from this decision stemmed the "Oceans"—often known as the "F" or "Tribal"-class. Oil fuel capacity of each was 200 tons, horsepower ranged from 21,000 to 27,000 and the speed was 33–35 knots. The twelve vessels in this class were all built to different private designs; some had three funnels, some had four, while the *Viking* is noted as the only six-funnelled ship built for the Royal Navy. As might be expected from such a miscellany of designs, oil consumption varied enormously, though all had a great appetite for fuel.

In consideration of the high cost of operating the "Oceans" there came a change of mind—albeit temporary—in 1908–09 and the "G" ("Basilisk")-class ships were built with reduced armament, a reduction in speed to 27 knots and a return to coal fuel, for there lurked an uncertainty of adequate oil supplies in time of war. But in the twenty "H" "Acorn"-class destroyers of 1909–10 it was oil fuel again.

*   *   *

With the decision to turn the Royal Navy from coal to oil burning, which was quickly emulated by leading foreign navies, there came a policy of building up large stocks as reserves in the event of an emergency. This caused the need for more tankships and a number were built specifically for this reason alone. Even so, during the ensuing war years, so many tankers were sunk that the supply of fuel oil for the Royal Navy was dangerously threatened and the Government appealed to some North Atlantic shipping companies to help in the carriage of oil in their ships. Cunard alone carried over 100,000 tons to Britain.

Anglo-American Oil Company Ltd.
Ocean-going fleet 1910

Steamships	Built		Built
Appalachee	1894	*Narragansett*	1903
Ashtabula	1903	*Ottawa*	1888
Cadillac	1909	*Potomac*	1893
Chesapeake	1895	*Saranac*	1908
Cheyenne	1908	*Schuylkill* (c)	1903
Cuyahoga	1902	*Seminole*	1903
Dakotah	1902	*Seneca* (c)	1901
Delaware	1893	*Suwanee*	1888
Genesee	1889	*Tamarac*	1908
Hudson (c)	1900	*Tioga*	1890
Impoco	1910	*Tonawanda*	1893
Iroquois	1907	*Tuscarora*	1898
Kennebec (c)	1902	*Weehauken*	1891
Lackawanna	1894	*Winnebago*	1901

(c) = case oil carriers.

Sailing ships	Built		Built
Alcides	1892	*Eclipse*	1902
Arrow	1902	*Glendoon*	1894
Brilliant	1901	*Juteopolis*	1891
Calcutta (tanker)	1892	*Lawhill*	1892
Comet	1901	*Lyndhurst*	1886
Daylight	1902	*Radiant*	1903
Drumeltan	1883	*Navahoe* (barge)	1908

Years of war

When war came, most of the 'teen years of the new century were filled with its horror. At sea, over 3,000 British ships were sunk and many shipping companies, buoyant in 1914, found themselves with greatly depleted fleets when war ended. Not so Anglo-American. In the early years their fleet actually continued to expand, five ships being acquired in 1915 of which one, *Mimosa*, was lost in the very same year. In the next year *Tamarac* was delivered and two more tankers acquired.

It was in 1916 that imports of motor spirit into Britain exceeded illuminating oil for the first time. This was due to the needs of the war machine—for motor transport and for the growing war in the air. Demand for more fuel came with the introduction of machines for mechanised warfare. The British secret weapon, the tank,[4] was fuelled from cans when it made its debut at Cambrai in 1916.

The worst year for the Anglo-American company was in 1917, when unrestricted warfare began. Three ships were lost, one of which was the *Narragansett* while on a voyage from New York to Britain. Another of unrestricted warfare at sea was petrol rationing in the United Kingdom, supplies dwindling rapidly as one ship in every four bound for Britain fell victim to the U-boats. All told, five Anglo-American tankers were lost during hostilities and when war ceased the company's fleet was eight units larger than in 1914 with the then major ships *Cadillac*, *Tuscarora* and *Saranac*, delivered in 1917–18, providing some 50,000 tons in extra carrying capacity.

In 1919, the Government Pool Board, formed in 1917 to co-ordinate the work of the oil distributing companies, was dissolved. Its formation had, in fact, disclosed that at the time the Anglo-American company was responsible for 54% of all the oil product sales in the country. In 1919 the first kerbside petrol pump in Britain appeared. The introduction of the hand-operated, one-gallon, bowser obviated the carrying of cans to and fro, spillage of petrol and having to use a funnel for filling. However, the pump was not in general use until the 1920s.

Acquired tankers 1914–1918

	Completed	Gross tons	
Cuyahoga	1914	4,586	Launched by Greenock & Grangemouth Dockyard Co. as *Inkisi*, but purchased by Anglo-American Oil Co. before completion. Measurements: 375 feet length × 53 feet breadth. 5,600 tdw.

The *Cuyahoga* was torpedoed on 5th July, 1917, off the NW coast of Ireland, while on a voyage from Liverpool to Philadelphia in ballast. Although seriously damaged, the tanker was put about with the intention of returning to port. She was again torpedoed and damaged by shell fire from the U-boat and finally had to be abandoned in sinking condition. Her crew were rescued by a patrol boat and taken safely to port. The ship sank 130 miles WNW of Tory Island, in position 55.12N 12.10W.

Earl of Elgin	1909	4,448	Built by Russell & Co., Port Glasgow, for W.I. Dobbie & Co., Glasgow. Measurements: 384 feet length × 49 feet breadth. 1915: (Anglo-American Oil Co.)

The *Earl of Elgin* left Plymouth on 5th December, 1917, bound from London to Belfast to load a cargo of empty barrels for New York. When about 12 miles from the Lizard a torpedo was fired at her, but passed beneath her, amidships. She reached the safety of Milford Haven and continued her voyage next day. All went well until the afternoon when a torpedo hit caused a terrible explosion. All hands were ordered to the boats as the ship began to sink, but heavy seas were running and washed right over the ship as she settled. Nineteen of the crew were lost. The *Earl of Elgin* sank in under four minutes, ten miles W½S from Caernarvon Bay Lightvessel on 7th December, 1917.

Mimosa	5.1905	3,466	Built by Short Bros., Sunderland, for Mimosa Steam Shipping Co. Ltd. (T. Stephens & Sons). Measurements: 352 feet length × 45 feet breadth. 1915: (Anglo-American Oil Co.). 4.9.1915: Captured and sunk by submarine *U.33*, 137 miles SW of Fastnet, 49.40N 12.00W (voyage: New York/Belfast and Liverpool—20,000 barrels of oil).

The crew took to the lifeboats and the Captain of *U.33* told the *Mimosa's* Captain he would inform the first trawler he saw of their plight. However, after six hours they were picked up, in a strange coincidence, by another Anglo-American tanker, the outwardbound *Comanchee*. In the morning of 6th September, they met up with the steamer *Norseman*, the crew transshipped, were landed at St Nazaire and later returned to Britain.

Winnebago	11.1915	4,666	Built by Sir James Laing & Sons Ltd., Sunderland. Measurements: 383 feet (oa)/370 feet length × 50 feet breadth. Engines: T3cyl. 12.3.1917: Damaged by submarine torpedo off Scilly Isles. Towed in. *1935: *Francunion VI* (Cie Venture-Weir SA); a fuel depot ship at Algiers. 1949: Scrapped Spezia.
Spiraea	8.1900	3,620	Built by Wm Pickersgill & Sons Ltd., Sunderland, for British & Foreign S.S. Co. Ltd., as *St Fillans*. Measurements: 361 feet length × 46 feet breadth. Engines: T3cyl. 1915: (Anglo-American Oil Co.). 29.2.1916: On fire in Manchester Ship Canal (Voyage: Philadelphia/Manchester—oil in barrels). Broken up at Morecambe.

The *Winnebago* of 1915, which twenty years later became a fuel depot ship at Algiers under the name of *Francunion VI*.

Tamarac	6.1916	5,042	Built by A. McMillan & Sons, Dumbarton. Measurements: 385 feet length × 50 feet breadth. Engines: T3cyl. 1935: Sold to British shipbreakers.

Silvertown	3.1873	5,046	Built by C. Mitchell & Co., Newcastle, as cable ship *Hooper*
			    for Hooper Telegraph Works Ltd., London.
			Measurements: 338 feet length × 55 feet breadth.
			Engines: C2cyl.
			Iron-hulled, three masted.
			1882: *Silvertown* (India Rubber Gutta Percha & Telegraph
			    Works Co., London).
			1916: (Anglo-American Oil Co.). Fitted with cylindrical
			    tanks for carriage of oil.
			1920: Used as bunkering vessel at Southampton.
			*1924: *Francunion II* (Cie. Venture-Weir SA).
			    Fuel depot ship, Algiers.
			1935: Sold to Dutch buyers; resold Italian shipbreakers.

Strathfillan	6.1906	4,353	Built by Wm Hamilton & Co., Port Glasgow, for Burrell &
			    Son, Glasgow.
			Measurements: 370 feet length × 52 feet breadth.
			Engines: T3cyl.
			1916: (Anglo-American Oil Co.).
			*1922: (Carlisle Sg. Co. (W. Stewart & Co., Glasgow)).
			1928: *Torbeath* (Waverley Sg. Co. Ltd., (T. L. Duff & Co.,
			    Glasgow).
			1931: *Elizabeth Moller* (Mollers Ltd., Shanghai).
			1944: (Ministry of War Transport).
			1947: (Government of Mysore) Broken up.

Tuscarora	1.1917	7,106	Built by Sir James Laing & Sons Ltd., Sunderland. Measurements: 425 feet length × 57 feet breadth. Engines: T3cyl. 9.9.1917: Damaged by submarine torpedo in North Atlantic, but reached port. 12.1.1935: Arrived Queenstown for breaking up.

On 1st September, 1920, when about 900 miles from the Azores, the crew of the *Tuscarora* sighted a ship in distress at about seven miles distant. It proved to be the new, wooden steamer *Elias Issaias* of 1,495 gt, a Greek-owned vessel, built to the design of an American war-built, standard-type ship and on her maiden voyage from Baltimore to Piraeus, laden with coal.

Some of the Greek crew had already taken to the boats and these were taken aboard the tanker. The master of the Greek ship, his engineer and three crew had remained aboard their vessel and it was decided to attempt to tow her to port. By late afternoon ropes were connected and towing started. Thirty minutes later it was signalled that the cargo ship was sinking and she was abandoned as the tow rope parted.

Then, despite the fact that she had been abandoned by her own captain, a party from the *Tuscarora* boarded the sinking ship and after their report, another towing attempt was made. The two ships were again connected up and towing commenced with the salvage party remaining on board. All went well until bad weather was experienced. On 3rd September, after the *Elias Issaias* had been towed 273 miles, the water was gaining fast, her decks were awash and she was in imminent danger of sinking. The tow was slipped, a boat returned safely with all hands to the *Tuscarora* and she proceeded on her voyage.

The Greek ship was not sighted again and it is presumed that she sank.

Cadillac	12.1917	12,074	Built by Palmers Shipbuilding & Iron Co. Ltd., Hebburn on Tyne. Measurements: 530 feet length × 66 feet breadth. Engines: Quad. Two decks and a shelter deck. 1.3.1941: Sunk by submarine (*U.552*) torpedo in North Atlantic, 59.44N 11.16W.

The *Cadillac* had her first major encounter with the enemy when she was only a few months old. In ballast, she left Plymouth on 5th April, 1918, in a convoy of fifteen ships under escort, westward bound for New York. All went well until the night of the 6th when the steamer *Knight Templar*, the lead ship of the convoy, was torpedoed.

In the absence of orders, the *Cadillac* maintained her speed and route, but steered a zigzag course. Later, there came an S.O.S. call from another ship which had been hit. No further incident occurred until next day, when there were seven other ships of the convoy in sight, the nearest being four miles away. The ships were then about 250 miles from Queenstown, Southern Ireland.

At midday a periscope was seen 300 yards off the *Cadillac's* bow and, within seconds, the track of a torpedo. A rapid helm order was given and as the ship swung to port the torpedo struck in No. 11 tank. Immediately after the explosion the periscope appeared less than 100 feet away and the *Cadillac* struck the submarine as momentum carried her round. The tanker's howitzer was brought to bear and for good measure four depth charges were fired over the submarine's position—and it was not seen again.

The *Cadillac* sent out a call for help. Though she had a large hole in her hull no damage had been done to the engines; she remained afloat and still capable of 10 knots. The same afternoon she was ordered to join an eastbound convoy that was coming up. Next day, ships in that convoy were torpedoed and the *Cadillac* was ordered to proceed alone to Plymouth. On 9th April she reached port and anchored in the Sound.

No drydock was available and only temporary repairs were made. She left Plymouth and arrived safely at Middlesbrough for repair on 2nd May.

In 1930 the midship section of the ship containing the tanks had corroded so badly with the carrying of benzol, petrol and similar cargoes that it was decided to insert a new midship section. She was sent to Hebburn for this work and was put into drydock, stern first, and cut into three sections.

The old fore and midship sections were undocked on 23rd April, the stern part was then sunk on to the blocks and the new midship section, which had been built on berth and launched on 27th March, was docked for joining. Then followed the forepart and on 29th May, 1930, the ship was undocked, with trials next day. This was pioneer work in ship surgery; the cost of reconstructing the *Cadillac* was half that of a new ship of the same size.

Saranac	1918	12,070	Built by Palmers Shipbuilding & Iron Co. Ltd., Hebburn on Tyne. Measurements: 530 feet length × 66 feet breadth. Engines: Quad. Two decks and a shelter deck. 25.6.1940: Torpedoed by submarine (*U.51*), then sunk by gunfire in North Atlantic, 48.24N 15.05W.

The *Saranac* was built too late to give any major war service, but she proved her worth soon after, when she performed a double salvage feat on a single round voyage, UK/USA/UK. The first was in 1919, when the Anglo-American tanker *Tamarac* was picked up in the Atlantic with her rudder carried away and sternframe damaged. She was brought safely into Milford Haven by the *Saranac*. Her second salvage commenced on 19th February, 1919, when she picked up a wireless call for help from the Government-owned, war-built steamer *War Hagara*, which reported that she had lost her propeller and was drifting in a severe storm, was pumping out oil to windward, had only one boat left and required a tow. *Saranac* answered the call and headed for the casualty, steaming all night through mountainous seas which continually swept her from bow to stern. At daybreak the disabled vessel was found, but the gale prevented a direct passing of a towing wire. Instead, a lifebelt connected to several hundred feet of line was drifted downwind from the ship. After many abortive attempts it

The tanker *Saranac* at Palmer's yard on the Tyne during the fitting of a new centre section in 1931.   *Esso*

was picked up and a towing connection made. The weather continued to be extremely bad and towing was carried out under constant difficulty. The *War Hagara* broke adrift and the long process of getting a cable between the ships had to be gone through anew.

For a time the towing speed was increased to five knots, the maximum considered safe, as *War Hagara's* windlass was useless, the whole engine smashed by the towing strain put on it and its frame badly cracked. The severe weather showed no sign of letting up and the convoy had to ease its speed down again, keeping steerage way only—and the towing bridle still held. Then, at last, the gale moderated somewhat and after 1,362 miles and eleven strenuous days of combined effort the ships arrived off Queenstown, Ireland, where Admiralty tugs took charge of the casualty.

Between the wars the *Saranac* was reconstructed in similar fashion to the *Cadillac*. She was docked at Hebburn on 17th January, 1931, and cut into three sections. The new section was launched on 3rd February, the forward and middle sections undocked on 10th February and the new mid-section docked the next day. The ship was completed on 20th March and she had her sea trials on 23rd March.

✻   ✻   ✻

The corrosion in tankers was a serious problem and the centre (tank) portion was usually unfit for further service after 12–15 years, although the fore and after portions were usually sound and capable of a further twelve years of service.

CHAPTER FIVE

The Years of Peace

UNTIL the end of the Great War Fawley lay untouched. A tiny, peaceful parish of Hampshire which included several hamlets, eight miles south-south-east of Southampton by water and five miles by country lane from Hythe. Among its cluster of cottages was *The Falcon* inn, and on the edge of the adjacent Ashlett Creek was, and still is, *The Jolly Sailor* inn, offering relief to the thirsty. Just south, Henry VIII's castle at Calshot gave dormant protection.

Far to the west, in New York, was the Atlantic, Gulf and West Indies S.S. Lines Inc., with traceable connections to 1844. Not only was this company in the shipping industry but it owned property and oilfields in Mexico.

At this time the motor car in Britain was rapidly increasing in numbers and the importation of motor spirit had already surpassed that of illuminating oils. Connected with these trends was the necessity for more and more roads. Factories were also beginning to be changed to oil energy and ships were being turned from coal to oil burning.

Here was an opportunity for the Atlantic, Gulf and West Indies S.S. Lines Inc. to extend their activities. The American company formed a new British company, the A.G.W.I. Petroleum Corporation Ltd., putting up 50% of the capital; the other 50% came from investors in Britain.

On 27th March, 1920 A.G.W.I. Petroleum Corporation Ltd. was incorporated, immediately acquiring 406 acres of the Hampshire countryside fronting Southampton Water, there to construct a refinery and oil tank farm. The sole rights of the cracking process were with the A.G.W.I. Petroleum Corporation, and benzol, for mixing with motor spirit, was to be supplied by the National Benzole Company, who were to market the products of the new refinery.

Work on the construction of the refinery began on 10th August, 1920. A depot had been set up at Totton, two miles up the River Test, for the transit of materials and stores. There was no rail link to Fawley and road access to the refinery was inadequate. At the site itself, lanes had to be widened and new roads laid. The ten miles of narrow, leafy lanes through the lush countryside on the edge of the New Forest from Totton to Fawley were mostly of rough gravel and could not stand up to constant use by heavy, loaded vehicles. The logical movement of materials for the new refinery was by water.

Just south from Fawley lay Ashlett Creek, with a quay in some disrepair. This was soon put in order and in came the small ships. By October, 1920, a five-ton steam crane was at work unloading lengths of rail track brought by sea from Totton for the construction of a two-foot narrow gauge railway. With trolleys pulled by horse and pushed by man, it soon linked quay to refinery. And the materials steadily arrived. Sailing ketches, motorised barges converted from sailing craft—a trend at that time—and even Thames barges tied up at the tiny quay bringing their cargoes of steel girders, piling, pipes, crates, drums and cement. In 1921 the first small steam locomotive was introduced, for by then a network of lines had been laid throughout the refinery.

As the refinery buildings spread in their seeming confusion of square and rounded shapes, their chimneys and uptakes probing here and there, a jetty was being constructed, 2,800 feet long. It stretched over marshland and shallows, on and on, then angling south-easterly and ending in deep water with a tanker berth giving thirty feet depth at low water and accommodation for coasters.

Meanwhile, in the United States, twelve tankers[5] had been built for the Atlantic, Gulf and West Indies S.S. Lines in 1920–21. Four were constructed by the Bethlehem Shipbuilding Corporation, three, *Agwisea*, *Agwilake* and *Agwipond* at Sparrows Point, Maryland, and one, *Agwibay*, at the Quincy Yard, Massachusetts. They were powered by quadruple expansion engines, and their measurements were 468 feet length and 63 feet breadth, giving 8,300 gross tons and 12,000 tdw. The Sun Shipbuilding and Dry Dock Company at Chester, Pennsylvania, built six, *Agwisun*, *Agwimoon*, *Agwimars* and *Agwiworld*, with dimensions of 429 feet length and 59 feet breadth, giving a gross tonnage of 7,035 and 11,300 tdw, and the larger *Agwihavre* and *Agwimex*, 8,850 gross tons, 480.5 feet length, 66 feet breadth and 13,800 tdw. The first four were given triple expansion engines; the other two quadruple expansion engines. The two largest ships of this huge order, *Agwistone* and *Agwismith*, came from Newport News Shipbuilding and Drydock Company, Virginia. They were twin-screw tankers driven by six-cylinder steam engines. The length was 500 feet, breadth 68 feet and tonnages 10,300 gross and 22,300 tdw.

On 18th June, 1921, the first tanker, the *Agwilake*, arrived at Fawley Jetty from the Tuxpan River, Mexico, to discharge 1,398 tons of Mexican crude oil, 5,843 tons of fuel oil and 2,677 tons of gas oil.

There was tank storage ashore for 99,000 tons. Products left the refinery by water in barges and coasters, and there was also a fully equipped deep water berth at which steamers could be bunkered day or night, irrespective of

Left: A.G.W.I.'s crude oil distillation plant at Fawley in the 1920s.

Opposite: The *Agwilake* at the Fawley jetty. She was the first tanker to berth there, arriving on 18th June, 1921.

Dr. F. Mayo

the state of the tide. The first ship to bunker from Fawley Jetty was the Swedish *Inga*, on 27th June, 1921.

With an ever-increasing number of cars being produced, more and more roads were being laid down and in April, 1923, it was decided to add an asphalt plant to the refinery complex; when completed the output was 150 tons per day. To load the asphalt (bitumen), an overhead ropeway was constructed on the jetty, wire cages containing up to five drums traversing the entire jetty for shipment to both local and overseas markets.

In 1922 a railway link had been started. The line was initially promoted by the A.G.W.I. Petroleum Corporation, building was continued by the London and South Western Railway Company, which at the grouping in 1923 became part of the Southern Railway Company, and it was opened on 20th July, 1925. The link began near Totton and followed the River Test, through Marchwood, then alongside Southampton Water, through Hythe to Fawley. The service was sparse and mainly for workers at Fawley, and

A.G.W.I. products became the major business. The line is still in use sixty years on; the main traffic is still oil. However, the small steam tank engines and carriages are long gone, for passenger carrying ceased in February, 1966, and the trains of long bogie tank wagons are hauled by diesel locomotives.

In 1923, the new and flourishing A.G.W.I. Petroleum Corporation was taken over by the British Mexican Petroleum Company Ltd.

In 1925 the *Dalmuir* was acquired by the A.G.W.I. Corporation. Once a sludge carrier for Glasgow Corporation, she was altered to an oil carrier for coastal work and then in 1926 was transferred to British Mexican Petroleum Company control.

In the same year of 1925, Anglo-American Oil Company acquired British Mexican Petroleum Company Ltd. The acquisition included part ownership of the A.G.W.I. Petroleum Corporation Ltd. Full ownership was achieved by Anglo-American in 1926.

Despite some damage by bombing, Fawley continued refining after the

Second World War began, although production was curtailed in 1942. At the end of 1943 refining ceased and Fawley became a bulk storage depot, used for transferring oil throughout the South of England. Fawley was later linked to the PLUTO concept (Pipe Line Under The Ocean) to feed the Normandy invasion forces with fuel. Just prior to the laying of the seventy-mile pipeline from storage tanks at Sandown Bay, Isle of Wight, to Cherbourg on D-Day plus ten, about twenty lines were laid between Lepe Beach, near Fawley, southwards across the Solent to Thorness Bay, Isle of Wight, and from there to Sandown Bay.

The Southampton bunkering scene

More and more shipowners were changing their ships from burning coal to oil fuel. The large passenger liners based at Southampton were rapidly being converted. Indeed, the first oil-burning ship to sail from Southampton was the *Olympic* of the White Star Line in June, 1920. Cunard had moved from Liverpool to Southampton in 1919 and began converting their ships, the

Fawley jetty, showing the aerial ropeway constructed for the shipment of bitumen in barrels. *Esso Dublin* is on the berth. *Esso*

The National Benzole Company's tanker *Ben Henshaw*, 308 gross tons, built in Norway in 1915, and the motor barge *Ben Johnson*, 183 gross tons, built in Holland in 1913, at Fawley jetty. Two more ships were built for National Benzole in 1923, the *Ben Reid*, 449 gross tons, and *Ben Robinson*, 290 gross tons.

Dr. F. Mayo

Aquitania in 1920, *Berengaria* the next year and the Blue Riband holder, *Mauretania*, in 1922.

Bunkering of fuel oil was obviously going to be big business and oil companies, anxious to be in at the beginning, quickly began arranging their facilities. Anglo-American Oil Company placed their ship *Silvertown* at anchor off Hamble Spit as a bunkering hulk in 1920 and she remained there until 5th September, 1924. In 1922, the *Genesee* was added, remaining there until 26th August, 1924. The Anglo-American Company was also planning a distribution depot in the Southampton area.

Early in 1921 the Anglo-Mexican Petroleum Company Ltd. purchased ten acres of ground on the Hamble waterfront, opposite Fawley, to erect an oil installation. A jetty 1,900 feet long was constructed, directly connected to three mooring dolphins. At that time the Anglo-Mexican Company merged with the Shell Company to become Shell-Mex Ltd., who then represented

Fawley refinery from the air in 1935. *Esso*

Anglo-Mexican and Shell Marketing Company Ltd. The Hamble installation was later able to bunker directly to ships via a pipeline across their jetty, and ships could be bunkered from barges. The Shell Company's tanker *Prygena* was a depot ship off Hamble for a time.

The Anglo-Persian Oil Company, in conjunction with their associated company British Petroleum Company Ltd., also placed their bunkering ship, *British Maple*, off Hamble. The *British Maple*, 8,039 gt, Tyne-built in 1898 as *Mount Royal* for Elder, Dempster and Company, had quite a history. She came under Canadian Pacific ownership in 1903 and in late 1914 was transformed into a dummy battleship, *Marlborough*. Next year she became the Admiralty oiler *Rangol*; she was later renamed *Mapleleaf* and in July, 1919, was sold to the British Tanker Company. Renamed *British Maple*, she arrived at Hamble on 6th June, 1922, as a fuel hulk of 11,650 tdw. There she remained until December, 1932, when she arrived at Rosyth for demolition.

The British Mexican Petroleum Company Ltd. was also extremely active in the bunkering business and could feature its barges fuelling the White Star liner *Olympic* in its advertisements. In early 1920 they secured rights to lay an oil pipeline from a site at Weston Grove, Woolston, east of the River Itchen and opposite the Docks. A long jetty owned by the London and South Western Railway Company was adjacent to a Government factory known as the Rolling Mills (built to produce steel for Russia, but instead turned over to the manufacture of shell and cartridge cases during the war) and was to be used to carry pipelines to the shore, then overland and up a gradient to storage tanks, a total distance of one and a half miles. The ground was also owned by the L.&S.W.R. and was next to the mills.

To keep the oil flowing upwards there was a pumphouse at Weston Grove in which were installed two of the largest Weir pumps ever built. Storage capacity at Weston Grove amounted to seven tanks totalling 52,500 tons. The installation was opened in 1923.

British Mexican had several dumb bunkering barges based at Southampton and they also fed the tanks at Weston Grove. Floating storage capacity of the barges was reckoned to total some 5,000 tons and oil came in British Mexican tankers which averaged about four calls each month to

The fuel depot ship *Silvertown* at moorings off Hamble. *Nautical Photo Agency*

moorings in Southampton Water. The barge fleet at Southampton was augmented with the self-propelled *Inveritchen* in later years. The anchorage area for the barges was opposite Hythe Pier and the tall, yellow, black-topped funnels of the barges were a feature of the port for many years. Eventually, with the run-down of the passenger liner services of the port in the late 1960s, bunkering requirements grew less and less, the remaining barges were sold and the Woolston depot closed.

During the Great War a train ferry link between Britain and France was introduced for military service, to connect with the French railway system. Three ferries were built, each to carry fifty-four wagons of war materials; sailings were from the little-known port of Richborough, on the estuary of the River Stour, near Sandwich, Kent, to Calais (thirty-five miles) and to

Left: Moving one of the storage tanks to County Wharf, Southampton.

Opposite: Fuelling a "pirate" bus in Regent's Park, London, during the General Strike of 1926.   *Esso*

Dunkirk (fifty-four miles). As a precautionary measure, another link was arranged from Southampton to Dieppe (130 miles).

In 1919 the Southampton train ferry operation ceased, although those from Richborough continued for some time. At Southampton the train ferry jetty, which was connected by rail spur from Southampton's West Station and equipped with a fuel tank installation, was closed down.

Meanwhile, an oil fuel distributing installation was being set up by Anglo-American Oil Company at the County Wharf, a mile or so up the Itchen, which flows through Southampton's industrial area. Anglo-American needed tankage and in early 1921 purchased the dormant installation at the Ferry site. The oil remaining in the tanks was barrelled up and sold; pumps, motors and piping were dismantled and all made ready for removal. The four tanks, 35 feet in diameter and 20 feet high, were lifted to flat barges and towed to their new site. In 1922–23 an open-piled jetty was built from County Wharf into the stream; it was called Pratt's Wharf.

Years of expansion

The first Anglo-American ocean-going motorship came in 1920, the *Narragansett* taking the name of the previous ship lost in 1917. She was the first post-war merchant vessel from Vickers after their wartime Admiralty building programme. Her sistership was named *Seminole*, after a tanker which had been in the fleet from 1904 until 1912. The *Narragansett*, launched on 27th November, 1919, was given a pair of Vickers patent oil engines; their use was not regarded as an experiment, for long research in the builder's engine works extending over fifteen years had forced them to the conviction that oil was more economically employed in the internal combustion engine than as fuel in the steam boiler. The first sea going motor tanker was the *Vulcanus*, built for the Shell Company in 1909 and equipped with Werkspoor engines which developed 350 bhp.

In the early 1920s other countries began adopting the American vehicle assembly line. More and more cars were built. New laws were passed for traffic control and a new pattern of life began to emerge. Anglo-American opened their first petrol service station at Paddington in 1920; next year the first private petrol station for the motorist opened at Putney; and the demand for showrooms, garages and cars, both new and secondhand, grew and grew. It had become obvious that retention of the Pratt's green two-gallon can was gradually becoming an economic liability. Huge depots were required for their storage and large staffs were necessary for examining, cleaning and refilling the cans, as well as for their repair and the replacement of leather washers for the caps. Other labour factors were the loading and unloading of the cans to and from wagon and cart; the carrying of the cans to garage and store; and from there to the customer. So the can was replaced and a long-necked petrol pump appeared, the name on the white globe at the top confirming it was Pratt's. And Pratt's Motor Spirit became a market leader.

More horses were being withdrawn at that time in favour of motor tank wagons and by 1925 the horse-drawn wagon had disappeared. Some steam wagons were introduced by Anglo-American in 1920 for fuel oil deliveries and these puffed along the roads until 1930.

The Valor Stove Company, which had been supplying petrol tins and oil

An early Pratt's pump installation, with a long-necked pump worked manually with a long crank handle. Note the cigarette!

heaters since 1911, was another acquisition in Anglo-American's immense expansion of the early 1920s. Anglo-American followed its acquisition with a vigorous advertising campaign directed at the "modern" housewife and at private and public schools. New importing plants were opened in 1921 at Hull, Avonmouth and Ellesmere Port for the growing fleet of tankers, and the Irish-American Oil Company was formed in 1922, enabling Anglo-American to further its operations in the then recently formed Republic of Ireland. A candle manufacturing business was also set up, its interests being consolidated in 1931 into the Standard Candle Company, which continued to trade until 1957.

But the major acquisition came in 1925 when the British Mexican Petroleum Company was purchased. British Mexican owned ten storage and bunkering plants, eight 10,000 tdw tankers, a petrol distribution organisation under the name of Redline and accompanying motor transport. British Mexican also had interests in the A.G.W.I. Petroleum Corporation and in

The "Ethyl" girls at Colchester in 1928.

1926 complete control of A.G.W.I. and its refinery was obtained by Anglo-American.

Motor car manufacturers continued to serve the public with the cars it demanded. In 1925, Henry Ford acquired a site at Dagenham, Essex, and in the following three years thousands of piles were driven into the marshland as the foundations of the first Ford motor car factory in Britain. The first vehicle rolled off its production lines in 1931.

Towards the end of this remarkable decade of expansion, Anglo-American introduced Ethyl to the motorist. In 1928 "Ethyl", personified as a young woman in tartan dress and wearing a stylish tam o'shanter on her head, became famous in a massive advertising campaign, advising motorists of the anti-knock properties in the new petrol. Seven million gallons of the new brand were sold in the first year.

There were 60,000 petrol pumps in use in 1930 for Britain's million cars, although not selling any one particular company's brand of petrol. By 1939 pumps had increased to 100,000 in number, supplying 830 million gallons of petrol being consumed yearly by the two and a half million vehicles on the roads.

Ocean tankers of the 1920s

	Completed	Gross tons	
Strathearn	1.1906	4,419	Built by Grangemouth & Greenock Dockyard Co., Greenock, for Burrell & Son, Glasgow. Measurements: 384 feet (oa)/370 feet length × 52 feet breadth. Engines: T3cyl.

The *Strathearn* was purchased by Anglo-American Oil Company in 1920 and four years later was disposed of to P. C. & G. C. Lemos who renamed her *Constantinos*. A year later she became *Kostantis Lemos* and shortly afterwards *Danaos*. In 1939 she moved from the Greek flag to Italy and became the *Moscardin* of the Soc. di Nav. "Polena", Genoa. She was put in the coal trade from Newcastle to Italy and when Italy entered the war on 10th June, 1940, was at Newcastle. She quickly put to sea but was stopped and escorted to Methil on 11th June. The *Moscardin* was officially seized on 27th June and handed over to the Ministry of War Transport for service as the *Empire Gunner*. On 7th September, 1941, she was in St Georges Channel on a voyage from Pepel (Freetown) to the Tees with iron ore when she was bombed and sunk in position 52.08N 05.18W.

Housatonic	1919	5,519	Built by Wm Hamilton & Co. Ltd., Port Glasgow, as *War Dogra* for the Shipping Controller. Measurements: 412 feet (oa)/400 feet length × 52 feet breadth. Engines: T3cyl. 1920: (Anglo-American Oil Company). 19.2.1941: Bombed and sunk 59.39N 07.24W (approximately), while serving as a Royal Fleet Auxiliary.

The *Seminole* of 1921, seen here, and her sistership *Narragansett* were the first ocean-going motor vessels in the Anglo-American fleet. *Esso*

The *Kennebec*, a war-built 'Z'-type standard tanker, was sistership to the *Housatonic*.   *Esso*

Kennebec	1919	5,548	Built by R. Duncan & Co. Ltd., Port Glasgow, as *War Mogul* for the Shipping Controller.

Measurements: 412 feet (oa)/400 feet length × 52 feet breadth.
Engines: T3cyl.
1920: (Anglo-American Oil Co.).
8.9.1939: Torpedoed and attacked by gunfire by submarine *U.34*, 49.18N 08.13W. Wreckage sunk by Royal Navy ship on following day.

The *Housatonic* and *Kennebec* were war-built standard ships of the 'Z'-type, designed for the carriage of heavy fuel oil. The intention was for forty of these ships to be built but of the twelve contracted for, six were completed and six cancelled, two later being built as dry cargo ships.

In the design, the expansion trunk was placed in a centre position on the weather deck, the usual side tanks being eliminated and creating a low deck on either side of the trunk. The *War Dogra* and *War Mogul* were acquired from the Shipping Controller on 16th February, 1920, and 13th February, 1920, respectively.

Narragansett	5.1920	6,889	Built by Vickers Ltd., Barrow.

Measurements: 425 feet length × 57 feet breadth.
Engines: Oil. Twin screws.
1933: Sold for breaking up.

The *Narragansett*, the first post-war tanker to be built for Anglo-American, was launched on 27th November, 1919, and ran trials on 5th May, 1920. Speed was guaranteed at 10½ knots and the daily consumption of oil was 9.6 tons. Her results in the Atlantic trade were extremely satisfactory and on one early voyage she ran from New Orleans to Liverpool at 11.1 knots. Both *Narragansett* and her sistership *Seminole* had a deadweight capacity of 10,500 tons.

Seminole	5.1921	6,923	Built by Vickers Ltd., Barrow.

Measurements: 425 feet length × 57 feet breadth.
Engines: Oil. Twin screws.
3.1936: Sold for breaking up "as lies" at Belfast.

On 13th December, 1927, the *Seminole* was on her way to Dingle oil jetty in the River Mersey to discharge 10,000 tons of petrol when she went aground on Pluckington Bank, near the Brunswick Dock, and could not be towed off. At low water some plates parted and some 2,000 or more tons of petrol flowed into the river, floating downstream towards Liverpool. There was immediate danger of a serious explosion and fire, considered so great that all available police were rushed to the landing stage to prevent people from smoking. Notices were placed on ferries warning passengers of the serious danger of striking matches, the Liverpool Fire Brigade laid out thousands of yards of hose and fire extinguishers were placed in readiness along the seven miles of dock quays. Naked lights were forbidden on river craft and dock sides. Some 1,200 troops were on board the 17,000-ton Anchor Line troopship *California* alongside the landing stage; she was moved. For some days the river and docks were held in a state of emergency, particularly in the area around the grounded ship but, eventually, a six-inch pipe was connected from the stranded *Seminole* to another tanker in the Brunswick Dock. The danger subsided as the petrol was transshipped.

Chesapeake	1.1928	8,955	Built by Workman, Clark & Co. Ltd., Belfast. Measurements: 477 feet length × 64 feet breadth. Engines: Oil. 12 knots. 1950: *Esso Aberdeen.* 28.9.1953: Arrived Faslane for scrap.

The *Chesapeake* was the first motorship built by Workman, Clark to be propelled by Workman Clark–Sulzer engines. Her hull was divided into twenty-two main and ten summer tanks. Launched on 24th November, 1927, she was the last vessel (Yard No. 494) to be built by the old firm of Workman, Clark & Company Ltd., and on her completion the shipyard, engine works and repair works all closed down. Within a few months the company was completely reorganised under the title of Workman, Clark (1928) Ltd., the first launching taking place on 16th October, 1928. This was the *Divis*, a small sludge carrier of 357 gt for the Belfast Corporation.

Schuylkill	5.1928	8,964	Built by Sir J. Laing & Sons Ltd., Sunderland. Measurements: 477 feet length × 64 feet breadth. 13,000 tdw. Engines: Oil. 12 knots. 1947: Sold for scrap.

The *Schuylkill* had an eventful end to her career. Sold for breaking up, she was originally intended for the Tyne, but was found too large to enter the shipbreaker's yard. Instead, she was taken to the Firth of Forth where P. and W. MacLellan Ltd. were to break her up. On 6th April she was torn from her moorings in a storm and blown across the Forth, running aground near the entrance to Charleston harbour, Fife. Refloated a month later, the *Schuylkill* was beached at the shipbreaker's yard at Bo'ness.

The *Appalachee*, completed in December, 1930, served in the Anglo-American fleet for just ten years, being torpedoed by a U-boat in the Atlantic on 2nd December, 1940.   *Esso*

The 1930s

In the early months of 1929 there were signs that all was not well in the financial world. The slight rumblings continued throughout the summer and in September there was concern in London over the failure of some companies. Within a week or so panic swept through the New York Stock Exchange, plunging the world into a period of economic blizzard that was to last through the early years of the 1930s. In Britain three million—one in six of the workforce—were unemployed by 1932. But these years, however economically dark, were of peace.

Two Anglo-American ships were delivered at the end of 1930; the *Cheyenne* in November and *Appalachee* in the following month. Both came from Palmers' yard on the Tyne where many tankers had been built over the years.

Standard Oil, the parent company, using its initials phonetically as Esso, produced something new in 1934, using the title to introduce Essolube, the first long-life motor oil, sold to the motorist in sealed glass bottles. At this time Esso globes began appearing at the top of petrol pumps, the old name Pratt's being withdrawn. With thousands of pumps to change, the old name lingered for a while but by April, 1935, it had disappeared.

In the early years of the 1930s, Anglo-American rationalised its distribution system. Over forty sales branches were reorganised into sales divisions; depots and terminals were reduced in number; and mechanical aids were introduced into offices.

The controlling interest in Cleveland Petroleum Products Company was acquired by Anglo-American in 1935 and in that year more national prestige came for Britain with Sir Malcolm Campbell's land-speed record of 301 mph. Then, on 27th May, 1936, the *Queen Mary* sailed on her maiden voyage to New York. A symbol of Britain's economic revival, she immediately gained the Blue Riband of the Atlantic. The middle years were the halcyon days of the 1930s, but colder winds were blowing in central Europe and there was an uneasy diplomatic situation as nations began re-arming. The Second World War was just over three years away.

A new lubricating oil carrier, *Comanchee*, was accepted into the Anglo-American fleet in 1936. She was capable of sailing up the Manchester Ship Canal.

A notable event in 1938 was the discovery of the company's first domestic oil supply at Dalkeith, just south of Edinburgh, in Scotland. The country's only producing well, it came into production in May, 1938, with a daily output of twenty barrels. It was still producing twenty-five years later and, although its contribution to overall needs was almost negligible, it nevertheless produced a total of several thousand tons.

Four tankers were transferred from the Panama Transport Company in 1939; three were placed in the Anglo-American fleet, the other being put under nominal ownership of the British Mexican Petroleum Company Ltd.

At the outbreak of hostilities in September, 1939, Anglo-American Oil Company, in common with all other oil companies, ceased to exist as an independent concern for all practical purposes. The whole of their resources and experience was placed at the service of the nation, with the government's Petroleum Board directing the entire oil industry in the United Kingdom. In fact, this Board was not wound up until June, 1948, but because of the economic situation the government kept both prices and imports controlled until 1953, and only then were branded names of petrol and products again allowed on sale.

Ocean tankers of the 1930s

	Completed	Gross tons	
Cheyenne	11.1930	8,825	Built by Palmers Co. Ltd., Newcastle. Measurements: 477 feet length × 64 feet breadth. 12,350 tdw. Engines: Oil. 12 knots. 15.9.1939: torpedoed and attacked by gunfire by *U.53* in 50.20N 13.30W. Abandoned. Wreck sunk later by Royal Navy destroyer.
Appalachee	12.1930	8,826	Built by Palmers Co. Ltd., Newcastle. Measurements: 477 feet length × 64 feet breadth. 12,350 tdw. Engines: Oil. 12 knots. 1.12.1940: Sunk by submarine *U.101* torpedo, 54.30N 20.00W while sailing in convoy HX 90 (United States–United Kingdom).
Comanchee	3.1936	6,837	Built by John Brown & Co. Ltd., Clydebank. Measurements: 450 feet length × 61 feet breadth. Engines: Oil. 1950: *Esso Plymouth*. 9.8.1962: Arrived Grimstad for breaking up.

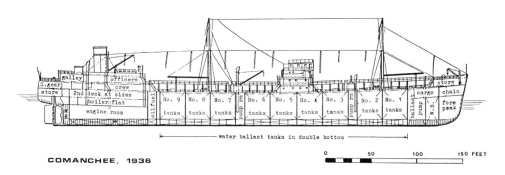

COMANCHEE, 1936

Acquired from the Royal Navy in 1920, the *Juniata* was used to distribute oil to depots on the British coast.   *Tom Rayner*

The *Comanchee* was built for the carriage of 10,300 tdw of lubricating oils in twenty-seven tank compartments, separated by two longitudinal bulkheads and by tranverse bulkheads. She had a cruiser stern and was also given a double bottom for water ballast to overcome the necessity of carrying water ballast in cargo tanks, as in earlier-designed tankers.

Her dimensions gave her a capability of negotiating the locks of the Manchester Ship Canal.

Distributing ships 1915–1939

During the Great War a number of coasters were acquired, and in the Government Disposal Scheme just after war ended the Royal Fleet Auxiliary tankers *Sprucol* and *Ferol* were purchased and renamed *Juniata* and *Osage* respectively. And as ships turned from coal to oil-burning, so more oil was carried to the bunkering depots.

In the Thames, tugs and lighters played a big part in the movement of oils upriver and a fleet of petroleum-carrying lighters was constructed in the early 1920s. Smaller estuarial craft were stationed in the larger seaport areas—the Clyde, Mersey, Humber, Southampton Water—moving oils for local storage. And motor barges thumped their ways along the canals of Yorkshire, Lancashire, Lincolnshire . . . all bearing the red, black-topped funnel of Anglo-American Oil Company Ltd.

	Completed	Gross tons	
Juniata	1.1918	1,137	Built by Short Bros. Ltd., Sunderland as *Sprucol* for the Royal Fleet Auxiliary Service.
			Measurements: 210 feet length × 35 feet breadth.
			Engines: Oil. Twin screws.

At the outbreak of war in 1914 the Admiralty embarked on a programme of tanker construction for the newly-formed Royal Fleet Auxiliary Service and over twenty of the 1,000 ton class were built. Seven were sold when war ended, and the *Sprucol* was purchased by Anglo-American on 31st March, 1920, and renamed *Juniata*. In 1940 she was taken up by the Royal Navy and sunk as a blockship at Scapa Flow. In July, 1949, she was raised, patched up at Water Sound, Orkney, and towed away to the shipbreaker's yard.

Osage	1914	1,010	Built at Devonport Dockyard as *Ferol* (Royal Fleet Auxiliary). Measurements: 200 feet length × 34 feet breadth. 1,125 tdw. Engines: Oil. 1.1920: (Anglo-American). Re-engined. 18.12.1940: Bombed and sunk 4 miles NE of Arklow Lightvessel, Co. Wicklow.
Luffworth	5.1911	279	Built by J. T. Eltringham & Co., Willington, Newcastle, as *Holzapfel I* for Steam Traders Ltd. and fitted with an experimental gas engine. Measurements: 126 feet length × 22 feet breadth. 1913: Re-engined C.2cyl—aft. 1915: (Anglo-American). *1934: (W. A. Andow & Co. Ltd., Newcastle). 1935: (Sea & Land Securities Ltd.). 1938: (Fellows S.S. Co. Ltd., Liverpool). 17.6.1940: Scuttled at Brest. Taken in prize by enemy.

Refloated by the Germans on 31.8.1940, the ship was purchased by Ed. Halm and Company, Hamburg, who intended to repair her at Bordeaux. Work was not commenced and she was scuttled again, at Rochefort in 9.1944. Refloated in 5.1949 and 10.1950: sold for scrapping.

Luffwell	9.1912	274	Built by Van Damme Freres & Adam, Baesrode, Belgium, as *Mate* for Steam Traders Ltd. Measurements: 120 feet length × 22 feet breadth. Engines: C.2cyl—aft. 1916: (Anglo-American). Fitted with tanks in hold to carry petroleum. 1.1935: Broken up.

The steam coaster *Luffwell*, built in Belgium in 1912, was fitted with tanks to carry petroleum.

Tom Rayner

Built on the River Dee at Connah's Quay in 1921, the *Allegheny* is seen here in Southampton Water.

Tom Rayner

Southwick	2.1917	443	Built by Swan, Hunter & Wigham Richardson Ltd., Sunderland. Measurements: 150 feet length × 26 feet breadth. Engines: T3cyl—aft. Case-oil carrier. *1925: (H. Harrison (Shipping) Ltd., Sunderland). 1927: (Harrison, Thornton & Co., Sunderland). 1931: (A. Chester (Springfield Shipping Co., Middlesbrough)). 1940: (G. W. Grace & Co. Ltd., London). 1946: *Rojo* (Rolf Johannesen, Oslo). 3.12.1948: Leaking, flooded after pump failure in heavy weather. Listed and foundered in North Sea on voyage Middlesbrough/Copenhagen with a cargo of steel.
Nuorla	1918	364	Built by Gebr. van der Windt, Vlaardingen, Holland as *Nautilus*. Measurements: 132 feet length × 23 feet breadth. Engines: T3cyl—aft. 1920: (Anglo-American). *1936: *Selma B.* (B. Bentzen, Copenhagen). 1939: *Ogre* (Kopredereja "Ogre", Latvia). 1947: *Balga* (Ministry of War Transport). 1948: *Ogre* (Operated by Hannan, Samuel & Co. Ltd., Fowey, for Minister of Transport (British flag.)) 10.1953: Broken up by G. Rees Shipbreaking Co. Ltd., Llanelly.
Eastwick	6.1920	518	Built by Swan, Hunter & Wigham Richardson Ltd., Wallsend. Measurements: 158 feet length × 26 feet breadth. Engines: T3cyl—aft. Case-oil carrier. 12.1948: Scrapped Grays, Essex.

Stourgate seen off the coast of Kent.   *Skyfotos*

Allegheny	7.1921	822	Built by J. Crichton & Co. Ltd., Connah's Quay, nr. Chester.

Measurements: 200 feet length × 32 feet breadth.
Engines: T3cyl—aft.
6.1962: Scrapped Boom, Belgium.

The *Allegheny* was launched from her builders' yard on 12th April, 1921, the largest vessel and first oil-burning steamer constructed on the River Dee. She was then towed to the builders' fitting-out dock at Saltney, where her propelling machinery was placed aboard and the ship made ready for sea.

Estuarial and river vessels

Bargate	1916	66	Built at Chester.

Measurements: 80 feet length × 17 feet breadth.
Motor tank barge for service in Southampton Water.
1925: (Risdon Beazley Ltd).
1955: (S. J. Clegg)
1972: Presumed scrapped.

After a fire, the *Bargate* was sold in the 1920s, repaired and then used as a sludge carrier, loading at a River Itchen wharf for dumping off the Needles. Her daily run included a call at the A.G.W.I. jetty where she took on acid tar waste from the naphtha-treating plant for dumping. When this work ended she was sold and became a workboat, which included pile-driving equipment.

Perfection	1916	73	Built by P. McGregor, Kirkintilloch, Scotland. Measurements: 64 feet length × 17 feet breadth. Motor tank barge for service on the Forth and Clyde Canal. 1956: Sold to the Admiralty.
Tetney	1909	47	Built by Cook, Welton & Gemmel Ltd., Beverley, Yorkshire. Measurements: 60 feet length × 15 feet breadth. 1917: (Anglo-American). Motor tank barge for service on the River Humber. 9.1956: Arrived Gateshead for scrapping by J. J. King & Co.
Silver Queen	12.1912	165	Built by H. & C. Grayson Ltd., Garston for S. C. Chambers & Co. Measurements: 95 feet (oa)/89 feet length × 18 feet breadth. 1919: (Anglo-American). For service on the River Mersey and coasting between Carnarvon and Barrow in the four summer months. 1927: Engines removed. Converted to a dumb barge.
Crown Diamond (tug)	1.1912	103	Built by C. H. Walker & Co., Sudbrook, Monmouthshire, as *BAHW 25*, for B. A. H. Walker & Co., Buenos Aires. Measurements: 95 feet (oa)/89 feet length × 18 feet breadth. Engines: T3cyl. 1920: (Anglo-American). 3.1950: Scrapped Grays, Essex.
Tensas	1911	643	Built by Union Normande, Rouen, France, as *Edith*. Measurements: 230 feet length × 27 feet breadth. A non-propelled oil barge. 1920: (Anglo-American).
Atoka	1914	581	Built at Rouen, France, as *Horace*. Measurements: 199 feet length × 26 feet breadth. A tank barge, 968 tdw. 1920: (Anglo-American). 1.1950: Reported scrapped.

The Southgate in Southampton Water on 4th July, 1949.   *G. A. Osbon*

Angloco	1921	73	Built by Rennie, Ritchie & Newport Shipbuilding Co., Wivenhoe. Measurements: 79 feet length × 19 feet breadth. Engines: Oil. Motor barge for service on Norfolk Broads, carrying petroleum in portable tanks from Oulton Broad to Norwich. 6.9.1956: Arrived Gateshead for scrapping by C. W. Donkin & Co.
Clydegate	1923	66	Built by Greenock & Grangemouth Dockyard Co., Grangemouth. Measurements: 64 feet length × 18 feet breadth. Motor barge for service on the Forth and Clyde Canal. *1956: (Alden Shipping Co. Ltd.).
Stourgate	5.1924	115	Built by J. Pollock & Sons, Faversham. Measurements: 85 feet length × 19 feet breadth. Engines: Oil. For service on the River Stour, Kent. *1955: (W. G. S. Crouch Ltd.). 1963: *Harriet Spearing* (W. G. S. Crouch Ltd., London).
Southgate	12.1925	143	Built by Amble Shipbuilding Co. Ltd., Amble. Measurements: 92 feet length × 19 feet breadth. Engines: Oil. Motor barge for service in Southampton Water. *1955: (H. G. Pounds, Portsmouth). 1956: *Cisterna* (P. Schipper, Holland). 1957: *Piet Schipper* (P. Schipper, Holland). Converted from a tanker and re-engined (oil). 10.5.1960: Foundered three miles from Haisborough Light, North Sea, after cargo of steel plate shifted on voyage from Antwerp to Boston, Lincs.
Fossgate	1925	49	Built by Henry Scarr Ltd., Hessle. Measurements: 85 feet length × 15 feet breadth. Engines: Oil. Motor barge for service on the Humber and Yorkshire/Lincolnshire rivers and canals. Carried oil in portable tanks. 5.9.1956: Arrived Gateshead for scrapping by J. J. King & Co.
Parkgate	11.1925	52	Built by W. J. Yarwood & Son, Northwich. Measurements: 71 feet length × 14 feet breadth. Engines: Paraffin motor. Motor barge for service in Southampton Water, carrying oil in portable tanks. 1955: *Esso Parkgate*. *1970: *Parkstan* (Southern Tanker & Bunkering Co.) 1975: *Bosham* (Bowker & King Ltd., London). 1985: Scrapped.
Lowgate	10.1925	75	Built by Henry Scarr Ltd., Hessle. Measurements: 81 feet length × 14 feet breadth (lengthened in 1935). Motor barge for service on the River Humber and Yorkshire and Lincolnshire rivers and canals.

Originally built for service on the Mersey and its associated waterways, the *Queensgate* is seen in Southampton Water in 1953.

G. A. Osbon

Caldergate	2.1926	138	Built by Amble Shipbuilding Co. Ltd., Amble. Measurements: 101 feet (oa)/97 feet length × 17 feet breadth. Engines: Oil. For coasting service, also stationed in Blackwall Reach, River Thames, bunkering gas oil to small vessels up to 200 feet. *1959: Sold, converted to hulk.
Tommy Pratt-kins (tug)	–	13	Measurements: 31 feet length × 9 feet breadth. Engine: Oil. A motor tug for service on the River Thames. Mostly used as a tender from Purfleet, carrying stores, ropes, lamps etc. to oil barge moorings in Bow Creek etc 6.1927: Vessel first registered with the Port of London Authority.
Castlegate	1.1928	87	Built by W. J. Yarwood & Son, Northwich. Measurements: 71 feet length × 14 feet breadth. Engine: Paraffin motor. Motor Barge for River Mersey and canal service, carrying oil in portable tanks. 1949: New engine (oil). *1955: *John Abbott*. 1956: Reported scrapped.
Queensgate	2.1928	87	Built by W. J. Yarwood & Son, Northwich. Measurements: 71 feet length × 14 feet breadth. Engine: Paraffin motor. Motor barge for River Mersey and canal service, carrying oil in portable tanks. *1958: Sold (H. G. Pounds, Portsmouth). Resold Holland, a barge.

| *Westgate* | 2.1928 | 48 | Built by Goole Shipbuilding & Repair Co. Ltd., Goole.
Measurements: 73 feet length × 14 feet breadth.
Engines: Oil.
Motor barge for service on River Thames and estuary.
  Frequently used for towing purposes.
1961: New oil engine.
*1966: *Brevet* (Bowker & King Ltd., London).
Now scrapped. |

Non-propelled tank barges built for use, under tow, on River Thames

For carrying petroleum in portable tanks:
>Built by R. Colby, Lowestoft. Yard Nos 22–27.
>Measurements: 78 feet length × 14 feet breadth.
>46 registered tons. 77 tdw.

Northampton	11.1920	*Anglesea*	3.1921
Radnor	11.1920	*Glamorgan*	4.1921
Montgomery	1.1921	*Merioneth*	4.1921

Three further vessels were built in later years:
>Built by Goole Shipbuilding & Repair Co., Goole.
>Measurements: 75 feet length × 14 feet breadth.
>57 registered tons. 90 tdw.

| *Berks* | 11.1927 |

>Measurements: 80 feet length × 22 feet breadth.
>96 registered tons. 160 tdw.

| *Shropshire* | 10.1926 | *Kent* | 4.1934 |

For carrying petroleum in bulk:
>Built by F. Braby, Deptford, London. Yard Nos 615–618.
>Measurements: 83 feet length × 21 feet breadth.
>102 registered tons. 150 tdw.

| *Cumberland* | 11.1921 | *Westmorland* | 2.1922 |
| *Northumberland* | 12.1921 | *Sutherland* | 7.1922 |

>Built by F. Braby, Deptford, London. Yard Nos 619–622.
>Measurements: 69 feet length × 20 feet breadth.
>69 registered tons. 115 tdw.

| *Leicester* | 9.1922 | *Hereford* | 12.1922 |
| *Worcester* | 11.1922 | *Monmouth* | 3.1923 |

Associates' activities

Apart from Anglo-American, there was a considerable expansion in foreign operations of Standard Oil Company of New Jersey's associated companies, particularly between 1927 and 1939 when the number of ships and their deadweight carrying capacity almost trebled. Much of the tonnage was acquired through the purchase of producing or marketing companies, but more significant was the number of new tankers constructed for the overseas affiliates during the period. A large proportion of the new vessels were ordered for a Danzig-based company which supplied many of the European markets and also carried crude oil from loading terminals in the

Americas to refineries in the United States. But, as economic and political conditions altered after 1927, so was the nationality of this fleet changed and other affiliated fleets, especially in the Western World and the Far East, expanded.

Of the foreign flag fleets in 1927, three were in the Western hemisphere. Since the dissolution of the Standard Trust in 1911 the Canadian affiliate, Imperial Oil Ltd., had enlarged its fleet to serve its refining and marketing organisations. In 1927 the company had fifteen ships under the British flag, of which more than half were engaged in the Great Lakes trade. The remainder carried crude oil from Peru, Colombia, Mexico and the United States to company refineries on both the Atlantic and the Pacific coasts of Canada. The two other companies owning tankers at this time were Compania Transportado de Petroleo, which had two small river and coastal ships under the Argentinian flag, and the International Petroleum Company Ltd., of Toronto, with two.

In the Eastern hemisphere ten offshoots owned tankers, both ocean-going and coastal; one, NV Nederlandsche Koloniale Petroleum Maatschappij, was using a small tanker under the Dutch flag to carry products from the Palembang (Dutch East Indies) refinery to nearby distributing terminals.

In Europe, eight associated companies in Belgium, Holland, Denmark, Germany, Norway, Sweden, Italy and France owned twenty-two ocean-going tankers which carried products to and from markets and sources in both hemispheres. The Danzig-based affiliate Baltisch-Amerikanische Petroleum-Import-Gesellschaft (B.A.P.I.C.O.) owned thirteen deep-sea tankers engaged in the transatlantic and coastal trades. Altogether, these affiliates in Canada, Argentina, Europe and Asia owned fifty-four tankers in 1927, with a deadweight tonnage of some 479,000, about the same tonnage as owned by Standard Oil's home-based affiliated fleets. In this same year a grand total of 960,000 tdw of shipping owned by the entire Standard Oil group ranked as the second largest tanker fleet in private hands, outclassed only by the Royal Dutch Shell group, which owned 145 tankers of 1,047,000 tdw under the British, Dutch and Mexican flags. The third company, Anglo-Persian Oil Company Ltd., owned eighty-three tankers totalling 735,000 tdw, all their ships under British registry. Collectively, these three large groups owned almost 2¼ million tdw, or some 30% of the world tanker tonnage.

Another company acquired, in 1928, was Creole Petroleum Corporation, which promptly ordered three Venezuelan-flag tankers to carry oil from Lake Maracaibo to a nearby terminal, the vessels operating under the management of Gulf Refining Company which was buying oil from Creole. Another acquisition was the one tanker of Beacon Transport Company Ltd., which flew the British flag.

In 1932, Standard Oil acquired through the Pan American Foreign Corporation the fleet of an affiliate, Lago Shipping Company Ltd., a British company whose twenty-one tankers were designed to carry crude oil from Lake Maracaibo to the refinery on the island of Aruba. In addition there was a tug, *Delaplaine*. Two of the larger vessels were immediately transferred to Standard Oil of Venezuela, but the remainder continued under the management of Captain Robert Rogers, the Aruba agent for Andrew Weir and Company, a British concern which had been managing the fleet.

A major addition to the parent company's complex family of tanker fleets was that of Anglo-American Oil Company Ltd. When Standard Oil Export Corporation acquired Anglo-American Oil Company's stock early in 1930, the company owned fourteen ocean-going and four coastal tankers plus, through its own affiliate, British Mexican Petroleum Company, a fleet of eight tankers for carrying oil to Great Britain and for supplying British bunkering stations in Europe.

By exchanging its ownership of Nederlandsche Koloniale Petroleum Maatschappij for a half-interest in the newly-formed Standard-Vacuum Oil Company in 1934, Standard Oil still further increased its involvement in shipping. Up to then Socony-Vacuum, [6] the other half-owner of the new company, had depended on its American and British affiliates and on chartered tonnage to carry products from Romania, Russia, Persia, Burma and California to its many markets in Asia, Australia and Africa. Socony began to build bulk terminals in the Indies in 1927 and depended on N.K.P.M.'s small tankers to supply products in bulk. By 1934, N.K.P.M. had three tankers and these were transferred in the following year to N.V. Nederlandsche Koloniale Tankvaart Maatschappij, while Oriental Tankers Ltd. was set up at the same time to build up a British ocean-going fleet for Standard-Vacuum.

In the years immediately preceding the depression, several of Standard Oil's foreign offshoots began to increase their fleets. The largest of the tankers built was International Petroleum's *C. O. Stillman*, a diesel-driven vessel of 22,270 tdw, a little larger than the parent company's *John D. Archbold*, built in 1921 and designed to carry both ore and oil. There were considerable additions to the B.A.P.I.C.O. fleet between 1929 and 1933, part of a twenty-ship building programme. The first two tankers, launched in 1929, were designed for carrying special products such as asphalt and lubricants; others were suited to transporting crude oil or, after cleansing, petroleum products. Of these, half the cost of a batch of six ordered in 1929

Ships of the Lago fleet fitting out at Belfast in 1927. Lying at the quay is *La Salina* and outside her is *Icotea*; in the background at the quay is *Lagunilla*, while the small vessel on the left is the *Inveritchen*.   *Andrew Weir & Co. Ltd.*

from Italian, German and British yards plus two ordered at the same time from American yards for Standard Oil's own fleet was paid for by the award of the Mixed Claims Commission for German destruction and utilisation of Romanian properties during the Great War. Another order was placed with Italian and German yards in 1930 for nine tankers, to be delivered within three years; one ship was delivered to Standard Oil's French associate. But all these new vessels were acquired at a time when the oil industry and its allied tanker trades were beginning to feel the effects of a world-wide depression, for late in 1931 it was estimated that a quarter of the world tanker fleet, 364 ships of some 3,300,000 tdw, was idle. Even Royal Dutch Shell's British company, Anglo-Saxon, were trying to delay the launching of twenty tankers that they had ordered to replace recent disposals. Several of Standard Oil's foreign-flag fleets joined with other companies to form an International Tanker Association in order that small payments could be made to old tankers laid up and so enable others to remain active at remunerative rates. The independent Norwegian owners were particularly hard hit, having forty tankers with a carrying capacity of 500,000 tdw idle in 1932. Gradually, however, the world situation improved and the number of idle ships declined, though many were sold for scrapping.

The decentralised management of tankers within the group's foreign-flag fleets created many problems, and when a surplus of tonnage in 1927 turned to a scarcity in 1928–29 the European affiliates were actually bidding against each other in a frantic effort to charter vessels. This kind of activity caused the parent company to realise that some central control of the marine business was necessary, despite the newly-adopted policy of decentralisation. A step in this direction was a plan for co-ordinating European tanker movements and an arrangement with a London broker to handle, exclusively, the chartering of outside foreign tankers. Standard Oil studied the possibility that Anglo-American, which in the past had handled the chartering of vessels through several brokers, might object to the move, but the change coincided with Anglo-American seeking a stronger position through becoming once again an affiliate of Standard Oil. These measures were not in themselves sufficient to introduce all the desired economies and during 1930 the pooling of all ocean-going tankers of the European affiliates was promoted. Oddly enough, Anglo-American objected to this pooling for two years, but in 1931 other affiliates became members of a European consortium. Profit or loss from the operation was shared by the members in proportion to the total cargo carried for each member.

Problems of taxation and management brought several changes in the ownership of these foreign-flag tankers between 1927 and 1939. Creole disposed of its "lake" tankers in 1932 in order that Lago Shipping might handle the transportation of all the crude oil of the two Standard Oil affiliates

The refinery at Aruba in 1936. Fourteen Lake Maracaibo shallow-draught tankers can be seen.
Andrew Weir & Co. Ltd.

from Lake Maracaibo, and in 1936 management of Lago Shipping was transferred to Anglo-American Oil Company Ltd. In the same year Imperial Oil, in order to reduce its liability for taxes, transferred its tankers to a separate company, Imperial Oil Shipping Company Ltd.

Another important change in ownership had occurred in 1935 when the increasing tempo of Hitler's Nazi politics made it unsatisfactory to have about half of the carrying capacity of the European fleet domiciled in Danzig, which could easily lose its neutral status if taken by Germany. In April, 1935, the B.A.P.I.C.O. fleet, under the Danzig flag, consisted of twenty-five tankers totalling 374,000 tdw, and until 1935 the favourable tax arrangements, the neutral position of the Free City of Danzig, and the low cost of operation fully justified the concentration of the large amount of tonnage in one company. A company statement recorded that "the present European political situation would make any European flag subject to most of the disadvantages presented by the Danzig registry." To what register should this Danzig fleet be transferred for safety in the event of war and for economical operations in time of peace?

Later, another statement proposed that "subject to being able to make a satisfactory agreement with the Panamanian Government on taxes and maritime regulations generally, especially with respect to complete freedom of nationality of licensed and unlicensed personnel and complete freedom to transfer the vessels to other registry when desired, the B.A.P.I.C.O. fleet should be transferred to Panamanian registry, it being contemplated that these vessels could be manned by German or other nationals, thereby maintaining equal efficiency". It was believed that in the event of a major war Panama and the United States might agree to the transfer of the ships to the registry of the United States in order to provide adequate protection for the Panama-flag tankers. Eventually, on 10th May, 1935, the B.A.P.I.C.O. fleet was transferred from Danzig registry—before all details of its Panamanian registry had been agreed. After being stateless for three weeks the ships were transferred on 31st May to Panamanian registry and the Panama Transport Company. The group was then prepared, in the event of war, to avoid the difficulties that had arisen over the German tanker fleet in 1914. The tankers were under the direction of the New York office and, as before, were part of the consortium arrangement, although they were still manned by German crews.

Altogether, there was a notable expansion in the total tanker fleet of Standard Oil's foreign affiliates between 1927 and 1939. The number of foreign-fleet tankers almost trebled, whereas the American home fleet did not quite double. An even larger increase had been planned for the foreign fleet, but construction was curtailed because of the increasing threat of war. Following an upturn in the condition of the petroleum market and a general recovery of business in 1934, new tankers were ordered in conformity with the company's aim of having about three-quarters of its foreign requirements covered by its own foreign tankers by 1942, and of relying on long-term chartering to assure a total sufficiency for 90% of normal needs. But uncertainties in Europe delayed the placing of contracts, with the result that only eight tankers had been delivered to European affiliates by September, 1939. Affiliates in the Western hemisphere were more fortunate, Panama Transport, Imperial Oil and Lago Shipping enlarging their fleets in 1937–38. All these additions were accompanied by the disposal of old vessels, and at the time Germany invaded Poland in September, 1939, the total foreign fleet numbered 148 vessels, of 1,388,000 tdw. This marked the high point for Standard Oil's foreign fleet, which then included two-thirds of the number of vessels and three-fifths of the tonnage of the whole group. From 1931 until the beginning of the Second World War, the European companies of the group joined in three agreements designed to provide for the more efficient use of their tanker fleets. As well as the 1931 agreement for a two-year pooling of tonnage, a second agreement, effective from the first day of 1933 and to run for five years, included Anglo-American. This agreement was

The White Star liner *Homeric* taking on fuel oil from the *Invergoil* in Algiers Roads in May, 1933.

Esso

revised five times to adjust to changing conditions, including those of rising freight rates. The third agreement, effective at the beginning of 1938, was not only revised several times but also provided the basis for arrangements by the British government during the war.

As the political situation in Europe deteriorated it became necessary to replace the crews of the German-manned vessels of the Panama Transport Company. Generally, the procedure was simple enough and in many instances the change was made when the ships arrived in American ports before the outbreak of war on 3rd September, 1939, but a number of crews had to be replaced on vessels held in foreign ports. By 31st August the German crews on seventeen of the twenty-seven ships so manned had been taken off, most of the vessels being re-manned by Americans, although there were four with British crews. In the September, nine more complements were replaced. By force of circumstance the tanker *Prometheus* was the last to undergo crew change, her German crew remaining aboard until 1st April, 1940, when an American crew took charge at St Vincent, Cape Verde Islands. The *Prometheus* had left Aruba on 7th August, 1939, with diesel and fuel oils

Built in Germany in 1933, the *Robert F. Hand* was quickly transferred to the Anglo-American fleet.

for St Vincent, where she arrived on the 29th. Discharge was completed on 2nd September, the day after German forces attacked Poland and the day before the declaration of the European war. The prospects that a vessel with a German crew could escape capture on the high seas were slim, and sailing orders were not issued. Finally, on 16th March, 1940, the tanker *Esso Trenton* sailed from New York carrying an American crew for the *Prometheus*. On 3rd April both vessels sailed, bound for Aruba.

The 1929–1933 programme

The large tanker programme, with orders placed through the Standard Shipping Company of New York in 1929–33, was in two parts.

The first orders for two ships to carry asphalt and oil in bulk were delivered from Palmers, on the Tyne. They were *Stanasfalt* (2,468 gt) and *Ebano* (2,623 gt). The *Stanasfalt* was delivered direct to Société Auxiliaire des Transports, Rouen, in April, 1929; the *Ebano*, delivered in October, 1930, joined the same French fleet later and was renamed *Petrophalt*. There was an order for a 15,000-ton oil carrier from Burmeister & Wain, Copenhagen, for the Standard Oil associate, Det Danske Petroleum A/S, to be named *Danmark*; two 19,000 tdw tankers from the Federal Shipbuilding Company of Kearny, New Jersey, for the American parent company, designed with superheated steam turbines of 4,000 ihp to give 11½ knots; and a further six vessels for Baltisch-Amerikanische Petroleum-Import-Gesellschaft..

Contracts for these six tankers were shared between British, German and Italian yards, five of the ships being based on the *Calgarolite*-type, a twin-screw motor tanker completed by Furness Shipbuilding Company, Haverton-on-Tees, in July, 1929, for Imperial Oil Ltd.

The second part of this huge shipbuilding programme was awarded in 1931, contracts for a further nine similar ships being split between German and Italian yards. All these tankers were 542 feet (loa) × 70 feet breadth and were driven by twin screws. Of these fifteen similar tankers, the French-flag *Marguerite Finaly* was delivered direct to Société Auxiliaire des Transports while two others were quickly transferred to other fleets; the *R. L. Hague* to the Italian flag and *Robert F. Hand* to Anglo-American in 1933. The remaining twelve ships were transferred to the Panama Transport Company when B.A.P.I.C.O. was reorganised in 1935 and of these the *D. L. Harper*, *F. J. Wolfe* and *George McKnight* joined the Anglo-American fleet and the *Victor Ross* went to the British Mexican Petroleum Company, all in 1939.

After seventeen years' service, the Sunderland-built *Tuscarora* was sold for breaking up in January, 1935.
Esso

The histories of these ships are shown in the postwar sections, as are those of the two American-flag, Federal-built ships *G. Harrison Smith* and *W. S. Farish* which, with the Panama-flag *F. H. Bedford Jr.*, were all transferred to Anglo-American (Esso) in 1950. All were named after leading personalities of the Standard Oil and Anglo-American companies. Histories of the remaining non-British ships are as follows:

	Completed	Gross tons	
Harry G. Seidel	10.1930	11,065	Built by Fr Krupp AG, Kiel. 1935: (Panama Transport Co.). 29.4.1942: Sunk by (*U.66*) torpedo, 11.50N 62.50W, 90 miles NW of Trinidad.
Heinrich von Reidemann	11.1930	11,020	Built by Bremer Vulkan, Vegesack. 1935: (Panama Transport Co.). 17.4.1942: Sunk by (*U.66*) torpedo, 11.55N 63.47W, 150 miles NW of Trinidad.

J. A. Mowinckel	11.1930	11,147	Built by Cantieri Riuniti Dell'Adriatico, Monfalcone.
			1935: (Panama Transport Co.).
			10.7.1942: Damaged by submarine (*U.576*) torpedo SE of
			    Cape Hatteras. Headed for Hatteras Inlet, but struck U.S.
			    mine. Beached, refloated and repaired.
			*1951: *Orionis*, then *Seacastle* (Soc. Nacionale del Mar,
			    Panama).
			1951: renamed *Audacious*.
			1953: *Platanos* (Puerto Miramar Cia de Nav. Panama).
			1954: Sold for breaking up.

Peter Hurll	11.1930	10,871	Built by Palmers Shipbuilding & Iron Co. Ltd., Newcastle. 1935: (Panama Transport Co.). 1948: *Esso Kobenhavn* (Dansk Esso A/S). 1963: Scrapped Denmark.

J. H. Senior	3.1931	11,065	Built by Nordseewerke, Emden.
			1935: (Panama Transport Co.).
			20.8.1943: Collision, damaged by fire (voyage: New York/
			    Clyde—gas oil).
			24.8.1943: Arrived Bay Bulls, Newfoundland (in tow).
			    Total loss. Laid up New York.
			1950: *Esso Picardie* (Standard Française des Pétroles).
			4.2.1955: Arrived Savona for breaking up.

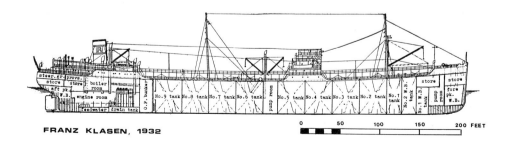

FRANZ KLASEN, 1932

Franz Klasen	7.1932	11,194	Built by Deutsche Werft, Hamburg. 1935: (Panama Transport Company). *1950: *Maggy* (Panamena de Transportes Petroles). 7.1960: Scrapped Savona.
R. L. Hague	7.1932	12,173	Built by Cantieri Riuniti Dell' Adriatico, Monfalcone. 1933: ("La Columbia" Soc. Maritima per Transport di Petrolio). 1945: renamed *Splendor.* 1951: renamed *Esso Italia.* 6.1959: Scrapped Trieste.
Orville Harden	3.1933	11,191	Built by Cantieri Riuniti Dell' Adriatico, Monfalcone. 1935: (Panama Transport Co.). 4.2.1945: Collision with *Ena* (Dutch, 1936/6229 gt) in Ambrose Channel, New York. Abandoned, partly submerged. Raised and repaired. 1950: *Esso Languedoc* (Standard Française des Pétroles). 1956: *Esso Orinoco* (Cie de Petroles Lago (Venezuela)). A hulk. 1961: Sold for breaking up.
Marguerite Finalay	12.1933	12,369	Built by Cantieri Riuniti Dell' Adriatico, Monfalcone for Soc Auxiliaire des Transports. 1939: *Esso Provence* (Standard Française des Pétroles). 26.6.1944: Scuttled at Marseilles. Raised and: 7.1946: Arrived Toulon for repairs. 16.9.1949: Trials, re-entered service. *1959: *Pacific Builder* (Cia Asiatic Panamense). 1961: *Pacific Navigator* (United Overseas Marine Corp., Panama). A storage vessel. 23.3.1961: Arrived Shimotsu. 1962: Broken up.

During the first few months of war, between October, 1939, and February, 1940, fifteen Standard Oil ships were removed from the United States flag and transferred to the Panama Transport Company and the Panamanian flag and in the subsequent four years several others followed. In July, 1941, eighteen tankers of the Panama Transport fleet were turned over to the United States Maritime Commission. Three of the vessels, *T. J. Williams*, *W. C. Teagle* and *Geo. H. Jones*, were selected for operation by Anglo-American and in August, 1941, were provisionally registered as British-flag ships. Altogether, during the years of the Second World War, some fifty ocean-going tankers were under Panama Transport ownership, of which twenty were sunk by enemy action and another lost as a result of explosion and fire after a collision. Just after war ended in 1945 the company houseflag flew on twenty-six tankers. In 1961 the company name began to be phased out and the ships transferred to various newly-formed companies, including Panama Transport and Navigation Company S.A.; Panama Transport and Shipping Company S.A.; and Panama Transport and Tanker Company S.A., all registered in Panama.

CHAPTER SIX

War Again

THROUGHOUT the 1920s and 1930s more and more factories and establishments had replaced their steam energy source of coal by oil. By the 1930s not only did the Royal Navy need huge supplies, but so did the Royal Air Force and the then mechanising Army.

More tankers had been constructed, their size governed by the limitations of the Suez Canal. Nearly 100 miles long, the canal at that time was available to ships drawing 34 feet of water, although the depth of the canal below the low water level was 40 feet. The width of the canal at low water was about 200 feet but at high water, and depending on the varying inclinations of the banks, the width was from 400 to 500 feet.

When war came again in 1939 Britain had 498 tankers of over 1,000 tons. Anglo-American Oil Company's ocean-going fleet comprised fourteen ships and another five listed under the subsidiary, British Mexican Petroleum Company Ltd.

At that time the largest tanker in the world was the C. O. *Stillman*, 13,006 gt and 22,270 tdw. Her overall length was 585 feet, breadth 75 feet 6 inches and draught 34 feet. Her twin screws were driven by oil engines. She was built by Bremer Vulkan, Vegesack, in 1928 for the International Petroleum Company Ltd., in 1937 moving to the Panama Transport Company.

Anglo-American Oil Company Ltd
Fleet 1939

Name	Built	Name	Built
m.v. *Appalachee*	1930	m.v. *Geo. W. McKnight*	1933
s.s. *Cadillac*	1917	s.s. *Housatonic*	1919
m.v. *Chesapeake*	1928	s.s. *Iroquois*	1907
m.v. *Cheyenne*	1930	s.s. *Kennebec*	1919
m.v. *Comanche*	1936	m.v. *Robert F. Hand*	1933
m.v. *D. L. Harper*	1933	s.s. *Saranac*	1918
m.v. *F. J. Wolfe*	1932	m.v. *Schuylkill*	1928

(British Mexican Petroleum Company Ltd)

Name	Built	Name	Built
s.s. *Beaconstreet*	1927	m.v. *Seminole*	1936
s.s. *Inverarder*	1919	m.v. *Victor Ross*	1933
m.v. *Narragansett*	1936		

Nine ships of the Anglo-American Oil Company's ocean tanker fleet were lost during the 1939–45 war, leaving ten of the pre-war ships remaining in the fleet in 1946.

Within one week of the outbreak of hostilities the *Kennebec* was sunk by a torpedo from *U.34* which was serving in the 2nd U-boat Flotilla in the South-west Approaches and was one of the U-boat wave which the German Navy had been sending into the Atlantic from 19th August, two weeks before war began, as a cautionary measure. Just one week later the *Cheyenne* was torpedoed by *U.53*, the wreck being sunk later by a British destroyer. In June, 1940, *Saranac*, one of Anglo-American's largest tankers, was lost.

December of 1940 was a bleak month. On the night of the 1st, *U.101* caught up with convoy HX 90 (Halifax NS to the United Kingdom) and sank three ships, damaging two more. One of the three lost was the *Appalachee*. And within hours the British Mexican tanker *Victor Ross* was sent down by *U.43*. She was in convoy OB 251, outward bound from Liverpool to the United States.

The *Saranac* was torpedoed by a U-boat in the Atlantic in June, 1940. Her sistership *Cadillac* was also sunk by U-boat torpedo the following year.   *Esso*

Serving under Admiralty orders, the *Housatonic* was bombed and sunk on 19th February, 1941, and on 1st March the *Cadillac*, sistership of *Saranac* and sailing in convoy HX 109 in the North Atlantic, was singled out by *U.552* and sunk.

Two British Mexican ships were lost in 1942, *Inverarder* in convoy ON 67 (United Kingdom–Halifax) on 24th February and *Narragansett* one month later on 25th March.

Of the ships remaining in the ocean fleet in 1946 the *Iroquois* was thirty-nine years old and was soon sent for breaking up, quickly followed by the *Schuylkill* which had been built in 1928. There remained her sistership *Chesapeake* (1928), the *Comanchee* of 1936, four ships which had been transferred to Anglo-American from the Panama Transport Company before the war and two ships, *Beaconstreet* and *Seminole*, which were transferred from the British Mexican subsidiary in 1944.

From 1st January, 1947, in a new operational arrangement, the remaining ten ocean-going tankers were placed under the management of Esso Transportation Company Ltd., formed by renaming Lago Shipping Company Ltd., which owned the fleet of tankers working in the Lake Maracaibo/Aruba service. Ownership of those shallow-draught tankers was now in the name of Esso Transportation Company Ltd. However, although

The *Geo. W. McKnight* is seen here as the *Esso Edinburgh* in 1954, the year she went to the scrapyard. *Skyfotos*

Esso Transportation Company Ltd. was managing the British-flag ocean tanker fleet, actual ownership of those vessels remained under the Anglo-American title.

A new funnel emblem was also introduced in 1947, in place of the red, black-topped Anglo-American funnel. It took the form of the Esso oval on a white band on a black funnel. The oval, edged in blue, had the word "Esso" in red.

The ten ships were:

	Completed	Gross tons	
Robert F. Hand	10.1933	12,197	Built by Fr. Krupp AG, Kiel, for Baltisch-Amerikanische Petroleum-Import-Gesellschaft. 1933: (Anglo-American). 1950: *Esso Newcastle.* *1955: Converted to an ore carrier and renamed *Alexander* (11,540 gt) (Cia. de Nav. Alexander (Panama). 1957: *Oligisto* (Cornigliano (Italy)). 5.1966: Scrapped Vado.
F. J. Wolfe	8.1932	11,244	Built by Bremer Vulkan, Vegesack, for Baltisch-Amerikanische Petroleum-Import-Gesellschaft. 1935: (Panama Transport Co.). 1939: (Anglo-American). 10.9.1942: Damaged by submarine (*U.96*) torpedo, 51.30N 28.25W, in convoy ON 127 (United Kingdom/North America). Continued in convoy in damaged state and: 19.9.1942: Arrived St. Johns. Repaired. *1953: *Locarno* (American European Tanker Co. (Panama)). 1957: *Morchella* (Cia. de Nav. Monte Estoril (Panama)). 1960: Scrapped.
D. L. Harper	9.1933	11,210	Built by Deutsche Werft, Hamburg, for Baltisch-Amerikanische Petroleum-Import-Gesellschaft. 1935: (Panama Transport Co.). 1939: (Anglo-American). *1954: *Hanseat* (E. Jung Tankschiff Rhederei, Hamburg). 1954: *Transpacific Hugo Stinnes* (H. Stinnes Schiff, Hamburg). 1957: *Aristid* (F. & W. Joch, Hamburg). 3.6.1960: Arrived Spezia for breaking up.
Geo. W. McKnight	1.1933	12,502	Built by Fr. Krupp AG, Kiel, for Baltisch-Amerikanische Petroleum-Import-Gesellschaft. 1935: (Panama Transport Co.). 1939: (Anglo-American). 3.5.1942: Damaged by submarine (*U.66*) torpedo, 11.18N 61.19W in convoy ON 87 (United Kingdom/North America). 1950: *Esso Edinburgh.* 26.7.1954: Arrived Blyth for breaking up.

In the summer of 1937 there were some disturbing incidents in the Mediterranean involving ships of several nations. In August, particularly, mysterious "pirate" submarines began torpedoing ships. On 6th August, unknown planes bombed the tanker *British Corporal* off Algiers; the Spanish Loyalist tanker *Campeador* was torpedoed and sank off Tunis on the 11th; in mid-August two more Loyalist ships were torpedoed by a "pirate" submarine in the eastern Mediterranean; two Russian

119

vessels were also sunk at the end of August, as was a British ship off the Spanish east coast. On 9th September a nine-power Conference agreed that their fleets be turned "loose" on the "pirate" submarines.

Also involved was the *Geo. W. McKnight* which was sailing through the Mediterranean with a Standard Oil cargo of crude oil when on 14th August she was shelled and set on fire twenty miles north-west of Cape Bon by two unknown torpedo boats.

She was then followed by an Italian destroyer which veered away as a submarine rose to the surface and fired eighteen more shells at the ship. The tanker, abandoned, then drifted away, a mass of flames.

She was later taken in tow by the British tanker *British Commodore* and with fires extinguished was put to safe anchorage off Cape Farina. From there she moved to Bizerta Roads where 10,000 tons of her 17,000-ton cargo was transshipped to the British vessel which then sailed for Havre. On 27th August the *Geo. W. McKnight* left in tow of the tugs *Hercule* and *Gladiator*, bound for Monfalcone for drydocking and repairs.

Beaconstreet	7.1927	7,467	Transferred from British Mexican Petroleum Co. Ltd., in 1944. 1950: *Esso Dublin.* 5.11.1953: Arrived Blyth for breaking up.
Seminole	4.1936	10,389	Transferred from British Mexican Petroleum Co. Ltd., in 1944. 1950: *Esso Hull.* 12.1958: Scrapped Trieste.

Earlier histories of *Beaconstreet* and *Seminole* appear in the British Mexican fleet appendix; those of *Chesapeake* (built 1928) and *Comanchee* (1936) in the pre-war section.

Of the eighteen tankers of Standard Oil of New Jersey's subsidiary, Panama Transport Company, which were turned over to the United States Maritime Commission at the request of the Commission in July, 1941, three were selected for operation under the control of the Anglo-American Oil Company and in August, 1941, were provisionally registered as British vessels. All three became war losses, two in 1941 and the other in 1942. As examples of the hazards that tankers faced in the Atlantic in those years of war their histories are detailed.

W. C. Teagle	7.1917	9,552	Built by Bethlehem Shipbuilding Corporation, Sparrows Point, Maryland. Measurements: 516 feet 7 inches (oa)/500 feet length × 68 feet breadth. 16,080 tdw. Engines: T6cyl. Twin screws. 9½ knots.

The war service of the *W. C. Teagle* lasted only two years but during that time she was given an unusual mission to perform. Towards the end of 1940 she had the task of dragging an anchor to deepen the channel across the Maturin Bar, at the mouth of the San Juan River, in the Gulf of Paria, Venezuela. She steamed back and forth, day and night, for twelve days, making a total of ninety-four trips.

Later, she was chartered to the United States Maritime Commission for British service, one of many American ships so placed after the Lease/Lend agreement. To prepare her for war work, the *W. C. Teagle* entered a ship repair yard at Baltimore on 15th August, 1941, for overhaul; to have degaussing gear fitted; to be armed and to change from Panamanian to British registry. Then on 22nd September her war service really began when she sailed from Aruba with a cargo of fuel oil for

The *Esso Dublin* was built as the *Beaconstreet* in 1927 for the Beacon Transport Company. Later she joined the British Mexican Petroleum Co. Ltd. and was transferred to Anglo-American in 1944.

Tom Rayner

Britain, joining a large convoy—SC 48—at Sydney, Nova Scotia, which left there on 5th October. On the 16th, eleven days out and only three from her destination, the ship was struck by a torpedo fired from submarine *U.558*. The tanker burst into flames, blazing oil covered the water and she began sinking. As the crew started to abandon ship she gave a sudden plunge by the stern, throwing the entire crew into the sea. For a moment the bow of the *W. C. Teagle* stood vertically out of the water . . . then the ship was gone. There was only one survivor, rescued by a British corvette.

Geo. H. Jones	9.1919	6,914	Built by Sun Shipbuilding Co., Chester, Pennsylvania.
			Measurements: 445 feet (oa)/430 feet length × 59 feet breadth.
			11,205 tdw.
			Engines: T3cyl. 10 knots.

In June, 1942, under the British flag, the *Geo. H. Jones* was on a voyage from Aruba to the United Kingdom with a cargo of oil and had joined a convoy at Freetown for the last leg of the trip. On 9th June engine trouble caused her to drop out of the convoy and next day, under orders from the Admiralty, she altered course for the Azores. In the early morning of 11th June she was struck on the starboard side, in the way of Nos 3 and 4 tanks, by a torpedo from the German submarine *U.455*. The tanker began to settle and was abandoned. As the boats pulled away a searchlight from the submarine was played on the ship's bow, in an attempt to read her name. At 2.30 a.m. *Geo. H. Jones* stood upright for a few moments, her stern out of the water, then she plunged beneath the waves.

At Newport News in January, 1942, the ship's No. 4 lifeboat had been fitted with a radio transmitter, and this was now used to send distress signals. Although designed with a range of 150 miles its messages were received at Valencia, Spain, some 600 miles distant. They were also picked up by another convoy, and H.M.S. *Lulworth*, by taking direction finding bearings on the signals, rescued survivors of the *Geo. H. Jones* on 16th June.

T. J. Williams	9.1921	8,212	Built by Oscar Daniels Co., Tampa, Florida.
			Measurements: 481 feet (oa)/465 feet length × 60 feet breadth.
			12,555 tdw.
			Engines: Quad. 9½ knots.

When war broke out in Europe, the *T. J. Williams*, under the American flag, was returning to the United States after delivering a cargo of gas oil to London. She duly arrived at Baytown on 10th

The *Esso Saranac*, built in 1941 as the *Empire Sapphire*, in the Manchester Ship Canal.

September and to the end of 1939 made six voyages from the Gulf of Mexico to New York carrying cargoes of heating oil. On 9th August, 1940, she was transferred from Standard Oil to the Panama Transport Company and made a dozen voyages under the flag of Panama. Then, following discharge at Halifax, she was refitted and armed at Newport News and transferred to British registry.

Loaded with aviation spirit, she left Baltimore on 2nd September, 1941, for the United Kingdom, joining convoy SC 44 at Sydney, Nova Scotia, on the 11th. Eight days later she was torpedoed by submarine *U.522* when east of Cape Farewell, Greenland. The *T. J. Williams* quickly settled and was abandoned, and when last seen, her stern was submerged and the main deck awash. Twenty-two survivors were rescued by a corvette and landed at Reykjavik, Iceland.

A few weeks after these three tankers were transferred to Anglo-American, another two were transferred. Both survived the war.

Beaconoil	9.1919	6,983	Built by Bethlehem Shipbuilding Corporation, Alameda, California, as *Devolente*. Measurements: 453 feet oa/435 feet length × 56 feet breadth. 10,665 tdw. Engines: T3cyl. 10 knots.

This tanker became *Beaconoil* of the Beacon Oil Company, Boston, Massachusetts, in 1923 and was transferred to Standard Oil in 1930. At the outbreak of hostilities in Europe she was tied up in the Patuxent River along with other company vessels, but she was quickly brought into service on 13th September, 1939, and worked in the American coastal trade until March, 1940, transporting oil from the Mexican Gulf and Caribbean ports to New York, Boston and Port Everglades. On 20th January, 1940, the *Beaconoil* moved to the Panama Transport Company and under Panamanian registry made her first wartime Atlantic crossing in March, from Aruba to Algiers.

The *Beaconoil* then worked in the Western Atlantic until September, 1941, and on the 17th of that month, manned by Canadians and under the Red Ensign, she sailed from Trinidad with a cargo of fuel oil for Milford Haven.

122

Thereafter the ship made a series of transatlantic crossings although reverting to the Panama flag in 1942. Again and again she crossed the danger zone, running the gauntlet of the U-boats, but came through unscathed, serving the Allied cause until the end of the war. In 1950 she was broken up at Baltimore.

Elisha Walker	9.1920	7,007	Built by Sun Shipbuilding Co., Chester, Pennsylvania, for Pan-American Petroleum & Transport Company, New York.
			Measurements: 446 feet (oa)/430 feet length × 59 feet breadth.
			11,365 tdw.
			Engines: T3cyl. 10½ knots.

The *Elisha Walker* was acquired by Standard Oil in 1935. On 25th August, 1939, the vessel arrived at Galveston for repairs, then loaded at Texas City and sailed on 2nd September, 1939, in coastal service. In November, 1939, she moved to the Panama Transport Company and with the exception of one transatlantic and four voyages to Tenerife from Caripito continued in the American coastal service until 30th August, 1941, when she was time-chartered to the United States Maritime Commission. On 17th September, 1941, she was transferred to British registry.

In September, 1942, the *Elisha Walker* left Curacao with fuel oil, sailed through the Panama Canal and down the west coast of South America, through the Strait of Magellan, then crossed the southernmost part of the Atlantic to Cape Town where she arrived on 23rd October. This roundabout route enabled her to avoid most of the danger areas of submarine activity. She then worked from the Persian Gulf to Ceylon, Mombasa and Australia. Her next loading port was San Francisco where, on 29th June, 1943, she reverted to Panamanian registry with more voyages to Australia, the Persian Gulf and the Indian Ocean before returning across the Pacific and through the Panama Canal to the Caribbean. Her arrival at Balboa (Canal Zone) on 18th September, 1944, marked the end of a circumnavigation of the globe, for it had been two years and six days since the tanker had sailed from the Canal en route for Cape Town.

The vessel's stay in home waters was short. She again crossed the Atlantic, making voyages to Oran from Abadan, and was then assigned to service in the Mediterranean. On VJ Day, 2nd September, 1945, she was back in the Persian Gulf, at the loading port of Ras Tanura. In 1949 the *Elisha Walker* was sold for breaking up at Baltimore.

Rebuilding the fleet

The fleet rebuilding programme began quickly when the war ended and early acquisitions were four British-built war standard tankers constructed for the Ministry of War Transport. They came under the classification of the "Ocean"-type and the "Norwegian"-type.

The "Ocean"-type were of the pre-war "Shell" design, sometimes known as the "Three Twelves"-type, the ships being of 12,000 deadweight tons and with engines producing 12 knots on a fuel consumption of 12 tons per day.

	Completed	Gross tons	
Esso Cadillac	1940	8,149	Built by Hawthorn, Leslie & Co. Ltd., Newcastle, as *Empire Bronze*.
			Measurements: 483 feet (loa) × 59 feet breadth.
			Engines: Oil.
			1946: *Esso Cadillac*.
			*1956: *Maribella II* (Chandris).
			1959: Broken up at Osaka.

Esso Saranac	1941	8,031	Built by Furness Shipbuilding Co. Ltd., Haverton Hill-on-Tees, as *Empire Sapphire*. Measurements: 479 feet (loa) × 61 feet breadth. Engines: T3cyl. 1946: *Esso Saranac*. 25.1.1959: Arrived Antwerp for breaking up.

The other two ships were steam tankers of the "Norwegian"-type, so named from the fact that they were based on the sisterships *Sandanger* and *Eidanger*, built by Sir James Laing and Sons Ltd., Sunderland, in 1938 for Westfal-Larsen and Company A/S, of Bergen.

Esso Cheyenne	1942	9,798	Built by Sir James Laing & Sons Ltd., Sunderland, as *Empire Coleridge*. Measurements: 504 feet (loa) × 68 feet breadth. 14,350 tdw. Engines: T3cyl. 1945: *Esso Cheyenne*. 15.4.1961: Arrived Boom, Belgium, for breaking up.
Esso Appalachee	1942	9,819	Built by Furness Shipbuilding Co. Ltd., Haverton Hill-on-Tees, as *Empire Dickens*. Measurements: 504 feet (loa) × 68 feet breadth. 14,350 tdw. Engines: T3cyl 1946: *Esso Appalachee*. In her last years she was based at Fawley and employed as one of Esso's large coasters, moving clean products to bulk storage plants around the coast. On 2.8.1960 she arrived at Faslane for breaking up.

A "Norwegian"-type standard tanker, *Esso Cheyenne* was built during the Second World War as the *Empire Coleridge*.

Formerly the *Empire Coast*, the *Esso Ottawa* was built in 1943 at Northwich.

Six coastal tankers were acquired from the Ministry of War Transport in 1946, four of the "Empire Cadet"-class and two of the "Empire Lad"-class. The "Empire Cadet" ships were a war standard-type building, the prototype being the Bulk Oil S.S. Company's *Pass of Balmaha*, of 1933. There were twenty-three in the class, from four builders. The ships measured 202 feet length (oa) and 31 feet breadth; triple expansion engines gave 9½ knots. They had counter sterns. Gross tonnage was 797 tons and deadweight capacity 850 tons. The four acquired were all built by Grangemouth Dockyard Company Ltd.

	Completed	
Esso Dakotah	1942	Ex *Empire Gawain*. 1962: Scrapped Boom, Belgium.
Esso Genesee	1943	Ex *Empire Harbour*. 1961: Scrapped Tamise, Belgium.
Esso Juniata	1941	Ex *Empire Lass*. *1956: *Argosity* (F. T. Everard & Sons). 1957: Lengthened to 230 feet 6 inches. 1969: Scrapped Bruges, Belgium.
Esso Tioga	1943	Ex *Empire Wrestler*. 23.9.1963: Arrived St Davids on Forth for scrapping.

The two "Empire Lad"-class ships were built by Rowhedge Ironworks Ltd, Rowhedge, near Colchester, and I. Pimblott and Sons Ltd., Northwich, respectively. Measurements were 135 feet length (oa) and 24 feet breadth. They had oil engines and tonnages were 300 gross and 340 deadweight capacity.

Esso Suwanee	1941	Launched as *Empire Garnet*, but completed as *Empire Lad*.
		1946: *Esso Suwanee*.
		*1960: (P. L. Den Breejen, Holland).
		1963: Converted to dry cargo (331 gt), renamed *U.S.A.* (Cia Comercio Nav. Alpes, Panama).
		1966: *Pejerey* (Antco S.A., Panama).
		1966: *Esterel* (Antco S.A., Panama).
		1968: *Westerend* (Colombo Shipping Co., Panama).
		1970: *Sunrise* (Albina S.A., Panama).
		1970: *Grace* (Albina S.A., Panama).
		1971: *Captain Stelios* (D. P. Gousetis, Greece).
		1975: *San Liberal* (C. Dagadakis, Greece).
		1977: *Kleopatra* (E. & G. Kottis, Greece).
Esso Ottawa	1943	Ex *Empire Coast*.
		25.4.1967: Arrived Bruges, Belgium, for scrapping.

Wartime tankers from an Esso design

Under the Merchant Shipping Act of 1936 the United States Maritime Commission was formed to rebuild the United States merchant fleet which, at that time, was composed chiefly of ageing ships which had been built in the frenzy of building at the end of and just after the 1914–18 war. The initial aim of fifty ships each year for the ensuing ten years was quickly seen to be far from sufficient in the rapidly deteriorating political situation of 1939–40, and in early 1941 huge orders were given to shipbuilders whose yards were not even constructed at the time the orders were placed.

Within the requirements were orders for seventy-two tankers, based on a design which the Sun Shipbuilding and Drydock Company of Chester, Pennysylvania, had been building for the Standard Oil Company of New Jersey. Dimensions were a length of 503 feet (bp) to an overall length of 523 feet 6 inches and a breadth of 68 feet. Gross tonnage was 10,448 and the deadweight capacity 16,613 tons. There were nine sets of tanks. Set No. 1 comprised one port and one starboard tank, the other eight sets each included a main centre tank as well.

In the planning, reciprocating engines were to be the driving power of many ships, but it was realised that to be so driven would be unsatisfactory for the faster merchant ships. It was then decided to step up the production of turbines and gears for the faster ships. But this brought another problem. Machine tools necessary for the production of gears were so scarce that a decision had to be made to install turbo-electric drive in the 14–15-knot emergency tankers to be built. In the event, machine tool production was also speeded up and by 1943 there was an adequate supply.

By the end of the war, 481 of a type designated by the United States Maritime Commission as T2-SE-A1 had been built. Commonly known as the T2, these workhorses of war carried their precious cargoes of fuel to industries and armies of the allies the world over. Shortly after war ended, many war-built emergency ships were sold under the Merchant Ship Sales Act of 1946, and 203 of the emergency tankers were sold out of American registry. Many were enlarged to become bulk carriers with larger mid-sections fitted and in 1950 a number were used as floating electricity generating plants in Norwegian ports and fjords when, due to a water shortage, the hydro-electric power source became threatened.

Of those tankers sold out of American registry, fifty-one moved to British owners and of those, nine were acquired by Anglo-American, all placed under the newly-named Esso Transportation Company Ltd. Eight were each given the Esso prefix and the name of a town where Esso representation was prominent; one sailed under the Cleveland Petroleum flag and bore the name *Cleveland*.

	Completed	Gross tons	
Esso Manchester	2.1944	10,448	Built by Sun S.B. & D.D. Co., Chester, Pennsylvania. Ex *Santiago*—'47. 8.1963: Scrapped Faslane.
Esso Purfleet	7.1944	10,448	Built by Sun S.B. & D.D. Co., Chester, Pennsylvania. Ex *Ridgefield*—'47. 8.1963: Scrapped Willebroek, Belgium.

A T2-type standard tanker, *Esso Manchester* is seen in Southampton Water in 1950.

Esso Fawley	9.1944	10,448	Built by Sun S.B. & D.D. Co., Chester, Pennsylvania. Ex *Turkey Island*—'46. *1955: Converted to a bulk carrier by Sasebo Heavy Industries. Measurements: 564 feet 6 inches (loa), 6,725 gt. Renamed *Atticus* (Cia. Nav. Lorca (Liberian)). 1957: *Andros Saturn* (Cia. Nav. Lorca (Liberian)). 1960: *Skiathos* (Cia. Nav. Vicalvaro (Greek)). 8.1963: Scrapped Aioi.
Esso Cardiff	8.1945	10,448	Built by Kaiser Co., Portland, Oregon. Ex *Halls of Montezuma*—'47. *1954: *Aquitanius* (Cia. Nav. Lorca (Liberian)). 11.1955: Converted to ore/oil carrier. Lengthened to 564 feet 6 inches, renamed *Andros Neptune* (Cia. Nav. Lorca (Liberian)). 1960: *Skopelos* (Cia. Nav. Vicalvaro (Greek)). 1960: *Transwarren* (Cia. Nav. Patagonia (Liberian)). 1962: *Niagara* (Sea Transport Inc. (U.S.)).

On a voyage from Ymuiden to Nassau, the *Niagara* met a severe gale on 28th January, 1965, in the Atlantic, losing some 400 square feet of plating. She limped into Ponta Delgada where temporary plates were fitted. The *Niagara* was then towed to Marseilles for drydocking, but it was found that repairs would not be economic. She was sold for scrap and arrived at Castellon on 29th October, 1965.

Esso Bristol	9.1944	10,448	Built by Sun S.B. & D.D. Co., Chester, Pennsylvania. Ex *Sandy Creek*—'46. *1954: *North Duke* (A. D. Pappadakis, New York). 1955: *Perseo* (SIOSA, (Italian)). 5.1963: Scrapped Vado.
Esso Birmingham	8.1944	10,448	Built by Sun S.B. & D.D. Co., Chester, Pennsylvania. Ex *Mauvilla*—'47. 12.1963: Scrapped Split.

The *Esso Glasgow*, the last T2-type tanker in the Esso fleet, was employed in the coastal service from 1957 until scrapped in 1971. *Skyfotos*

| *Esso Glasgow* | 12.1944 | 10,448 | Built by Sun S.B. & D.D. Co., Chester, Pennsylvania. Ex *Wauhatchie*—'47. |

In 1956 it was decided that a new midsection should be fitted in the *Esso Glasgow* to enable her to carry a number of different grades of fuel for entry into the British coastal trade. The new section was laid down in December, 1956, by Harland and Wolff Ltd., at Belfast. In the new year the old midbody was removed and sent to Faslane for scrapping, where it arrived on 8th March. The new mid-section, 310 feet in length, was launched on 14th March and fitted in April. The *Esso Glasgow* left Belfast on 10th August, 1957, and began her work in the coastal distribution service.

On 12th January, 1963, in snow and fog in the River Humber, the *Esso Glasgow* was involved in a collision off Spurn Head with the local pilot cutter, *J. H. Fisher*, which sank. The cutter, 461 gt and built in 1931, was owned by the Humber Pilots Steam Cutter Company Ltd., and fortunately there were no casualties.

And on 3rd January, 1967, Southampton Water was the scene of a spectacular blaze following explosions on the *Esso Glasgow* as she lay berthed at Fawley. After the fire she moved to Husbands Shipyard at Southampton for temporary repairs, then moved on to Wilton Fijenoord, at Rotterdam, for permanent repairs.

The *Esso Glasgow* continued in the coastal service until 1971 when she arrived at Bilbao on 18th July, for scrapping.

| *Esso London* | 11.1944 | 10,448 | Built by Sun S.B. & D.D. Company, Chester, Pennsylvania. Ex *Champion's Hill*—'46. 19.6.1958: Arrived Split for scrapping. |

The remaining vessel of the nine T2 ships acquired by Anglo-American in 1946–47 was placed under the nominal ownership of the associated Cleveland Petroleum Company Ltd., but it was managed, as were the others, by Esso Transportation Company Ltd.

| *Cleveland* | 7.1944 | 10,448 | Built by Kaiser Co., Swan Island, Portland, Oregon. Ex *Forbes Road*—'47. 1953: *Enrico Insom* (Enrico Insom, Italy). 1959: Refitted at La Spezia Navy Yard as an Italian fleet oiler. Renamed *Sterope* (Pennant A.5368). |

The Cleveland Petroleum Products Company was founded in 1920 by two Manchester business men to market white spirit in the north-west of England.

It commenced trade with just two lorries and in a short time had a following of scores of enthusiastic dealers in Lancashire. Seven years later later the firm was formed into a limited company and in the following year began retailing motor spirit.

In 1930 a national sales and distribution system was set up and at the same time the company introduced alcohol into its petrol, as an alternative to lead as an additive.

By 1934 a brand name, "Cleveland Discol", had been introduced and in the same year a Frazer Nash/BMW sports car, running at the Brooklands race track with the new brand of fuel, was the first car to cover 100 miles in less than an hour.

In 1935 Anglo-American obtained a controlling interest in the company and in 1938 the name was changed to Cleveland Petroleum Company Ltd.

No great changes were made for two decades, but in 1958 Esso acquired the whole of the share capital, soon afterwards introducing the "Cleveland Super Discol" brand of petrol. Yet another brand, "Cleveland Premium", then came on the market, bringing the product range in line with Esso. In 1964 the bulk distribution plants of both companies were combined, as were the vehicle maintenance depots. Just one year later the distribution truck fleets were also integrated, with deliveries made by the group fleet. Cleveland's "Flying C" motif appeared in 1967, but within a few years it was apparent that the Cleveland banner served no real purpose and the complete integration of the company into Esso was made in 1973.

One further T2-type tanker was transferred to British flag Esso in 1955.

	Completed	Gross tons
Esso Avonmouth	8.1945	10,729

This was another United States war-built standard tanker of the T2 SE A1-type, built by the Sun Shipbuilding Company, Chester, Pennsylvania as *Fort Massiac*.

In 1949 she was acquired by Standard Oil and placed under the Panama Transport Company flag as *Esso Valparaiso*. In 1955 she was transferred to British registry as *Esso Avonmouth* and worked from Fawley for five years until laid up on 2nd June, 1960, at Falmouth.

She was soon sold to Cia. Athlos Nav., S.A. under the Greek flag as the *Athlon* and an early job was at Bergen where she arrived on 18th December, 1960, for temporary use as an electricity generating plant.

As with so many of the T2-type tankers, she was enlarged in 1962, being fitted with a new midship section by Navali di Taranto. Her length was then 578 feet 8 inches and her deadweight capacity 23,980 tons. She worked as a bulker until 14th March, 1975, when she arrived at Bilbao for breaking up.

Transfers from the American flag

In 1950, four older ships were transferred to Anglo-American, three from the parent company fleet, Standard Oil Company of New Jersey, registered at Wilmington, Delaware. The two Federal-built ships under yard

The *Esso Liverpool*, seen here off Fawley in 1950, had a lifespan of forty-one years, being scrapped in 1962. *G. A. Osbon*

Built as the *Fort Massiac* in 1945, the T2-type tanker *Esso Avonmouth* did not join the British flag until 1955.   *Skyfotos*

numbers 113 and 114 were sisterships. These transfers were to "fill the gap" whilst new tonnage was under construction.

	Completed	Gross tons	
Esso Liverpool	9.1921	12,590	Built by Newport News Shipbuilding & Drydock Co., as *John D. Archbold*.

Measurements: 572 feet 6 inches (oa)/ 555 feet length × 75 feet breadth.
22,600 tdw.
Engines: T6cyl driving twin screws.

The *John D. Archbold* was nearly thirty years old when transferred to the British flag to fill a gap pending the advent of the "Esso Oxford"-class then building. She was renamed *Esso Liverpool*.

In 1953 she was then sold to Steamship Enterprises of Panama Inc (Marini & Brichetto, Genoa) who deleted "Esso" from her name.

On 8th January, 1957, she left the Queen Elizabeth II Oil Dock at Eastham and was on her way down the River Mersey bound for Venezuela when she collided with the British and Continental S.S. Company's *Ousel* (1,533 gt, built 1922) which was at anchor near Rock Ferry Stage awaiting entry to the Manchester Ship Canal. Four tugs tried to beach the *Ousel*, but she sank. The *Liverpool*, with only slight damage, continued her voyage. On 16th September, 1957, she was laid up at Genoa and was eventually scrapped there in 1962.

The *John D. Archbold* and sistership *William Rockefeller* were regarded as giants of the world tanker tonnage when they were completed in 1921 for Standard Oil of New Jersey. Indeed, there were very few tankers of like capacity at that time. Two of the nearest size ships were under the British flag, *San Fernando* and *San Florentino*, owned by Eagle Oil Transport Company Ltd., both built on the Tyne, 530 feet in length and 13,000 gross tons. It is interesting to see how these four large tankers of the day fared. Three were lost in the war, the first, *San Fernando*, in 1940 when sailing from Halifax, Nova Scotia, to the United Kingdom in convoy HX 49, she was torpedoed by *U.47* and sank in position 50.20N 10.24W. Her sistership *San Florentino* when about 1,200 miles ENE of Newfoundland on 1st October, 1941, was hit by three torpedoes from *U.94* but apparently with no effect for she continued on her way. Next day she was torpedoed again by *U.94* and this time broke in two and sank in position 52.42N 34.51W. The American-flag *William Rockefeller* was torpedoed by *U.701* on 28th June, 1942, off Cape Hatteras, North Carolina in position 35.07N 75.07W.

The *John D. Archbold* did worldwide voyaging throughout the war years and came through unscathed. For the first two years she worked mainly in the Western Atlantic, delivering crude oil to the East coast refineries of the United States.

On 23rd April, 1942, the War Shipping Administration took her over and in the following November she began making a series of North Atlantic crossings from Halifax, Nova Scotia, to Glasgow. This lasted for a year and in 1943 the *John D. Archbold* was ordered to the Pacific area. Here, she carried oil for the U.S. Navy from Curacao through the Panama Canal and in the long Pacific supply lines to the fighting areas; to Funafuti in the Ellice Islands; to Majuro in the Marshalls; Eniwetok; Esperito Santo in the New Hebrides; to Bora Bora in the Society Group where she lay offshore and discharged her cargo through two eight-inch shore lines, a quarter mile in length. Oil was also transferred from the *John D. Archbold* direct to U.S. Navy oilers.

Finally, she arrived at Melville, Rhode Island, on 27th November, 1944, and New York two days later, having left there on 4th November, 1943, and not having berthed at a port in the United States in that period.

On 8th May, 1945, she steamed into Glasgow, just in time to celebrate V.E. Day. During the 1939–45 war the *John D. Archbold* made seventy cargo voyages and carried nearly ten million barrels of oil.

	Completed	Gross tons	
Esso Belfast	10.1930	11,752	Built by Federal Shipbuilding & Drydock Co., Kearny, New Jersey, as *G. Harrison Smith*. Measurements: 525 feet (loa) × 74 feet breadth. 20,600 tdw. Engines: Steam turbines to single screw. 1950: *Esso Belfast*. 4.1958: Scrapped La Seyne.
Esso Southampton	11.1930	11,787	Built by Federal Shipbuilding & Drydock Co., Kearny, New Jersey, as *W. S. Farish*. Measurements: 525 feet (loa) × 74 feet breadth. 20,600 tdw. Engines: Steam turbines to single screw. 1950: *Esso Southampton*. 10.2.1958: Arrived Split, in tow of tug *Hercules*, for scrap.

The fourth ship flew the Panamanian flag of the subsidiary Panama Transport Company. She was British-built.

Esso Bedford	11.1930	10,844	Built by Furness Shipbuilding Co. Ltd., Haverton Hill-on-Tees for Baltisch-Amerikanische Petroleum-Import-Gesellschaft, as *F. H. Bedford Jr*. Measurements: 542 feet (loa) × 70 feet breadth. 17,460 tdw. Engines: Oil. . 1935: (Panama Transport Co.). 1950: *Esso Bedford*. 16.6.1954: Arrived Bremerhaven for scrap.

CHAPTER SEVEN

A Change of Policy

The expansion of Fawley refinery

IN 1939 three-quarters of the oils used by Britain were from overseas, petrol, diesel fuel and lubricating oils being imported in a refined state through the marketing companies in Britain. But in the postwar years a new policy emerged. At that time Britain was desperately short of United States dollars and a new scheme was designed to overcome the major problem of meeting the nation's need for twenty million tons of petroleum products each year, and at the same time easing the strain on dollar resources by reducing Britain's dollar outflow. The plan was for Britain to have her own refineries, bringing in crude oil mainly from the fast expanding oilfields of the Middle East and available at sterling prices.

The site for the first refinery was chosen at Fawley, Hampshire. And what better site could there be? Midway along the South coast on the shores of Southampton Water; with double tides, sheltered, and with water deep enough to accommodate the world's largest ships, it was perfectly placed as a distributing centre. And there was already a small refinery there, built in 1921.

In June, 1949, the earthmoving machines moved in, clearing, digging and grading vast areas of gravel sub-soil for the immense construction to come. The first tree was cut on 4th July; the ground broken in August. Then came the concrete mixers and concrete. Thousands of tons of foundation and countless concrete piles. Workshops sprang up: offices from which to administrate; storage tanks in their hundreds, silver and glistening, regimented in rows and groups with miles of accommodating roads in symmetrical criss-cross patterns between the rows. Concrete foundations for enormous processing plants were laid, those for the heaviest unit, the catalytic cracking plant, being twelve feet deep. This huge plant—"cat cracker"—converts heavy gas oil into high octane motor and aviation gasolene components and other gaseous products, its fifty-six feet diameter regenerator reclaiming the catalyst for further use and its thirty-five feet diameter reactor being where the cracking reaction takes place. Other plants were placed. The crude distillation unit which separates the crude oil to gas oil for the "cat cracker",

133

Fawley refinery nearing completion in 1951.

Esso

light fuel and residual oils; the light ends unit separating light gases from the catalytic unit; a unit for reducing the sulphur content of raw kerosene; and plants to produce tractor fuel, converting butylene into a high-octane liquid, copper chloride sweetening processors . . .

Then up went the chimneys and uptakes of many differing heights, all contributing to the Wellsian scene of minarets, pagoda-like shapes, lines of silver horizontal pipes and batteries of vertical ones, all connected and inter-connected to the field of tanks. And at night a thousand lights with flames from the waste-gas uptakes, 350 feet high, flickering and licking heavy cloud and producing a sombre redness and eerie effect.

The opening ceremony on Friday 14th September, 1951, was performed by the Prime Minister, the Rt. Hon. C. R. Attlee. The refinery had taken

134

twenty-seven months to build, was rated sixth largest in the world and was then the largest in Europe. Fawley was "on stream".

At the end of the decade three large plants, conveniently adjoining Fawley refinery, were opened by other companies in the developing field of petro-chemicals. One was supplied with butadiene for the production of synthetic rubber; another produced polyethylene plastic and needed ethylene supplies and the third also needed ethylene to produce ethylene oxide, a basic raw material for several petroleum chemicals.

A change of name

In Britain, in 1951, the Anglo-American Oil Company was primarily a marketing organisation, importing finished products for distribution and sale. It had been convenient in working practice that the separate concern, Esso Transportation Company Ltd., had been given the responsibility for the provision of tonnage and management of the tanker fleet ever since its formation in 1947. However, in 1951, when the new refinery at Fawley was ready to begin production, the Anglo-American Company became a major manufacturer of petroleum products and the whole scope of its activities changed. The transportation task greatly increased; more ships were required, not only to feed the new refinery but also in the distribution and marketing of its products.

It was therefore decided to re-assume control of the tanker fleet and to this end a Marine Department was set up within the company to be responsible for the management and operation of the fleet, maintenance and repair of the ships, new construction, and the chartering of vessels. And with these new arrangements came the decision to change the name of Anglo-American Oil Company Ltd. to Esso Petroleum Company Ltd. With the exception of the Maracaibo ships of the old Lago Shipping Company Ltd., practically all the ocean tankers, coasters and small estuarial vessels were gradually transferred to the newly-styled Esso Petroleum Company Ltd., under its new Marine Department for fleet management. The old management name was slowly phased out, the last two vessels, *Esso Westminster* (built 1954) and *Esso Windsor* (built 1958), being transferred in 1959.

A new arrangement had also been made by the parent company in the United States, for from 1st January, 1950, the United States-flag ocean tanker fleet of Standard Oil Company (New Jersey) was transferred to a new subsidiary, Esso Shipping Company, incorporated in Delaware, and its ships were re-registered at Wilmington, Delaware. The purpose was to centralise all marine operations that had been carried on by the Standard Oil Company (New Jersey) since 1944.

Fawley Marine Terminal

Concurrent with the construction of the refinery was the building of the Marine Terminal, a 3,200 feet long jetty with berthing accommodation for four ocean tankers of 28,000 tdw broadside to the river. There was a 5,000 feet causeway approach which involved piledriving across marshy ground. On it were two trestles, each of 1,900 feet, to carry pipes for both the incoming crude oil and outgoing products. The two crude oil pipes were thirty-six inches and twenty-four inches in diameter. Some 95% of the products from Fawley were to be shipped by sea, with a traffic movement of 250 ships each month.

Appropriately, it was the *Esso Fawley* which became the first tanker to berth at the Marine Terminal. Her arrival date was 15th August, 1951, one month before the official opening of the refinery. But the tankers grew larger . . .

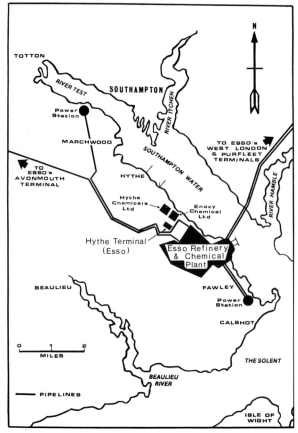

A map of the Southampton area showing the location of the Fawley refinery and, opposite, an aerial view of Fawley marine terminal. *Esso*

136

In June, 1955, a contract was obtained to supply fuel to seven of Britain's power stations over the following ten years. The plants were at Littlebrook, Tilbury, Barking and Brunswick Wharf on the Thames; and at Poole, Plymouth and Portishead. The amount of fuel involved was thirty million tons.

Towards the end of the 1950s the "Esso City"-class ships and vessels of the "Esso Lincoln"-class were beginning to be superseded by a class of six "County"-class tankers, 860 feet in length and with a planned deadweight capacity of 73,000 tons. Then two of the six were increased in breadth which, in turn, lifted the capacity to 96,000 tons. The forty-nine feet draught of these large vessels was eight feet more than that of Cunard's *Queen Elizabeth* and to accommodate them special dredging operations were planned at the approaches to the Nab Tower and in Southampton Water.

More accommodation at the Marine Terminal became necessary and in the summer of 1956 the order was given for the construction of an ocean tanker berth, No. 5, followed a few months later by an order for an additional coaster berth, No. 9, for a 5,000 tdw ship. The new No. 5 berth was opened in 1959; the jetty was then 4,400 feet long.

The dredging programme began in November, 1961. It was in three phases. The first was to cut a deeper channel, 500 yards wide and 2,100 yards long through the Nab Shoal from the Nab Tower to Nab End Buoy. Then, in phase two, the western approaches to Southampton Water were deepened from thirty-seven feet to forty-three feet (low water) at the West Bramble Buoy. The third phase was to dredge at Fawley Marine Terminal to enable tankers of 120,000 tdw to lie there at any state of the tide. More than seven million cubic feet of spoil was dredged from the approach channel and half this amount, gravelly and ideal for land reclamation, was dumped at nearby Ower Lake at the site of the Central Electricity Generating Board's new power station. From midnight on 24th August, 1963, fully laden tankers of 120,000 tdw were able to berth at Fawley, entering through the newly-dredged Nab channel and the wider approaches to the Brambles. One week later on 31st August, the 81,138 tdw tanker *Esso Lancashire*, drawing forty-seven feet of water, berthed fully laden at Fawley and became the largest ship ever to enter Southampton Water. But still the tankers grew larger . . .

At the end of the 1960s tankers were being constructed with double the carrying capacity of the "County"-class ships and further modification was given to the Fawley Marine Terminal to accommodate the giants. Plans were drawn up to give No. 5 berth the capability of accommodating partly-laden tankers of 190,000 tdw by the construction of another dolphin, 175 feet long, at the southern end. On 27th February, 1970, *Esso Cambria* became the first of the 250,000 tdw-class to use the Port of Southampton. She arrived from Ras Tanura and six tugs were used to berth her at Fawley Marine Terminal.

By 1972 there were nine berths, five for ocean-going tankers and four for short sea and coastal ships, the latter on the landward side of the outward-facing ocean tanker berths. At the end of 1986 berth accommodation was:

	Berth No	
Ocean	1 2 3 }	Used for discharging and loading clean products; can accommodate tankers to 30,000 tdw.
	4	A back-up berth to No 5 berth, used in similar fashion and with the same limitations.
	5	Use for crude oil discharge and can accommodate VLCCs up to 300,000 tdw capacity, but to a 49 feet draught only and with no more than 165,000 tons of cargo on board.
Coaster	6	Loading clean and black oils and bitumen. Cargoes to 5,000 tdw.
	7 8 }	Import/export of chemicals up to 5,000 tdw.
	9	Import/export of chemicals including ethylene, to 5,000 tdw.

Two fire-fighting tugs are permanently based at the Marine Terminal. The *Gatcombe* and *Vecta* (269 gt) are owned by Red Funnel Tugs, Southampton, and were constructed in 1970 by Richard Dunston Ltd., Hessle. During 1982 the Marine Terminal had 2,400 tankers at berth. The discharge rate is up to 10,000 tons an hour, while all grades of petroleum and oils are loaded at from 200 to 1,500 tons per hour.

The distribution factor in the 1950s

In the early postwar days the distributing pattern had not changed. Nearly all products were imported from overseas and discharged to storage terminals at coastal ports. From there the smaller coastal tankers transferred them to lesser storage plants and so to the consumer. The average delivery to a petrol station was then some 300 gallons. In the distribution pattern of 1948 there were no fewer than 472 terminals and bulk plants.

But all this was to alter. Fawley opened in 1951, and by 1952 the pattern of distribution was already showing great change. The 1948 number of terminals had been halved to 225 by the elimination of numerous small plants. With the increasing demand for oils and the reduction in the number of plants, those remaining had not only to be enlarged to greater capacity but had also to be automated to enable the distributing road tanker to have a faster turnround. In parallel with the small plants the road tanker had decreased in number from 1,636 in 1948 to some 1,200 in the early 1960s, yet this reduced road fleet could carry about twice as much. Oil products were not only distributed by road but by train and pipeline. Special tank wagons

In the 1950s, the *Esso Appalachee* was employed in coastal distribution.   *W. D. Harris*

with increased capacity over earlier pre-war types were made into 60 mph freight trains. The quantity carried was doubled by the early 1960s.

But there was still much work for the coaster, ranging in size from 280 tons to more than 16,000 deadweight tons. Some of the coasters were specifically designed to carry a special product; some were for special services, and there were some which had a dual capacity, for either coastal or bunkering work. The four largest ships—ocean-going—were introduced for coastal distribution between Fawley and the larger of the company's terminals. These giants of the coastal fleet comprised two British-built and two American-built tankers.The former were the war-built sisters *Esso Appalachee* and *Esso Cheyenne*, each with a deadweight of some 14,800 tons. The other two were slightly larger T2-type turbo-electric tankers, *Esso Avonmouth* and *Esso Glasgow*, both of 16,500 tons.

In 1957 the Esso coastal fleet, numbering more than forty vessels, carried over eight million tons of oil products.

When Esso's refinery at Milford Haven opened in 1960 the new plant fed the West coast while the Fawley refinery fed the South and East coasts. From Fawley the distribution network stretched along the South coast, westwards to Plymouth, eastwards to Dover and across the English Channel to the Channel Islands. It also took in London, the major terminal at Purfleet and the Salt End terminal at Hull. Another terminal was at Tynemouth and there were bulk plants in Scottish ports, including Dundee, Aberdeen and Inverness. Coasters from Milford Haven fed the North Devon and South Wales storage plants; northwards they carried to Caernarvon and to Dingle, on the north bank of the River Mersey. At Ellesmere Port, further upstream, was a terminal with a 100 feet barge wharf. Another terminal, at Mode Wheel—the inland end of the Manchester Ship Canal—had two berths, 521 feet and 413 feet long. Milford Haven refinery also fed the bulk plants at Douglas on the Isle of Man, Belfast and Londonderry in Northern Ireland, Ayr and the Clyde, where there was a terminal at Bowling.

The increase in product output also brought further need of expansion in the distribution fleet, and 26,000 tdw ships, previously on the Middle East run, became coastwise vessels and were used to transport various products from the refineries to certain coastal distribution centres.

Then in the early 1960s came the pipelines, the first stretching some eighty miles from Fawley to Severnside. Another went to the North Thames Gas Board at Southall, and shorter lines ran from Fawley to Southern Gas at Hythe and to the Central Electricity Generating Board's power plant at Marchwood.

Coastal ships of the 1950s

	Completed	Gross tons	
Esso Abingdon	5.1952	446	Built by Henry Scarr Ltd., Hessle.

Measurements: 168 feet (loa) × 32 feet 6 inches breadth.
Engines: Oil.
*1966: *Babingdon* (Bowker & King Ltd.).
1975: (Belcon S. and T. Co. Ltd.); arrived Milton Regis, Kent, 9.7.75 for scrapping.

Designed specifically for the carrying of bulk products on the River Thames, the *Esso Abingdon* could carry 500 tons of petroleum spirit in seven tanks—the maximum permitted under Port of London Authority regulations in 1951.

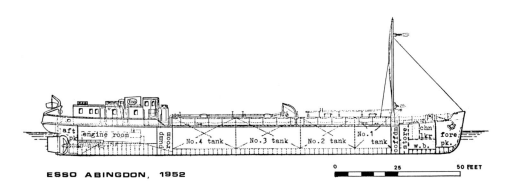

ESSO ABINGDON, 1952

141

The coastal tanker *Esso Hythe*, one of three sisterships built in 1958–59.   *Skyfotos*

| *Esso Poole* | 12.1955 | 754 | Built by Henry Scarr Ltd., Hessle. |

Measurements: 196 feet (loa) length × 34 feet 7 inches breadth.
*1968: *Mary J.* (Celtic Coasters Ltd, Dublin).
1984: Broken up, Haulbowline.

Launched on 23rd June, 1955, the *Esso Poole* on completion inaugurated a daily service from Fawley Refinery to the new Central Electricity Generating Board station at Marchwood and also did bunkering work at Southampton Docks. Her deadweight tonnage was 1,070 and she was driven by an 8 cylinder diesel oil engine.

| *Esso Preston* | 3.1956 | 1,965 | Built by Hall, Russell & Co. Ltd., Aberdeen. |

Measurements: 299 feet (loa) × 42 feet breadth.
Engines: T3cyl.
A bitumen/oil tanker, 2,790 tdw.
31.1.1975: Grounded off Whitegate and sustained some damage. Laid up at Cardiff, then sold for breaking up.
1.4.1975: Arrived Aviles, Spain, in tow.

The *Esso Preston* was the most highly-specialised ship in Esso's coastwise fleet. A vessel of 1,965 gross tons, she looked like an ordinary coastal tanker, but whereas most modern coasters were diesel driven, the *Esso Preston* was an exception, being steam driven—and for a very good reason. The ship was designed and equipped for the bulk transportation of bitumen, as well as for the carriage of oil. The thick, sticky bitumen[7] was loaded at a temperature of 280–300 degrees and remained heated during voyages by a bank of steam-heated coils in each of the five cargo tanks.

In her later years she was on a near-regular run supplying fuel oil to the oil-burning power station at Barking, on the River Thames—a service she took over after the demise of the two previous ships on the service, *Esso Chelsea* and *Esso Fulham*.

On 31st January, 1975, the *Esso Preston* was approaching Whitegate (Cork Harbour, Republic of Ireland) on a voyage in ballast from Belfast, when she grounded off the port. Subsequently refloated, she was found to be holed in Nos 1, 3 and 4 cargo spaces. On 2nd February she sailed for Cardiff, where she arrived the next day. Laid up for a short time, she entered the Mountstewart Dry Dock on 16th February for examination. The inspection found severe damage to her internal pipework in addition to the hull damage. Considered not worthy of repair, the vessel was sold for breaking up and towed to Aviles by the tug *Sea Bristolian*.

Esso Brixham	11.1957	758	Built by Philip & Son Ltd., Dartmouth. Measurements: 196 feet (loa) × 34 feet 6 inches breadth. Engines: Oil. Intended for bunkering work at Liverpool in addition to coastwise voyaging. Carried 1,080 tdw in eight tanks. *1979: *Brixham* (Tyne-Tees Waste Disposals Ltd. (Panama flag). 1980: (Capella Finance & Trading Co.; resold B.D.K. Engineering Co. Ltd.). 5.1980: Scrapped Middlesbrough.
Esso Tilbury	1957	15	Built by Thames Launch Works, Twickenham. Measurements: 40 feet (loa) × 11 feet breadth. Motor tug for service on River Thames.
Esso Woolston	2.1958	856	Built by Henry Scarr Ltd., Hessle. Measurements: 209 feet (loa) × 35 feet breadth. Engines: Oil. *1982: *Kinbrace* (Salvesen Offshore Services Ltd.) (oil pollution recovery vessel). 15.10.1985: Arrived Santander for breaking up.
Esso Lyndhurst	4.1958	856	Built by Henry Scarr Ltd., Hessle. Measurements: 209 feet (loa) × 35 feet breadth. Engines: Oil. 1981: *Bunker I* (Saudi Bunkering Transport Co. Ltd.) 1982: (El Hawi Shipping, Saudi Arabia).
Esso Hythe	5.1959	856	Built by Henry Scarr Ltd., Hessle. Measurements: 209 feet (loa) × 35 feet breadth. Engines: Oil. 1981: *Rim* (Tristar Shipping Ltd., Lebanon).

The *Esso Woolston*, *Esso Lyndhurst* and *Esso Hythe* were sisterships, except for machinery. They were built for coasting and bunkering work, mainly at Southampton Docks. Their capacity was 1,300 tons in eight tanks.

Canal and river craft

For the river and canal fleet three motor barges were built in 1956 for work on the rivers Humber and Trent and the Aire and Calder canal. All came from the Thorne yard of R. Dunston Ltd., and each was given one 16 feet and 4 × 14 feet storage tanks. Hull measurements were 127 feet length × 17 feet 6 inches breadth; tonnage was 170 gross. An oil engine gave 7 knots. All three were sold in 1964 to J. H. Whitaker Ltd., Hull.

Esso Leeds	Built 6.1956.	1964: Sold, renamed *Humber Queen*.
Esso Nottingham	Built 8.1956.	1964: Sold, renamed *Humber Prince*.
Esso Saltend	Built 9.1956.	1964: Sold, renamed *Humber Princess*.

On the River Thames, large quantities of refined products and much of London's fuel moved on the tideway each day. Years ago the fuel cargoes of the barges were of wood and later coal. When oil became the chief fuel it was still carried by the Thames barge, but for oil cargoes the barges had become tank barges. Non-propelled, they resembled the open-hatch, traditional Thames cargo lighter generally known as a barge, except that they were decked over. And whereas the 1871 Petroleum Act merely required spirit to be carried "in a covered barge built of iron", modern laws stipulated that petroleum barges should be custom-built and their manhole hatches hermetically sealed. Spirit-carrying craft had also to identify their cargoes by flying a metal flag, red in colour and with a white centre.

Esso maintained a number of upstream bulk plants along the tideway, at Greenwich, Silvertown, Bromley East, Fulham, Battersea and Hammersmith, and supplies for them were carried from the company's terminals at Thames Haven, in the estuary, and Purfleet in their own lighters.

There was certainly no glamour to this continuous operation. Strings of barges were towed beneath numerous road and rail bridges, carrying cargoes to wharves and depots, often to the very heart of London and beyond. The towing tugs had to be powerful, for if the upstream destination was a lengthy haul full advantage of a flood tide had to be taken in order to deliver a cargo to its discharge point in one passage and in daylight. Even then they were only allowed to proceed if the cargo could be discharged immediately on arrival.

A group of swim-headed barges fitted with portable tanks was delivered by Henry Scarr Ltd., Hessle, in 1951. They were for use under tow in the River Thames and estuarial waters. Measurements were 97 feet length × 24 feet breadth, giving a gross tonnage of 131. The deadweight capacity was 140 tons.

Esso Hertford	Esso Sussex	Esso Buckingham
Esso Oxford (1953: renamed Esso Hampshire)		
Esso Middlesex	Esso Kent	Esso Norfolk
Esso Cambridge (1953: renamed Esso Dorset)		
Esso Essex	Esso Surrey	

Another ten were completed in 1961:

Esso Humber	Esso Tyne	Esso Thames
Esso Avon	Esso Severn	Esso Mersey
Esso Tees	Esso Forth	Esso Clyde
Esso Trent		

Two motor tugs, also for work on the Thames, were delivered in 1953–54 from W. J. Yarwood and Sons at Northwich, Cheshire. Measurements were 76 feet length (oa) × 19 feet 6 inches breadth, giving 77 gross tons. Crossley diesel engines gave 10 knots. They became a familiar sight plying the river regularly with oil barges until sold in 1966.

The motor tug *Esso Greenwich* heading downstream through the London bridges with five barges in tow.

Esso

	Completed	
Esso Greenwich	1953	*1966: *Silvergilt* (Silvertown Services Ltd.).
		1971: *Kitara* (J. P. Knight Ltd., Rochester).
		1973: (H. Pounds, Portsmouth). Laid up.
		1978: *Metrec* (Metrec Ltd., Newhaven). Re-engined and rebuilt.
Esso Reading	1954	*1966: *Silverclad* (Silvertown Services Ltd.).
		1971: *Kokota* (J. P. Knight Ltd., Rochester).
		1973: (H. Pounds, Portsmouth). Laid up.
		1977: *Chrianie IV* (Christiani & Nielsen).

Finally in this decade came the small, 8 gross tons *Esso Recovery II*, for use in oil reclamation work. Built by Mechans Ltd. in 1960, her measurements were 28 feet (loa) × 10 feet breadth. (A previous oil reclamation barge, *Esso Recovery*, was built by E. Newell and Company Ltd., Misterton, in 1941. She had measurements of 45 feet length (oa) and 16 feet breadth, giving 60 gross tons. She had oil engines, was fitted with a bow door and worked in Southampton Water.)

Maracaibo tankers

Four Maracaibo shallow-draught tankers were brought to Britain from Venezuela in 1956. This type of ship had evolved from the necessity of having to top-up ocean-going tankers on the seaward side of a bar across the entrance to Maracaibo Lake. After the war, dredging overcame this barrier, and many of the Maracaibo tankers became redundant.

The ships were trunk-decked, with a bridge astride the trunk just forward of midships. They were somewhat akin to the early Admiralty tankers designed for bunkering work and were given a great beam.

During the war ten of these ships were constructed in the United States for the newly-formed Creole Petroleum Corporation, Panama, a subsidiary company of the Standard Oil Company of New Jersey, and it was four of these that were transferred from the Panamanian flag to the Esso Petroleum Company and the British flag in 1956. The ships were refitted in early autumn of that year by Brigham and Cowan Ltd. and at Palmers (Hebburn) yard for the United Kingdom coastal service, sailing out of Fawley with oil to those electricity generating stations which the Central Electricity Generating Board had converted from coal to oil burning, particularly on the River Thames.

	Completed	
Esso Lambeth	9.1943	Ex *Caripito* 1956.
		27.9.1965: Arrived Hamburg for breaking up.
Esso Wandsworth	11.1943	Ex *Guarico* 1956.

On the foggy night of 23rd September, 1965, the *Esso Wandsworth* was bound from Thames Haven with fuel oil for Littlebrook power station, at Dartford, on the River Thames.

At 10.50 p.m., when in the vicinity of the Ovens Buoy, Lower Hope Reach, she was in collision with the Dutch motor vessel *Moerdyk* (11,127 gt, 1965), which was outward bound from the Royal Docks for Havre and Vancouver.

The *Esso Wandsworth* was holed in the port side of No. 1 tank, being cut through to the centreline, with the cargo tank, ballast tank, pump rooms and store rooms flooded. There was also extensive deck damage and some 800 tons of her cargo was lost into the river. The vessel was beached on the mudflats upstream of the buoy, with four tugs in attendance.

The *Moerdyk*, holed in the forepeak and split on her starboard waterline, anchored off Alpha Jetty, Cliffe, for inspection. She later proceeded to Rotterdam, discharged her cargo and was repaired by the Rotterdam Dry Dock Company.

The *Esso Wandsworth* was refloated on 26th September and towed to Purfleet where she was discharged. She then went back downriver, first to Tilbury Repair Jetty and then to Commercial Wharf, Gravesend, where work commenced on cutting away some of the damaged structure. On 12th October, while this was in progress, there was the blinding flash of an explosion, flames shot into the air and dense smoke rose over the Gravesend waterfront as fumes and oil, sprayed across the ship's bridgefront in the collision, were set on fire by sparks from a cutting torch. The fire was extinguished later the same day by the fire brigade and firefighting tugs, and a week later the ship was drydocked at Tilbury. Here, the resultant examination showed that the vessel could not be economically repaired and she was declared a constructive total loss. On 11th December the tanker was towed just a mile upstream and delivered to the shipbreaker's yard at Grays, Essex, for demolition.

Esso Chelsea   5.1945   Ex *Amacuro* 1956.
                                    30.6.1969: Arrived Bruges for breaking up.

Esso Fulham   6.1945   Ex *Trujillo* 1956.
                                    10.6.1970: Arrived Bilbao in tow of tug *Aznar Jose Luis* for breaking up.

The ten ships built for the Creole Petroleum Corporation were constructed in two yards, seven in 1943 by Barnes-Duluth Shipbuilding Company and three in 1945 by Bethlehem-Sparrows Point Shipyard Inc., Maryland. They were 335 feet in length and 60 feet in breadth. The draught was 15 feet and the tonnage 3,401 gross. Deadweight capacity was 5,500 tons and twin screws were driven by triple expansion engines. The *Caripito* and *Guarico* came from the Duluth yard, *Amacuro* and *Trujillo* from Sparrows Point.

The shallow-draught tanker *Esso Chelsea* seen in 1959, three years after having been brought to Britain from Venezuela.   *G. A. Osbon*

The *Esso York* with large fenders on her port side after having been modified for lightening work in 1969.
Skyfotos

The histories of the remaining six ships are varied. The other Duluth-built ships were *San Joaquin, Temblador, San Cristobal, Guiria* and *Valera*, and of these, *Valera* was the first to go, sunk on 7th March, 1944, by a torpedo from the submarine *U.518* in the Caribbean, in position 11.30N 76.27W. Three, *San Joaquin, San Cristobal* and *Guiria*, went to the Compania de Petroleo Lago, Venezuela (a subsidiary of Standard Oil of New Jersey) during the period 1948–50 and had the prefix Esso added to their names. The *Esso Joaquin* then moved to Petroleos Mexicanos in 1959 and as *Pemex A* sank on 21st January, 1960, on a voyage in ballast from Campeche to Coatzacoalcos, in position 18.11N 94.13W, in the Gulf of Campeche, Mexico. On 27th October, 1961, *Esso Guiria* arrived at Hamburg to be broken up, while *Esso San Cristobal*, which in 1960 became *Witwater*, owned by Challenger Ltd., Trinidad, broke in two on 13th December, 1968, off Colon (Canal Zone) on a voyage from Las Minas to Cristobal with diesel and heavy oil. The next day the forepart sank in position 09.25N 79.49W and on the 16th December the after-part dragged anchor and went aground. The remaining ship of the group, *Temblador*, went to Canadian owners in 1960 and by 1978 had been relegated to the status of a barge, operating on the Great Lakes.

Nothing very spectacular happened to the *Mara*, the first of the Bethlehem ships. She, too, joined Compania de Petroleo Lago—in 1954—and also took the *Esso* prefix. On 23rd February, 1965, she arrived at Valencia for breaking up.

148

Esso "Oxford"-class 1953–1955

This class of handy-sized tankers came out in the early 1950s. They were constructed to a specially adapted American design, all-welded and fitted with thirty cargo tanks. The crude oil carrying capacity was 26,700 tons. A feature at that time was the unusually high rate of discharge, about 3,000 tons per hour.

The overall length was 630 feet, breadth was 83 feet and the gross tonnage around 17,500. Two steam turbines geared to a single shaft gave 17 knots.

Built by Cammell Laird and Company Ltd., Birkenhead

	Completed	Gross tons	
Esso Oxford	12.1953	17,539	*1972: *Golden Robin* (Warwick Shipping Ltd., Bermuda). 30.9.1974: Aground, Douglas Island, off Dalhousie, New Brunswick. Three portside tanks were ruptured and about 100,000 gallons were spilled. Refloated. 25.11.1974: Arrived Castellon for breaking up.
Esso Cambridge	9.1954	17,551	*1968: *Stephanie Conway* (Cosmopolitan Shipping Co. S.A., (Liberian)). 1971: *Tripoli* (Mainland Shipping Co. (Liberian)). 1974: Renamed *Destiny*. 6.3.1975: Laid up at Piraeus. 10.1976: Scrapped Piraeus.

The *Esso Oxford* in the River Clyde.   *Esso*

Built by Vickers-Armstrongs Ltd., Barrow

Esso Westminster	2.1954	17,554	*1972: *Kikis* (Laomedon Shipping Co. Ltd., Cyprus).
			1973: Renamed *Windjammer*.
			1973: *Windtides* (Coscol Tankers Inc., Liberia).
			13.11.1975: Arrived Santander for breaking up.
Esso Canterbury	7.1954	17,543	

Oil was discovered by an Esso affiliated company at Zelten, Libya, in 1959 and on 6th August, 1961, an oil pipeline was completed and tested, from Zelten northwards some 120 miles to Marsa el Brega in the Gulf of Sirte. Two days later oil began flowing, reaching Marsa el Brega on the morning of 17th August where a temporary pipeline led to the *Esso Canterbury*, lying offshore at temporary moorings. She sailed with the first cargo of Libyan oil on 12th September and arrived at Fawley eight days later. King Idris officially opened the pipeline on 25th October, 1961.

In 1968 *Esso Canterbury* was sold to Camelot Shipping Ltd. and was renamed *Golden Jay*. On 14th May, 1972, on a voyage from Los Angeles to Venezuela in ballast there was an explosion and she sank 200 miles south of Mazatlan, position 20.10N 106.34W.

Built by Vickers-Armstrongs Ltd., Newcastle

Esso York	4.1955	17,570	Became a lightening ship, modified on the Tyne in January, 1969.
			11.7.1981: Arrived Bombay for breaking up.
Esso Exeter	7.1955	17,554	

The *Esso Exeter* started her career with a flourish, for when launched on 5th January, 1955, she moved stern-first across the river instead of turning and hit the premises of British Paints at Bill Quay, causing some damage to their boiler house.

All went well for a decade until 11th January, 1965, when on leaving Purfleet, in ballast, for Milford Haven, she collided with the Norwegian motor ship *Medicine Hat*, 4,259 gt/1960, on charter to Canadian Pacific. The *Medicine Hat* came off worse, being beached, and then two days later suffering a fire in a hold. This was extinguished and the ship refloated. Only bow damage was suffered by the *Esso Exeter*.

Early in 1968 the tanker was sold to Atlantic Agency Corp., Woodbridge, New Jersey, and placed under the Western Oil Transport Inc., Monrovia, as *Good Hope*. She was sold again in 1972 to Amerada Hess Shipping Corp., Monrovia, and worked around the U.S. Gulf ports until she arrived at Kaohsiung in July, 1982, for breaking up.

CHAPTER EIGHT

Esso and the Suez Emergency

THE years of the 1950s were not peaceful in the Middle East, yet it remained the richest oil-bearing area in the world. Its emergence as a major factor in the world oil balance had been sudden and spectacular, for while the world oil industry claimed to be about a century old, the Middle East as a really large producer had developed in a mere decade.

In the 1950s the six main producing states were Iran (formerly Persia), Iraq (formerly Mesopotamia), Saudi Arabia, Kuwait, Bahrain and Qatar, and between 1945 and 1955 their oil output rose six-fold from 27 to 162 million tons a year. This expansion was some three times that of the world output as a whole and raised the Middle East's share from 7% to nearly 25%. The proven reserves remained scarcely tapped, with fewer than 1,500 wells drilled in the whole of the Middle East compared with many times that number in the United States. But whereas the average daily output of a well in the Middle East was 580 tons, it was only thirty-six tons in Venezuela and a mere two tons in the United States.

At this time Europe was by far the largest of the Middle East's customers. The whole of Europe's supplies in 1955 came either from the Persian Gulf via Suez or through pipelines to ports in Syria and the Lebanon and thence by tankers through the Mediterranean.

Following several years of political strife Egypt nationalised the Suez Canal Company and seized control of the Canal on 26th July, 1956, sparking off a crisis of world magnitude. The events that followed culminated in a joint British–French ultimatum to Egypt, and when this was rejected troops were landed to restore the Canal status to that of an unrestricted international waterway. Instead, the Canal was blocked by Egypt and at the same time the Iraq Petroleum Company's pipelines from Kirkuk were cut. Thus, with the sole exception of the Arabian-American Oil Company's "Tapline" to Sidon—which was barred to Britain and France—the normal supply routes for 90% of Europe's total oil consumption were suddenly closed.

At 03.20 hours on the morning of 31st October, 1956, only forty minutes before the expiry of the Anglo-French ultimatum, a tanker on voyage charter to Esso cleared Port Said and headed west through the Mediterranean. As luck would have it, no other Esso ship at that moment was nearer than thirty-six hours' steaming from Suez.

At 21.30 hours on the same day, well over a thousand miles to the west and 110 miles east of Gibraltar, the *Esso Cambridge* was steaming through the Mediterranean at 16 knots, bound for Suez and the Persian Gulf where she was to load crude oil at Mena al Ahmadi for the refinery at Fawley. It was a routine trip . . . she had made the same voyage several times before . . . The ship's radio crackled . . .

MASTER ESSOCAMBRIDGE
VIEW ADMIRALTY INSTRUCTIONS 30TH NOW PROCEED PERSIAN GULF VIA CAPEOFGOODHOPE CALLING CAPETOWN FOR REPLENISHMENT BUNKERS WATER REACH RASTANURA FOUR DAY MARGIN DRINKING WATER TO CAPACITY ADVISE ESTIMATED REQUIREMENTS STOP STEAM AT MAXIMUM SPEED CONSISTENT WITH SAFETY ACKNOWLEDGE ADVISE POSITION AND TIME COURSE ALTERED ALSO E.T.A. CAPETOWN.

ESSOSHIP

It was no longer routine. The long-threatened emergency had become fact, the Suez Canal was being blocked at that very moment. The *Esso Cambridge* altered course and turned back for Gibraltar and the long haul round the Cape of Good Hope. But that was only the beginning, for an

The tanker *Esso Cambridge* was steaming through the Mediterranean on 31st October, 1956, when she found herself caught up in the Suez emergency.

urgent cargo of crude oil required loading at the Syrian port of Banias. No other Esso ship was readily available and again the tanker altered course, to head for Syria. But it was already too late: Syria would not release the oil and within twelve hours pipelines from the Iraqi oilfields to the eastern Mediterranean ports of Banias and Tripoli were sabotaged and the pumping stations destroyed. The *Esso Cambridge* stood by for further orders and was then directed to the long westabout route round Africa, at maximum speed. Entering the Atlantic she was nearly diverted again, this time to the Caribbean.

The new situation affected many companies as well as many national governments, and when it concerned the supply of oil to Britain it also involved Esso, the effect stretching from boardroom to depot; departments, divisions, districts, areas and terminals worked day and night to bring order out of sudden chaos. The story of the *Esso Cambridge* is merely one example of what was done to keep oil flowing to Britain's largest refinery; to garages and industry; to farms and to airlines, ships and homes. Fortunately, a correct interpretation of the political scene in the Middle East during the summer had led Esso to build up stocks of crude oil and petroleum to the maximum, and the emergency came with the tanks at Fawley full and standby supplies at the ready throughout the United Kingdom. This helped to bridge the immediate gap in delivery from overseas, although by the time the British government introduced rationing the nation's stocks were depleted to well below normal. Luck also played a part to the extent that no Esso tanker, owned or chartered, was caught in the Suez Canal and no cargo was lost. Above all, the initial weeks of crisis proved the incalculable advantage of Esso being part of a worldwide organisation, for it afforded great flexibility of operations, and supplies were quickly forthcoming from the Standard Oil Company (New Jersey), at a time when the United States policy on the situation had not been defined.

The situation facing Esso on the morning of 1st November was complex. The company had been buying over 90% of crude oil for its refinery from the Middle East. Normally, about two-thirds of this would be shipped from ports in the Persian Gulf through the Canal to Fawley, a voyage which, at 14½ knots, would take about nineteen days. The remaining one third used to be sent through the Iraq Petroleum Company's pipelines to the East Mediterranean port of Banias and transported from there by tanker. Banias to Fawley was a nine-day run. But both these routes were now closed and the company had nearly one million tons of shipping heading for or returning from Middle East ports at that moment. The only way left of obtaining supplies from the Middle East was via the Cape of Good Hope. The other possible source—through the Trans-Arabian pipeline—was no longer open to either Britain or France.

A comparison of distances and times gives the full implication of the situation:

Route	Distance (miles)	Time (days at 14½ knots)
Banias–Fawley	3,150	9
Mena al Ahmadi (Persian Gulf)– Fawley (via Suez)	6,200	19
Mena al Ahmadi–Fawley (via Cape of Good Hope)	11,100	32

In other words, from the moment a tanker left the refinery in ballast for the Persian Gulf, every ton of crude oil loaded there would, on the round voyage, take four weeks longer to reach Britain than before. A vast increase in tanker tonnage would be required to transport the same quantity of crude oil from the Middle East over nearly twice the distance. But the tonnage did not exist. The oil was available; the tankers were not.

Nevertheless, the company was not unprepared. For some time all ships had carried a three month supply of stores, extra bunkers had been taken on and charts for the Cape of Good Hope were aboard. Crude oil stocks at the refinery were the highest ever held. The priority task was to organise the new pattern of supply from Esso in the United States which, combined with the reduced amount of oil possible from Kuwait, could keep Fawley refinery running to maximum capacity possible under the circumstances.

But it was not as easy as it sounds. Taps cannot be turned on and off at will in a refinery, nor can a refinery be shut down and re-started at frequent intervals. And there are minimal limits of feed to each plant below which it is uneconomic and sometimes dangerous to go. The new situation required solutions to two main problems. First, how to re-programme the refinery for reduced throughput and, second, to adjust its processes to take account of the difference in quality between Middle East and Western crude oils and in particular the marked variations in their sulphur content. The large Fawley refinery was built primarily to process crude oil from the oilfields of Iraq, Kuwait and the neighbouring states. Now it had to deal with many different grades of crude, each producing products in different ratios. Moreover, the high sulphur content of Middle East crude oil had originally dictated the incorporation of special plant at the refinery for its treatment. Now the situation changed. Crude oil from the United States Gulf was low in sulphur, but required special treatment. And there was still a considerable quantity with different characteristics moving round the Cape of Good Hope for which it was necessary to change operating techniques and sequences of processing, and to make alterations in flow plans. In addition, it was necessary to adjust the balance of the manufactured products as new priorities demanded. The company had to put in operation the government scheme for the reduction of supplies of products to dealers and consumers.

When the main supply routes of oil to Europe closed, the shortage that resulted was sufficiently serious to threaten the whole structure of the economy. Aid was quickly sought by Esso and obtained from their associates across the Atlantic. First, the "spare" oil had to be found and Esso companies began a systematic search. Substantial supplies were found in Texas; purchases were increased in Arkansas and Louisiana and excess production was located in Colorado, Kansas, Oklahoma and as far away as the Rocky Mountains and 2,000 miles from the nearest available seaport. Under normal circumstances oil from the Rockies would be for domestic consumption only, since the great distance and cost of its transport would make it impractical for export. But these were not ordinary circumstances and one of the most unusual oil movements in the history of the United States was put in motion. From the oilfields in the Rockies the crude oil was carried some 1,000 miles by pipeline to a barge terminal near St Louis, on the Mississippi River. Transferred to barges, it was then carried on a long, twisting voyage of 1,100 miles downstream to the Esso Marine Terminal at Avondale, near New Orleans. Avondale itself was yet another example of the emergency measures taken by Esso. Put into "mothballs" only a year earlier, it was brought back into service to handle the additional volume and to relieve the heavily-burdened ports of the Gulf of Mexico.

Even so, arranging delivery of the other new supplies created further difficulties. The pipeline system transporting oil hundreds and sometimes thousands of miles from the interior to Esso's Texas seaboard terminals at Baytown and Harbor Island was not designed for such an increased throughput, and huge bottlenecks occurred. In addition, although Texas oilfields had the capacity to produce substantial quantities above their normal output, the Texas Railroad Commission was not at first prepared to increase the already agreed output, although after five months a large increase for the month of March was allowed. The Texas Railroad Commission had come into being in 1891, its original purpose being to prevent discrimination and other abuses on the State railways. With an increase of ferries and buses in the early years of this century, the commission took on the regulation of road transport, and a little later the regulation of the rapidly expanding oil and gas pipeline systems which, in 1917, were defined as common carriers. Because of its experience with the pipeline systems it was given the responsibility of administering state oil and gas conservation laws passed in 1919. The powers of the commission were absolute with neither state nor federal government able to overrule it.

Although remaining responsible for railways, road transport and pipelines, the regulation of oil and gas production became its most important function.

Every producer in the state was required to detail every phase of drilling and production from each well, the commission meeting once a month to decide how much oil could be produced in the following month. Each well in the state had a daily withdrawal rate, the orders expressed in terms of the number of days' production allowed in the month.

The emergency created an overall need for ships, for it was one thing to have the availability of supplies, but quite another to transport them some 5,000 miles by sea from the Gulf of Mexico to Fawley. To meet this need a high proportion of the British Esso fleet was diverted to lift the oil while the remainder, the fastest ships, went south for the long run round the Cape of Good Hope. At times it was necessary to send ships to Las Palmas to await further orders so that when supplies became available they could be diverted either to the Persian Gulf or the United States Gulf. So rapidly was this redeployment carried out that by the end of November tankers which had been diverted from the Middle East had picked up 442,000 tons of crude oil in the United States Gulf ports and 166,000 tons in Venezuela. That was the measure of success achieved by Esso's efforts in the first, and most difficult, month of crisis. And by the first week of December supplies were again coming in from the Persian Gulf via South Africa.

On 7th December the United States government established a Middle East Emergency Committee, a group of experts from fifteen major oil companies. Operating under the auspices of the Oil and Gas Division of the United States Department of the Interior, it had no executive authority; it could make recommendations, but not decisions.

An example of the type of arrangement the M.E.E.C. made possible was the diversion of the year-old 56,000 tdw tanker *Sinclair Petrolore*, 35,477 gt. Carrying 52,600 tons of oil from Kuwait, the vessel was rounding the Cape of Good Hope, bound for Philadelphia, on the very day the committee started operating. Esso reached agreement with the Sinclair Oil Corporation and the tanker was diverted to Britain, discharging her cargo at the Fawley refinery on Christmas Eve and becoming the largest tanker ever to dock in a United Kingdom port.

By the end of December, 1956, Esso group companies in the United States had found over a million tons of "spare" oil for shipment to Europe. Only six weeks later, by mid-February, a grand total of more than six million tons of oil and products had been sent from the United States, of which the group headed by Standard Oil (New Jersey) had provided more than half the volume. When political tension eased, and after protracted negotiations, the Suez Canal was cleared by a United Nations salvage operation and re-opened to all shipping on 9th April, 1957.

CHAPTER NINE

The 1950s

AVIATION development from experimental stages to supersonic flight occurred in less than a lifetime. Apart from the aeroplane itself, the fuel and the methods of its supply underwent many changes in order to meet the everchanging demands.

Almost from the beginning, when the first frail bird machines bounced into flight, Anglo-American products were used. In those early days the fuel supplied was petrol, stacked on primitive airfields in the familiar green, two-gallon cans of "Pratt's Perfection Spirit" and then poured carefully through chamois leather filters into the aeroplane tanks. In its growing years of infancy the aeroplane flew faster and faster, records were set, only to be broken over and over again. There were also the daredevils whose early stunts were held in awe. Competition and advertising were well to the fore.

In 1903 the Wright brothers, Wilbur and Orville, flew a distance of 852 feet in the first controlled flight of a heavier-than-air machine at Kitty Hawk, North Carolina. Only six years later, on 25th July, 1909, Louis Blériot flew across the English Channel from Calais to Dover and Anglo-American proudly exhibited at the Motor Show Aero-Naphtha as a motor spirit specially prepared for aero engines. The first air race from London to Manchester was held in 1914 and won, using Pratt's Spirit, at the remarkable speed of 69 miles per hour. Anglo-American products also assisted the first British aviator to loop-the-loop and fly upside down.

Although the evolution of aviation fuel was temporarily checked by the advent of the Great War of 1914–18, aerial warfare developed at an amazing rate. When war began Germany had 470 aircraft, France 500, Russia 400 and Britain 130, but there followed a great surge in British production. The Royal Flying Corps gave a tremendous service on the battle fronts using great quantities of Pratt's Aviation Spirit. On 1st April, 1918, the Royal Flying Corps and Royal Naval Air Service, which had come into being on 1st July, 1914, and by 1918 operated over 2,900 planes as well as shore-based airships, amalgamated to become the Royal Air Force.

Three years after armistice five hundred passengers a week were passing through London's "Airport" at Waddon, near Croydon, to and from Paris, Brussels and Amsterdam. The "Flying Liner", as the aircraft was dubbed, was able to taxi across the airfield to an Anglo-American Golden Pump and take on Pratt's Aviation Spirit for its return flight.

For half-a-century up to the 1950s, and even after the huge "strato-cruiser" airliners had entered service, petroleum spirit remained the fuel for aviation. It was not so very different from that which was being used as fuel for motor vehicles, except that it was of a higher octane and produced with much greater care under very stringent conditions of quality control.

But when the jet engine came the demand for piston-engine aviation fuel, Avgas as it had become known, plummeted almost to zero overnight. Introduction of the first jet aircraft to go into civil service, the de Havilland Comet, led not only to air travel as a common conveyance, even for routine purposes, but also to a change from petrol to kerosene as aircraft fuel. Aviation kerosene (Avtur) it was called: basically a simple fuel, it could be used just as safely in home-heating installations as in the airliners and military aircraft for which it was primarily intended. Its main difference from standard domestic paraffin was the care with which it was manufactured, one essential requirement being that its freezing point be low enough to avoid any possibility of its freezing in high-flying aircraft.

Fuelling a de Havilland Moth from a mobile bowser in 1926.

The "City"-class

There were twelve ships in the "City"-class of tanker, around 36,000 tdw, delivered between 1957 and 1960 with orders shared between British, German, French and Italian yards. The lead ship of the class came from AG Weser, Bremen, in July, 1957, and the twelfth, and last, from CRD Adriatico in May, 1960. All were propelled by two steam turbines connected to a single shaft giving a speed of 16½ knots. The length overall was 696 feet and breadth 90 feet.

Built by AG Weser, Bremen

	Completed	Gross tons	
Esso Guildford	7.1957	23,960	*1969: *Delphic Runner* (Dorian S. S. Corp. (Liberian)). 12.10.1974: Laid up Piraeus. 29.4.1976: Arrived Bilbao, in tow for breaking up.
Esso Winchester	2.1958	24,026	*1969: *Winchester* (Tiha Inc. (Liberian)). 1970: *Hoegh Transporter* (L. Hoegh & Co.). Converted to car carrier at Rijeka. (21,670 gt). 9.2.1979: Arrived Kaohsiung for breaking up.

Built by Howaldtswerke AG, Hamburg

Esso Salisbury	12.1957	24,008	*1972: *Terrytwo* (Terrytwo Shipping Corp. (Liberian)). 24.4.1975: Arrived Kaohsiung for breaking up.
Esso Bristol	6.1958	23,972	1964: *Esso Nicaragua* (Esso Transportation Co. Inc., Panama). 7.10.1977: Arrived Kaohsiung for breaking up.

Built by Arsenal de Brest

Esso Norwich	5.1959	23,997	1962: *Esso Balboa* (Esso Transport & Shipping Co. Inc., Panama). 1963: Lengthened and deepened. Measurements: 771 feet 3 inches (loa) × 90 feet 5 inches breadth. 30,187 gt. 50,500 tdw. *1969: *Eland* (Oil Transportation Company Inc. (Liberian)). 1971: *Eressos* (same). 1974: *Messenger* (same). 1.1975: Arrived Kaohsiung for breaking up.

Built by Vickers-Armstrongs Ltd., Newcastle

Esso Durham	9.1958	23,862	

On 26th January, 1961, the *Esso Durham* left Fawley for Mena al Ahmadi but before reaching Gibraltar suffered a serious explosion which blew a hole in her side. The *Esso Durham* was escorted to Gibraltar by the Liberian-flag Shell tanker *Philine* at a speed of 4 knots and anchored in Gibraltar Bay on 30th January.

It had been thought that the accident was a boiler blow-out but it was later identified as a gas explosion while cleaning tanks. Such was the force that the ship's sides in way of No. 4 tank were blown out between decks and below the waterline.

After drydocking, the *Esso Durham* lay at Gibraltar pending a decision as to her future and it was decided that as the damage was so extensive she would be reconstructed on somewhat similar lines to the *Esso Portsmouth*. The reconstruction plans included an insertion of two additional tank

The first of the "City"-class, the *Esso Guildford* of 1957, at Malta.

sections—a length of 40 feet—and increasing the deadweight capacity by 2,000 tons. The bridge and accommodation were also moved aft from the midships position.

The ship was then cut in two at Gibraltar, the after part leaving there in tow on 30th September, 1961, and the forepart on 3rd October, both for Cadiz where they were joined with the additional tank section by Astilleros de Cadiz.

			Measurements: 733 feet (loa) × 90 feet breadth. 25,673 gt. 40,929 tdw.
			*1967: *Durham* (Petroleum Transport Inc. (Liberian)).
			1971: *Pyrgos* (same).
			1972: *Courier* (Helmos Shipping Inc., (Liberian)).
			31.7.1975: Arrived Kaohsiung for breaking up.
Esso Portsmouth	7.1959	24,125	Measurements: (new): 733 feet (loa) × 90 feet breadth. 25,715 gt. 40,300 tdw.
			*1972: *Winson* (Winson Tankers Ltd., Panama).
			21.1.1975: Aground, 11.28N 114.23E on North Danger Reef, South China Sea (voyage: Galveston/India— wheat).
			6.8.1975: Refloated but:
			7.8.1975: Foundered in bad weather, 11.41N 115.19E, while in tow.

On 8th July, 1960, the *Esso Portsmouth* arrived at Milford Haven dressed overall, for she was the first ocean-going tanker to berth at the marine terminal of the new Esso refinery. She had 32,000 tons of crude oil to discharge from Kuwait. Early next morning while the ship was discharging, a structural failure of an unloading arm on the jetty caused a spillage of oil. This quickly ignited and there was a massive explosion.

Fire and rescue services managed to extinguish the flames but not before the ship's hull structure was heavily buckled and her midships accommodation completely gutted. Fortunately the bulk of the cargo was saved and after its discharge the ship was placed on buoys in the harbour for survey. This

160

revealed that the shell plating was damaged over the whole length of the ship. Deck plating, tanks and bulkheads were ripped open and the midship superstructure damaged beyond repair; even its aluminium panelling having melted in the intense heat. Nevertheless, it was decided that the *Esso Portsmouth* could be repaired and at the same time modernised and enlarged, reforming her to the modern "bridge and accommodation aft" configuration.

After temporary repairs to make her seaworthy, the *Esso Portsmouth* left Milford Haven in tow on 26th July, arriving in the Tyne on 6th August where she went into Palmers, Hebburn drydock for examination by Swan, Hunter. Eventually, a new midship section, 200 feet in length, was built by Vickers-Armstrongs, Walker, who were her builders, and after the damaged centre part of the ship had been cut away, the new midbody was grafted into the two remaining end sections, this work done by Swan, Hunter. Riveters and welders fitted new longitudinal frames, stiffeners and shell plating, with the outfitting work carried out by Palmers, Hebburn.

In December, 1961, the ship was ready for service and in the second week of the month, with her new "all aft" profile, put to sea, bound for the Persian Gulf. It had taken a year, and more than 4,000 tons of steel, to rebuild a "new" ship from the old casualty.

The German-built *Esso Salisbury* off Portsmouth when new in 1957.　　　　　　　*Esso*

SAILING SHIP TO SUPERTANKER

Built by Cantieri Riuniti dell' Adriatico, Trieste

	Completed	Gross tons	
Esso Southampton	12.1958	23,457	1962: *Esso Jamaica* (Panama Transport and Tanker Co. Inc., Panama).

In 1963 the *Esso Jamaica* was sent to Mitsui Zosen KK at Chiba for the insertion of an additional 80 feet in the hull, giving measurements of 773 feet 3 inches (loa) and 90 feet 5 inches breadth. Tonnages were increased, to 29,262 gt and from 35,580 to 49,850 in deadweight capacity. The draught became 41 feet 8 inches. At the same time a bulbous bow was fitted and the speed was subsequently increased by 1 knot. The ship left the Chiba yard on 12th December, 1963.

> *1969: *Nepco Advance* (Transoceanic Tankers Inc., Panama).
> 29.1.1977: Arrived Kaohsiung for breaking up.

Esso Coventry	7.1959	23,275	1963: *Esso Trieste* (La Columbia SMA).
			1975: (Esso Italiana).
			7.1976: Scrapped Masan, Korea.

Built by Cantieri Riuniti dell' Adriatico, Monfalcone

Esso Windsor	6.1958	23,581	1963: *Esso Genova* (La Columbia SMA).
			*1969: *Hoegh Trader* (L. Hoegh).
			2.1970: Converted to a car carrier at Rijeka.
			16.12.1978: Arrived Kaohsiung for breaking up.
Esso Liverpool	11.1959	23,720	1964: *Esso El Salvador* (Esso Transport Co. Inc., (Panama)).
			1970: *Esso Punta del Este* (Esso Standard Oil Co. (Uruguay) S.A.).
			5.2.1977: Arrived Kaohsiung for breaking up.
Esso Dublin	5.1960	21,627	1964: *Esso Honduras* (Esso Transport Company Inc., (Panama)).
			25.6.1976: Arrived Kaohsiung for breaking up.

The *Esso Portsmouth* after being rebuilt following an explosion and fire at Milford Haven.

CHAPTER TEN

Milford Haven—and the 1960s

MILFORD HAVEN on the Pembrokeshire coast of West Wales is regarded as one of the finest natural harbours in Britain. It extends for some ten miles and varies between one and two miles in width. Another attraction is its natural beauty, with numerous tiny creeks and inlets and clusters of houses forming attractive villages.

The Haven has a varied nautical history. Ships have traded along its shores for centuries, carrying the products of the area, loading excavations from its limestone quarries and anthracite from nearby pits. The tide rises twenty-five feet inside the Haven, yet many of the old wooden traders would load direct from the beaches, for there were many safe anchorages.

The Great Western Railway came to Pembrokeshire in 1850, reached the village of Johnston, just south of Haverfordwest, and there split into two lines, each leading to a terminus; at Milford Haven and at Neyland. Milford Haven's new commercial docks were finally completed in 1888 at great cost and also with the idea of inducing some of the transatlantic trade away from Liverpool. But this did not happen. The first ship to enter the dock on 27th September, 1888, was the steam trawler *Sibyl*, and so it was that the docks were to become the centre of a fishing industry. The fleet grew to huge proportions, but then sadly declined.

Pembroke is on the south bank of the Haven, two miles away from Pembroke Dock. Prosperity of the area began with the transfer of the naval dockyard from Milford in June, 1815, and the first two ships, the 28-gun frigates *Valorous* and *Ariadne*, were both launched on 10th February, 1816. Warship construction at Pembroke was to continue for over a century, the last vessel being completed in 1925. The yard lasted some 112 years and in 1926 was closed.

When war broke out again in 1939 work began on the dockyard installations to enable it to undertake refit and repair work once more. During the war years ships returned to the Haven just as they had done in the 1914–18 conflict, not only patrol craft and convoy escorts but countless hundreds of merchantmen, gathering in their grey numbers to make the concerted effort out into the St George's Channel, then north-about and away across the Atlantic.

SAILING SHIP TO SUPERTANKER

When peace came in 1945 the ships departed and for a decade the Haven lay quiet. But oil was to wreak a tremendous influence on the tranquillity of Milford Haven. In the early 1950s the 17,000 gross ton tankers had appeared, these giants of the day capable of carrying 26,000 tons of crude oil. But Esso ships carrying 35,000 tons were being ordered, and monsters to carry 80,000 tons were being considered. The ships needed deep water. And where better than the natural harbour of Milford Haven?

Land for new oil installations near Herbrandston was acquired by Esso on 14th November, 1955. Construction of a refinery was begun in July, 1958, a condition being that the refinery be landscaped. And so it was skilfully blended with the slopes from the water, although in the unrelenting wind trees on the open coast were sparse.

Milford Haven refinery seen from the south side of the haven. Berthed alongside the jetty is the Liberian-flag *Esso Okinawa*. *Esso*

British Petroleum followed, but on the south side at Popton Point, on East Bay, where the old Victorian fort was turned into offices for an ocean terminal, then capable of accommodating tankers to 150,000 tons dead-weight. Named Angle Bay Terminal, it was officially declared open on 20th April, 1961, to feed the British Petroleum refinery at Llandarcy.

After British Petroleum came the Regent Refining Company, who in 1962 decided on a site for a refinery at Pwllerochan. The eventual five-berth Texaco (Regent) jetty east of Angle Bay could accommodate ships to 275,000 tons deadweight. The refinery was opened by Queen Elizabeth, the Queen Mother, on 27th October, 1964. And a mile or so away, at West Pennal, the Pembroke electric power station pointed its 714-foot chimney skywards. With fan turbo-generators, it was opened as the largest oil-fired power station in Europe.

On the north side of the Haven two more oil majors established themselves. A mile or so eastwards from Milford Haven and to the west of Wear Point, Gulf Oil Corporation purchased a 460-acre site for a new refinery and petrochemical complex. Construction started in early 1966 and the plant was opened by the Queen two years later. Tanker accommodation was built for three vessels, the centre jetty berth capable of taking ships to 120,000 tdw. Amoco (U.K.) Ltd. also constructed a refinery and a three-berth jetty on the north side, east of the Esso jetty, at Gellyswick.

Milford Haven had become a major port of Britain in only two decades. When Esso began its refinery construction there was not even a harbour administration authority and this was established by Parliamentary Act in 1958. One of the first schemes was its dredging projects. The first part, commenced in 1966, was to widen the entrance between St Ann's Shoal and Mid-Channel Rocks and to straighten the channel from Thorn Island to the Esso Terminal. Dredging also gave a facility for ships of fifty-seven feet draught and up to 170,000 deadweight tons to move from the entrance to the Texaco terminal on every tide. Yet even as this was being implemented, plans for tankers to 270,000 tons deadweight were being prepared. The second phase of the dredging programme was therefore begun, for deeper dredging and even more straightening and widening of the channel. By the end of 1970 a ship of sixty-two feet draught was able to enter on every tide and some of over 65 feet could enter on a lesser number of tides.

By the second half of the 1950s, with the United Kingdom's need for still more energy and more products from oils, the possibility arose of a gap between supply and demand. The Esso refinery at Fawley had reached its maximum practical size and increasing demand could leave a deficiency in refinery capacity. Another refinery was considered necessary.

Complex surveys were made of many possible sites around the country, the essential requirement being to berth and discharge very large tankers at all

An aerial view of the Esso refinery at Milford Haven looking south-east towards Angle Point. The marine terminal is on the right of the picture. *Esso*

states of the tide. At Milford Haven the conditions proved to be ideal. There was a natural depth of water of between forty-eight and sixty feet in the approach channel and at the site of the proposed berths. And although the location had no great local marketing potential, land and freshwater were readily available, soil conditions were good for the erection of heavy plant, and electrical and rail facilities could be arranged.

Construction of the new refinery commenced on 2nd July, 1958, when a mechanical excavator moved the first of millions of cubic feet of earth at the site. A plan of the local hills, valleys and contours was studied to ensure that spindly uptakes, chimneys and assorted erections so familiar in refining processes did not clash too harshly with the natural beauty of the area. In the construction of the refinery and the regrading of 350 acres of the 1,270 acres,

166

almost one million tons of earth was moved and some seven and a half miles of new roads were laid.

Opened by the Duke of Edinburgh, the new refinery came "on stream" in November, 1960. It was designed to process in the first instance four and a half million tons of crude oil each year, but its design allowed for future expansion. The oil would be brought by ocean tankers, berthing at a marine terminal equipped with the most modern aids for the quick and safe handling of both ships and oils. The first necessary process, and one which no refinery can be without, is distillation and at the new refinery the distillation plant was half as big again as the largest of the three at Fawley, with a capacity of three and a half million gallons a day. Around it were built various treatment plants—catalytic reforming units and hydro-sulphurisation plants—to bring partly refined products to the highest standard of quality. Office blocks were built, maintenance and repair buildings were constructed, laboratories set up and storage tanks erected for both crude and refined oils. Output of the many products involved the use of many different processes, although the principal products were petrol and turbo-jet fuels, diesel oils and marine and industrial fuel oils.

The "T" shaped marine terminal is 4,300 feet in length and extends 3,500 feet from the North shore of the Haven. There are five berths, Nos 1–4 seaward and No. 5 on the inside, East of the approach road. Accommodation for tankers is:

Berth No. 1 to 190,000 tdw
Berth No. 2 to 300,000 tdw
Berth No. 3 to 36,000 tdw
Berth No. 4 to 20,000 tdw
Berth No. 5 to   5,000 tdw

The year 1963 was the first year in which both Esso refineries, Milford Haven and Fawley, worked at full capacity, almost all the crude oil imported for them coming from Libya and the Middle East. In 1964 the envisaged expansion at Milford Haven refinery was met, the annual crude oil capacity being increased from 4.5 million to 6.3 million tons. Just under half of the oil came from Libya, one fifth came from Kuwait and a similar amount from Iraq, the remainder from Saudi Arabia and Venezuela. In addition, the refinery at Whitegate, County Cork, Eire, in which Esso held a 40% interest, processed nearly two million tons.

At the end of the 1960s it was considered that the oil demand in Britain would continue to grow and that further oil refining and petrochemical capacity would be needed through the 1970s and into the 1980s. But within a year or so all this had changed. The optimism of the 1960s soon disappeared after the Middle East oil crisis of 1973 when a substantial increase in the price of oil led to an economic slowdown. Worse was to come in 1979 and 1980 with further steep oil price increases followed by a worldwide economic recession. In 1981 total demand for oil in the United Kingdom was down to some 72 million tons, 9% lower than in 1980 which was, itself, 15% lower .an in 1979. Much of this decline in the demand for heavy fuel oil was due to .. comprehensive switch to gas or coal for heating and for the generating of electricity, and there were also big changes in the pattern of the oil products required. During 1981 Esso invested vast sums in its two refineries to adapt to this change in demand for lighter products and for products requiring more processing at the refineries. But it also caused large surpluses of shipping, refining and distribution facilities in the heavier products range. In 1982 the British oil demand was about the same as in 1981. But this was some 60% of the 1973 figure and the need was evident to trim excess refinery capacity. At Fawley the capacity was reduced by over 20%, but at Milford Haven the refinery was brought to a standstill in April, 1983, as overall trade for the year through Milford Haven, once Britain's busiest oil port, dropped four and a half million tons below the 1982 figure.

In July, 1984, it was announced that the refinery portion of the plant at the site had been sold to Arab interests, the Ajman-Saudi Refining Company, based in the United Arab Emirates. Within a few months negotiations failed, and a new scheme was agreed with the single-named Ajman Refining Company Ltd. (Arcol) in August, 1985. Under this arrangement the refinery was to be dismantled and some 40,000 tons of equipment cleared from the site and shipped to Ajman. Dismantling of the plant was to be done to enable carefully-marked pieces to be packed into forty-foot containers for shipment from Pembroke Dock. The larger and more ungainly items were to be loaded to heavy-lift vessels from a specially-built jetty at Milford Haven.

At Ajman the plant was to be re-assembled, with the reconstructed refinery planned to begin operating during 1988, handling 100,000 barrels of oil each day. The crude oil for processing will be supplied by neighbouring countries, Ajman being one of two members of the United Arab Emirates without a commercial oil or gas discovery. The trend toward increased oil refining by Middle East oil exporters followed the lead set by Saudi Arabia, where some half-million barrels per day of refining capacity was scheduled to come "on stream" in 1985.

The Milford Haven site, however, remains as an Esso distribution centre with its marine terminal and its share of the Mainline Pipeline system continuing to be used as part of the marketing operation.

Tugs berthing the *Esso Demetia* at the Milford Haven refinery on 22nd July, 1973, at the end of her maiden voyage. *Esso*

The "Esso Fawley"-class

When built, these ships of just over 18,000 deadweight tons were the largest in Esso's coastal fleet, distributing refined products from the Fawley and Milford Haven refineries. They became frequent users of the Dingle tanker buoy berth in the River Mersey.

Five tank spaces were subdivided to give fifteen tanks, two of which were for segregated water ballast. Each cargo tank was given its own suction line connecting to four manifolds in the cargo pump room, so that four different grades of cargo oil could be discharged simultaneously. If necessary, two pumps could discharge from a single tank.

Two oil engines were geared to a single controllable pitch propeller. Controls for this and for a bow thrust unit were through a console in the bridge housing. Speed was 16.25 knots. Measurements: Length 553 feet 7 inches (oa)/508 feet (bp), breadth 72 feet. Built by A/B Lindholmens Varv, Gothenburg:

	Completed	Gross tons
Esso Fawley	9.1967	11,064
Esso Milford Haven	1.1968	10,902

A third sistership, *Esso Slagen*, completed by Lindholmens in October, 1968, was for Esso Norske, Oslo. She was slightly different in that she was equipped for part carriage of bitumen.

The Dingle Tanker Buoy berth was completed in August, 1967. It consists of four mooring buoys where a tanker can moor from bow and stern near a moored "Hose barge" with six hoses which connect to the discharging tanker. The hoses reach to the river bed where they join with steel pipes to shore tankage at Dingle Bank. Dingle Tanker Buoy is about half a mile offshore of Dingle Bank tank storage complex and adjacent to Herculaneum Branch Dock, where importation of oil began in 1892.

Coastal ships of the 1960s

	Completed	Gross tons	
Esso Tynemouth	2.1960	525	Built by J. Bolson & Sons Ltd., Poole. Measurements: 171 feet (loa) × 28 feet breadth. 688 tdw. Engines: Oil. 9½ knots. *1978: *Celtic Lee* (Celtic Coasters Ltd.). 3.12.1979: Steering gear failed, struck quay, holed, capsized and sank while berthing at Cork (voyage: Whitegate/Cork-diesel fuel). 14.1.1980: Refloated, sold and repaired. 1982: *Maldea* (Marine & Industrial Energy Cleaners Ltd.). 1984: *Drysdale* (Irish Waste Ltd., Belfast).

One of two sisterships for British coastal work, the *Esso Fawley* was built in 1967.   *Skyfotos*

Esso Ipswich	11.1960	1,103	Built by J. L. Thompson & Sons Ltd., Sunderland. Measurements: 231 feet (loa) × 36 feet breadth. 1,576 tdw. Engines: Oil. 9½ knots. *1981: *Maldivo Valour* (Maldives Shipping Ltd.). 1984: *Fulidhoo* (Central Atolls Shipping (Pte) Ltd., Maldive Islands).
Esso Dover	3.1961	490	Built by J. Bolson & Son Ltd., Poole. Measurements: 176 feet (loa) × 27 feet breadth. 556 tdw. Engines: Oil. 10 knots. *1980: *Cherrybobs* (Cherry Marine Ltd.).

Towards the end of 1980 *Cherrybobs* was acquired by the St Helena Shipping Company for service at St Helena. She was renamed *Bosun Bird* and her new job was to load fuel at Ascension for St Helena. There she lay as a floating fuel store, her oil not only used for the island's domestic purposes, but for the motorship *St Helena*, the island's link with Europe. Until then oil had been imported in drums from South Africa for there is very little demand for it in the tiny mountainous island.

Esso Jersey	5.1961	313	Built by Scott & Sons Ltd., Bowling. Measurements: 123 feet (loa) × 24 feet breadth. Engines: Oil. 9 knots. *1972: (T. Holden). 1974: *Edwharf* (Edgells Wharf, Southampton); converted to an effluent carrier, renamed *John S. Darbyshire*. 1977: *Kielder* (Effluent Services Ltd.). 3.7.1984: Arrived Hull for scrapping.

The coastal tanker *Esso Caernarvon* passing Dungeness, with the Dungeness power station rising above the low coastline. *Skyfotos*

Esso Caernarvon 7.1962 1,103 Built by J. L. Thompson & Sons Ltd., Sunderland.
Measurements: 231 feet (loa) × 36 feet breadth.
1,570 tdw.
Engines: Oil.
*12.1985: *Caernarvon* (C. Crawley Ltd., Gravesend).

In 1985 Esso made Avonmouth its main distribution centre for South Wales and much of the south-west and on 5th August, 1985, the *Esso Caernarvon* made the last delivery to the Esso Wharf, in the Ely River adjacent to Penarth Dock in South Wales. The wharf, the last trading berth on the Ely River, was officially closed on 14th September, 1985.

Esso Purfleet 1.1967 2,838 Built by Furness Shipbuilding Co. Ltd., Haverton Hill-on-Tees.
Measurements: 323 feet 6 inches (loa) × 47 feet breadth.
4,430 tdw.
Engines: Oil.
*8.1983: *Prima Jemima* (Prima Tankers Ltd., Gibraltar).

Built for the carriage of lubricating oil and other refined products in a highly automated cargo system, with fuel lines connecting independently to tanks. Twelve grades of oil could be carried.

Between 1962 and 1964 a number of 60-foot steel pontoons were built at North Woolwich for work in yachting and boating centres around the British coast. They were really Esso floating service stations, with a capacity for

5,000 gallons of diesel oil, petrol and two-stroke mixture. For the convenience of yachtsmen they were also able to offer fresh water, marine stores and some consumable stores.

Esso Chale Bay
Esso Langstone Bay (renamed *Esso Poole Bay II*)
Esso Pegwell Bay
Esso Seaford Bay
Esso Thames (renamed *Esso Poole Bay*)
Esso Weymouth Bay
Esso Torbay

The "Esso Lincoln"-class

While the "City"-class ships were under construction, another four of bridge-aft design were ordered. These, however, were larger, with a deadweight carrying capacity of 52,000 tons on dimensions of 743 feet (loa), breadth 102 feet and a draught of 37 feet 5 inches. Two geared turbines, developing 19,000 shp, gave 17 knots. Each ship had 35 tanks. Two were ordered from the Tyne and the other pair came from Amsterdam.

The *Esso Dover*, seen here in the English Channel, was acquired in 1980 by the St Helena Shipping Company for service at St Helena, in the South Atlantic. *Skyfotos*

The *Esso Cardiff*, here seen in her earlier years, was fitted with special fenders for lightening VLCCs after the closure of the Suez Canal in 1967. *Skyfotos*

Built by Vickers-Armstrongs (Shipbuilders) Ltd., Newcastle

	Completed	Gross tons	
Esso Edinburgh	2.1963	30,981	28.10.1976: Arrived Kaohsiung for breaking up.
Esso Newcastle	12.1963	31,200	3.1977: Converted by Sasebo Heavy Industries Co., Sasebo, Japan, to a floating separation, gas-treating and storage facility for crude oil production. Deck house, funnel and engines removed and a new spar deck fitted above the main deck. Renamed *W. P. No. 1*. 1980: Renamed *Exxon Santa Ynez* and moored 3½ miles offshore at the Hondo Field, off Santa Barbara, California, attached to a single anchor leg mooring system 1½ miles from the production platform.

Built by Nederlandsche Dok en Scheepsbouw Maats., Amsterdam

Esso Lincoln	9.1962	31,720	20.2.1965: Struck Avocet Rock, 14.22N 42.43E on voyage Jabbal Dhanna to Milford Haven and sustained severe damage although refloated on 26.2.1965. 9.11.1976: Arrived Kaohsiung for breaking up.
Esso Cardiff	5.1963	31,720	10.10.1983: Arrived Ulsan, South Korea, for breaking up.

When the Suez Canal was closed in 1967 there came the introduction of the large crude-carrying tanker to work from the Persian Gulf around the Cape of Good Hope. These large ships outstripped the capacity of the discharging terminals of Europe and the oil companies saw it as necessary to fit out one or two tankers as lightening ships, taking oil from the larger tankers in various anchorages, particularly off the south coast of England at Lyme Bay. When a satisfactory draught was met the larger ship moved on to her discharge port. *Esso Cardiff* was fitted with special fenders for this work.

The aim of naval architects ever since the age of the steamship began has been to reduce water resistance to ships. Experiments proved that this could be done by a specially designed bow—a bulbous bow, in which the forward frames are swelled out at the forefoot into a bulb which reduces the dipping movement. It also sets up a new wave system which affects the normal bow wave and reduces the energy expended in making the primary bow wave.

In the summer of 1964 Esso sent a number of their tankers for the fitting of bulbous bows. The work was spread over the July–December period, with each ship taking about fifteen days. Six ships of the 48,000 tdw type were handled by Palmers Hebburn Works of Vickers-Armstrongs, beginning with *Esso Cardiff* on 10th July, while five of the 26,000 tdw type went to the Swan, Hunter yard at Wallsend, beginning with the *Esso Exeter* on which work was completed on 4th August.

Postwar Purfleet

When war ended in 1945, Anglo-American's repair, reconstruction and new building programme for its Purfleet terminal on the River Thames enabled it to grow steadily and so meet the challenge of expanding industry. Many changes were made in plant, in processing and in its facilities.

Then, in January, 1953, came disaster as the river overflowed its banks during a North Sea tidal surge. On two previous occasions, in 1897 and 1911, abnormally high tides had flooded the works, but the damage in 1953 to plant and machinery was by far the worst, partly because the developed area was very much larger than in earlier times, the river water flooding the complex to a depth of seven feet and putting much of it out of action. However, all was put right in due course and in successive years grease, additive and rust-ban plants were added and distillation units for producing solvents were erected.

Concurrent with these changes No. 1 and No. 2 jetties were completely rebuilt to accommodate the bigger tankers of the day. Situated between the jetties, close to the shoreline, were the massive wooden structures which, for years, had been the loading berths and moorings for the company's fleet of river tank barges. Another part of the complex was the bitumen terminal, once the property of Ebano, a German asphalt company which came into Anglo-American hands in 1930. Just upstream of this installation, nudging the frontage of the old-established Royal Hotel which had in one form or another been on the site since 1769, was Harrison's Wharf. Here barges were hauled out and repaired; later it became a tank-cleaning berth.

In the 1960s Purfleet grew in size and importance as the company policy of concentrating storage at fewer, but larger, terminals evolved. It played its part in handling some of the 2,000 tankers which used the Port of London annually and, in 1962, handled a large part of the coastwise imports of oil into London, which totalled around four million tons. Much of Esso's share was "base oil", shipped in from Fawley. From this, and apart from gasoline, kerosene, diesel and fuel oil stored in bulk, the Purfleet plant manufactured and blended up to 700 grades of lubricating oils and greases, the end-product then being shipped out by barge, coastal tanker and road vehicle. In quantity alone the comparative figures of actual products handled over the years are impressive; from fifty million gallons in 1919 to 450 million gallons in 1962 and 600 million gallons in 1966.

The Esso terminal at Purfleet seen from the air in the 1970s. *Esso*

Looking aft along the deck of the motor barge *Esso Abingdon* as she passes through the Pool of London on her way upstream during the winter of 1958.   *Esso*

A decade later, in the ever-changing pattern of distribution, a pipeline link connected Fawley with Purfleet. Trade was also in recession and a combination of these facts was enough seriously to affect the river and tank barge operations at Purfleet. Left with rapidly diminishing trade in this sector, the old barge loading berths were no longer required and were demolished.

In retrospect the handling of heating and lighting oils almost a century ago was a relatively simple matter. Once ashore it was transported by horse and cart, and sales were by the can-full. Today, operations at the Purfleet terminal have become complex and of infinite variety. Black oil for storage is now discharged at Powell Duffryn's adjacent oil jetty, which once belonged to Cory. From here it is loaded into small tankers and taken away for bunkering purposes. Light oils are brought ashore at No. 2 jetty, often from chartered foreign-flag coastal tankers. No. 1 jetty is used infrequently, its mooring buoys having been removed, although the occasional tanker may be seen here when a sudden shortage of a particular product requires a topping-up supply. Even for this Esso prefer their own tankers with fast discharge rates, the berth having a draught limit of twenty-six feet before vessels touch bottom at low tide. A fast discharge of deeper-laden tankers brings them to the limit and they can beat the tide. Otherwise, with the thirty-two foot draught river limit, the company is cautious in chartering large coastal tankers for the run unless it is sure of their actual discharge rate. Nevertheless, many products are still despatched from Purfleet terminal by coastwise tanker, and by a huge fleet of road vehicles.

Launching of the *Esso Yorkshire* at Malmo, Sweden, on 11th September, 1963.   *Esso*

The "County"-class

Included in the huge tanker-building programme of the 1950s–60s were orders for six vessels to reach an estimated 84,000 tdw. Three ships were ordered from the German builders A. G. Weser at Bremerhaven, two were from Kockums, Malmo, and the remaining one from the Verolme yard at Rozenburg. At first the ships were planned for a 73,000 tdw capacity and the carrying capacity was then increased to 85,000 tdw by giving more depth to the ships, while the last two of the group, *Esso London* and *Esso Yorkshire*, were widened, with a resulting capacity of 96,000 tdw.

The first ship completed was the *Esso Pembrokeshire*. At the time she was the largest merchant ship ever built on the continent of Europe, exceeding the displacement of the famous Norddeutscher Lloyd passenger liner *Bremen*, of 1929.

Esso Warwickshire before her conversion for work in the North Sea.   *Skyfotos*

The ships had dimensions of 861.5 feet length overall, a breadth of 112.7 feet and a draught of 48 feet 3 inches but, as stated above, the last two were widened to 125 feet 3 inches. In these there were twenty-six tanks as compared with thirty-five in the first four. Two steam turbines provided 26,500 shp and were geared to a single shaft to give 17 knots. The trial speed of the *Esso Lancashire* reached 18.19 knots. Facilities for the crew included a swimming-pool and an air-conditioned cabin for each crew member.

Another innovation was that a bulbous bow was designed into the hull shape of the *Esso London*—certainly the first time that a large bulb had been adapted for use on a British-flag tanker. The plans of the *Esso London* were amended twice for an increased carrying capacity and as Yard No. 1340R (revised) she took the water on 14th November, 1963.

	Completed	Gross tons	
Esso Pembrokeshire	11.1961	48,898	Built by A. G. Weser, Bremen. 24.10.1975: Arrived Kaohsiung for breaking up.
Esso Hampshire	5.1962	48,141	Built by Verolme Dok en Scheepsbouw Maats. N.V., Rozenburg. 15.9.1975: Arrived Kaohsiung for breaking up.
Esso Warwickshire	12.1962	48,049	Built by A. G. Weser, Bremen. 1983: (Esso Exploration & Production (UK) Ltd.). 1984: (Esso Petroleum Co. Ltd.)

This ship was chosen for conversion to enable her to take on crude oil from the Esso/Shell Brent oilfield offshore installations, east of the Shetlands, from a specially designed buoy facility known as the Brent Spar Buoy. The 56-day ship conversion work was done by Western Shiprepairers, Birkenhead, where she arrived on 23rd April, 1976, and the first oil from the North Sea Brent oilfield was discharged from the *Esso Warwickshire* at Fawley on 18th December, 1976.

Esso Lancashire	1962	49,397	Built by Kockums Mekaniska Verkstads AB, Malmo. *1975: *Petrola XXVIII* (J. S. Latsis, Greece). 1976: *Petrola 28*. 22.5.1975–14.1.1977: Laid up Piraeus. 25.1.1977: Arrived Barcelona, in tow, for breaking up.

(Improved "County"-class)

Esso Yorkshire	1963	52,544	Built by Kockums Mekaniska Verkstads AB, Malmo. 20.11.1975: Arrived Kaohsiung for breaking up.
Esso London	2.1964	53,342	Built by A. G. Weser, Bremen. *1975: *Petrola XXVII* (J. S. Latsis, Greece). 1976: *Petrola 27* 1.6.1982: Arrived Split for breaking up.

These tankers were to have fairly short lives, for in 1975 the Nissho-Iwai Company Ltd., of London, purchased three of the ships, for demolition in Taiwan. The vessels involved, *Esso Pembrokeshire*, fourteen years old, *Esso Hampshire*, thirteen years old, and *Esso Yorkshire*, only twelve years of age, were comparatively young in shipbreaking terms. Two more, *Esso Lancashire* and *Esso London*, were also sold in 1975 to John S. Latsis and raised the Greek flag, leaving only the *Esso Warwickshire*, which continued moving crude oil from the Brent Terminal to Fawley.

The *Esso London* beats her way through a Force 10 gale in the Bay of Biscay in March, 1965.   *Esso*

CHAPTER ELEVEN

The Giants

ESSO'S huge construction programme of the 1950s and 1960s ended with the *Esso London* in 1964, but tankers much bigger than this ship were already under construction and in August, 1965, orders for many huge tankers began to be placed.

The first of the British-flag giants, *Esso Mercia*, was launched on 18th August, 1967, at the A. G. Weser yard, Bremerhaven, and began a class name of old British kingdoms. When completed in 1967 she was the largest tanker ever built in the yard.

At that time, two tankers of 193,000 tdw were building at the Chantiers de l'Atlantique yard at St Nazaire, the British-flag *Esso Anglia* and *Esso Paris* of Esso Standard S.A. Française. Two more, the British-registered *Esso Bernicia* and *Esso Norway* (Esso Transport Company Inc., Panama) were under construction by Howaldtswerke-Deutsche Werft, Kiel. Added to these ships were thirteen tankers of about 250,000 tdw each on order for Esso at various European yards.

	Completed	Gross tons	
Esso Mercia	1967	87,002	Built by A. G. Weser, Bremerhaven. Measurements: 1,010 feet (loa including bulbous bow) × 146 feet breadth. Speed 16½ knots. 169,496 tdw.

The first ship to be equipped with a German-built steam turbine where a propeller speed of 80 rpm with 30,000 shp was obtained using special dual-torque path reduction gearing. A single main boiler was fitted but an auxiliary boiler for ancillary work was capable of getting the ship to port in an emergency. There were thirteen cargo tanks. Equipment included two bicycles for crew proceeding fore and aft.

Early in 1977 she was sold to become a non-powered storage barge for positioning at Tapis, Malaysia.

11.2.1978: Following conversion left Sakaide in tow for
Malaysia.
8.3.1978: Suffered an explosion 05.31N 105.01E.
7.1978: Arrived Tapis Terminal, Malaysia.
1983: (Petronas Petroleum Nasional Berhad) (Esso
Production Malaysia Inc.).
Sold for breaking up and:
25.9.1984: arrived Singapore en route for Taiwan.

181

Esso Anglia	9.1969	97,082	Built by Chantiers de l'Atlantique, St Nazaire. Measurements: 1,056 feet (loa including bulbous bow) × 157 feet breadth. 193,361 tdw.

The *Esso Anglia* was launched on 15th May, 1968. On 4th July, 1969, she was on trials but boiler trouble caused her to put back to port. The vessel was eventually handed over on 9th September, 1969. On 14th December, 1978, *Esso Anglia* arrived at Kaohsiung for breaking up.

A sistership to the *Esso Anglia* was *Esso Paris*, launched on 28th January, 1969, by the same builder for Esso Standard S.A. Française. She, too, was broken up at Kaohsiung, arriving there on 14th December, 1978.

Esso Bernicia	1968	96,903	Built by Howaldtswerke-Deutsche Werft, Kiel. Measurements: 1,062 feet (loa including bulbous bow) × 155 feet breadth. 193,658 tdw. 31.3.1979: Arrived Kaohsiung for breaking up.
Esso Scotia	7.1969	127,158	Built by A. G. Weser, Bremerhaven. Measurements: 1,141 feet 9 inches (loa including bulbous bow) × 170 feet breadth. 253,962 tdw.

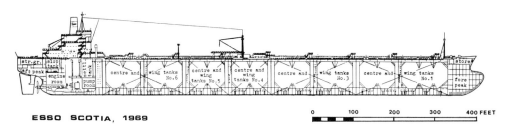

ESSO SCOTIA, 1969

At the time of launching on 31st March, 1969, the *Esso Scotia* was the largest vessel in the world to be launched from a slipway, as opposed to being floated out from a drydock. The hull was all-welded and there were eleven cargo tanks, these being handled by four turbine-driven centrifugal pumps, each having a capacity of 3,000 tons per hour (sea water) and two steam reciprocating stripping pumps, each of 300 tons per hour capacity. The upper deck was continuous to the bow where a short foremast which accommodated the foghorn and lighting was placed. The draught was 65 feet 5 inches.

Propulsion was by steam turbine, driving a propeller through reduction gearing at 80 rpm and giving 16 knots.

Officers and crew were accommodated aft, each in a single cabin. All cabins were air-conditioned as were the messrooms and other amenities. A swimming-pool was on the boat deck. At her launching the total steel weight to be moved was 36,600 tons.

From trials off the north-east coast of Spain the *Esso Scotia* sailed for Ras Tanura.

The *Esso Scotia* was broken up at Kaohsiung where she arrived on 6th June, 1981.

Esso Cambria	12.1969	127,158	Built by Verolme Dok en Sheepsbouw N.V., Rozenburg. Measurements: 1,141 feet (loa including bulbous bow) × 170 feet 2 inches breadth. 253,962 tdw.

The *Esso Cambria* was the first of the 250,000-ton tankers to berth at Fawley, on 7th February, 1970. She came from Ras Tanura, although part of her cargo of light crude oil was discharged at Milford Haven.

The launching of the *Esso Cambria* in Holland on 10th May, 1969.

The *Esso Northumbria* in the turbulent English Channel. *Skyfotos*

On 30th August, 1970, she stranded for a time off Jazirat Island, Persian Gulf, 26.15N 55.15E, but refloated, unaided, on 2nd September with some bottom damage.

The *Esso Cambria* arrived at Masan, South Korea, on 1st October, 1981, for breaking up.

Esso Northumbria	5.1970	126,543	Built by Swan, Hunter Shipbuilders Ltd., Wallsend.

Measurements: 1,143 feet 3 inches (loa including bulbous bow) × 170 feet 3 inches breadth. 254,277 tdw.

Named by Princess Anne on 2nd May, 1969, the *Esso Northumbria* presented a problem by her sheer bulk, for a considerable portion of the opposite riverbank had to be cut away. All-welded in construction, she was given a raked stem, pronounced bulbous bow and modified cruiser stern of the "clearwater" type. The sternframe was of cutaway "ham" type and the rudder of semi-balanced design. An overall discharge rate of 10,000 tons per hour could be made by means of four turbine-driven centrifugal main cargo pumps. Propulsion was by geared turbines to a single screw to give 16 knots.

She left on trials on 8th February, 1970, with some 200 people, including research specialists, on board with a drydocking at Lisbon. However, due to turbine trouble, she was not handed over until 14th May, then sailing on to the Persian Gulf. On the return leg of her maiden voyage from Kuwait, she became the third 250,000 tdw tanker to use the Esso refinery at Fawley, where she arrived at the modified and strengthened berth on 23rd July. On 7th May, 1982, she arrived at Kaohsiung for breaking up.

Esso Hibernia	12.1970	126,539	Built by Swan, Hunter Shipbuilders Ltd., Wallsend. Measurements: 1,122 feet (loa including bulbous bow) × 173 feet 10 inches breadth. 254,277 tdw. 4.12.1970: Left Tyne for Lisbon on maiden voyage. 24.10.1982: Anchored off Langkawi Island and on 5.1.1983 moved to the Johore River for lay-up. 25.4.1983: Arrived Kaohsiung for breaking up.
Esso Ulidia	10.1970	126,538	Built by Harland & Wolff Ltd., Belfast. Measurements: 1,143 feet 3 inches (loa including bulbous bow) × 170 feet 3 inches breadth. 254,011 tdw. 11.5.1970: Floated at Belfast. 1.1983–3.1983: Laid up in Johore River. 20.4.1983: Arrived Kaohsiung for breaking up.
Esso Caledonia	9.1971	126,535	Built by Harland & Wolff Ltd., Belfast. Measurements: 1,143 feet 3 inches (loa including bulbous bow) × 170 feet 3 inches breadth. 250,011 tdw.

Floated on 2nd June, 1971, the *Esso Caledonia* was completed three months later. When she arrived at Southampton on 18th September, 1971, she was, to that date, the largest ship ever to berth in Southampton Docks, where she occupied three berths—Nos 34, 35 and 36 on the Itchen Quays. Six tugs assisted her to berth. The ship arrived direct from her builders for adjustments after running trials and berthed on a draught of twenty-nine feet. The depth of the *Esso Caledonia* from keel to main deck was 84 feet and her superstructure rose another 116 feet. Steel weight was some 34,800 tons and there were 26½ miles of piping and 66 miles of electric cable in her construction.

Laid up in Johore River in April, 1982, she arrived at Masan, Korea, on 19th July, 1982 for breaking up.

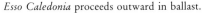

Esso Caledonia proceeds outward in ballast.

Esso Demetia	5.1973	125,293	Built by Kockums Mekaniska Verkstads AB., Malmo. Measurements: 1,117 feet 2 inches length × 170 feet 2 inches breadth. 258,979 tdw.
Esso Dalriada	7.1973	125,331	Built by Kockums Mekaniska Verkstads AB., Malmo. Measurements: 1,117 feet 2 inches length × 170 feet 2 inches breadth. 259,042 tdw. *2.1984: *Seal Island* (Seal Island Shipping Corp., Liberia).

The 1960s and 1970s were the years of the building of the world's largest oil carrying fleet, with huge tankers, ever growing in size, to carry 200,000, 300,000 and then over 500,000 tons of crude oil.

Tankers were well over the 100,000 deadweight tons mark in the early 1960s. Many were constructed in Japanese yards and incorporated endless new features. Tower bridge structures seven decks high were introduced, which contained all the accommodation and gave a wide field of vision. Moreover, as each tower was constructed as a separate component it was devoid of noise, vibration and heat. It was merely lifted to fit on the hull.

In 1957 the capacity of a tanker had not quite reached the 100,000 deadweight tons mark. The largest tanker in the world was the *Universe Leader* of D. K. Ludwig's Universe Tankships Inc., 51,400 gross tons and a deadweight capacity of 85,500 tons. But even as this ship was delivered, other

The VLCC *Esso Demetia* berthed at the Fawley marine terminal. Such supertankers were designed to bring crude oil on the long haul around the Cape of Good Hope.   *Esso*

yards were completing larger ships. Five years later, in 1962, the *Nissho Maru*, 74,868 gross tons, was placed in service for the Idemitsu Tanker Company of Tokyo; in 1966 the *Tokyo Maru* of Tokyo Tanker Company reached 94,360 gross tons to carry 159,800 tons of crude oil from Ras Tanura to Yokohama. But her record was shortlived, for the *Idemitsu Maru* of the same company was launched on 6th September, 1966, and, measured at 107,133 gross tons, could carry 209,143 deadweight tons. She left Yokohama for Mena Ahmadi on 13th December, 1966, on her maiden voyage.

In the United Kingdom towards the end of the 1960s the main oil companies had also reached the 200,000 tons load-capacity tankship. Shell had sixteen "M"-class 206,000 deadweight-ton ships, twelve under the Red Ensign and two each on German and Netherlands Antilles registry. British Petroleum's tanker fleet included twelve built in the early 1970s, most placed under their BP Medway Tanker Company and BP Thames Tanker Company, while the Esso Petroleum Company had eight under the British flag.

Four of these Esso VLCCs were built in Britain, the contract from Esso secured by a joint tender from Harland and Wolff Ltd., Belfast, and Swan, Hunter Group at Wallsend. They were designed to carry 250,000 tons of crude oil.

In order to complete their contracted buildings at Belfast, Harland and Wolff had to construct a new building dock and assembly shop which would enable ships of one million tdw to be built. On 25th January, 1968, Harland and Wolff announced that the contract for construction of the dock had been awarded to George Wimpey and Company Ltd. Completion was scheduled for 30th November, 1969, although the dock would be sufficiently advanced earlier than that to allow work to begin on the first of the tankers, the building of the ship and dock to run concurrently. The first dock operation came on 1st May, 1969, when a weldment for the first tanker was placed.

When finished, the dock was the largest in the world, with an acreage of twelve and three-quarters and a considered capability of accommodating all the Cunard "Queens" at the same time. It was situated at the head of Musgrove Channel where a cofferdam of 60,000 tons of rockfill was built to enclose a fitting-out berth. Then water and mud were pumped out; a base of rock fill was spread; and 250,000 tons of concrete worked in, together with 6,000 piles. A dock gate of 1,400 tons replaced the cofferdam. The completed dock was measured at 1,800 feet in length, 300 feet in width and 40 feet in depth. To work the dock a crane was installed, 300 feet high and 450 feet wide, straddling the dock. On three hooks a lift of 840 tons was possible, with the crane providing its own 1,485 hp diesels driving generators. The first Belfast-built ship, *Esso Ulidia*, was floated on 11th May, 1970; the second, *Esso Caledonia*, on 2nd June, 1971, and during their building the massive bow section, 52 feet high, 67 feet long and 135 feet wide, was placed and reckoned to be the largest single lift ever made in the United Kingdom. It weighed 730 tons.

The largest British Esso ships, *Esso Demetia* and *Esso Dalriada*, were delivered in 1973. Both were from Kockums yard, Malmo, and were close on 260,000 tdw carrying capacity.

These were the Very Large Crude Carriers—the Supertankers—built to help fulfil the world's requirements of oil and constructed for the long haul around the Cape of Good Hope.

Half a Million Tons

Tankers are broadly classified to four types. Those between 6,000 and 45,000 tdw are referred to as handy-sized tankers, and medium-sized ships are those with a carrying capacity between 45,000 and 160,000 tdw. Above 160,000 tdw and up to 320,000 tdw are the Very Large Crude Carriers

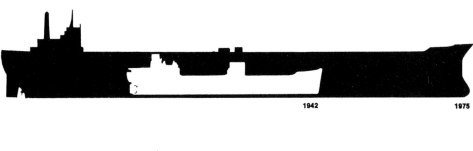

1942   1975

1942

1975

Tanker growth in the 30 years following World War II

(VLCCs) and above that are the Ultra Large Crude Carriers (ULCCs). The two giant types carry nothing but crude oil, "Handies" are mostly used for the products, while the medium-sized ships carry crude and oil fuel. There are other types of special design for the carriage of liquefied natural gas (LNG) or liquefied petroleum gas (LPG), and there is also the chemical carrier.

In the VLCC range *Esso Demetia* and *Esso Dalriada* were the largest tankers of the British Esso fleet, but there were far bigger carriers under other Esso flags. Two came into the ULCC category, *Esso Atlantic* and *Esso*

Pacific; when built, they were the third and fourth largest ships in the world. Both came from Hitachi Zosen's Ariake yard and were launched on 10th February, 1977, and 13th June, 1977, respectively. They worked from Juaymah Terminal, Saudi Arabia, to Aruba and sometimes to European ports and from San Nicolas Bay to the United States. Measurements of the ships were 1,334 feet length oa—almost the height of the Empire State Building in New York—and breadth 233 feet. Two steam turbines, double reduction geared and developing 45,500 shp, gave 15½ knots and the propeller was as high as a three storey building. The crude oil capacity of 516,893 tons could, if necessary, have met Japan's oil needs for half a day. But they did not have the largest carrying capacity; nor were they the first ships of over 500,000 tdw carrying capacity.

From orders dating back to September, 1972, construction of the world's first half-million ton oil carrier was begun in January, 1975, at Chantiers de l'Atlantique, St Nazaire. Flotation took place from her building dock in May, 1976, and on 25th June the ship was at France's oil terminal, Antifer, near Havre, to officially receive her name, *Batillus*. Her sistership, *Bellamya*, followed from the same yard. Both tankers measured 1,359 feet in length and 206 feet 8 inches breadth. The gross tonnage was 275,267 and the capacity 550,001 and 553,662 deadweight tons respectively. Four steam turbines to twin screws developed 64,800 shaft horsepower to give sixteen knots. The two ships were for Société Maritime Shell, Paris.

Yet these giant ships were to be eclipsed in carrying capacity by two ultra-large crude carriers for the Compagnie Nationale de Navigation, also of Paris. Twin-screw ships of similar dimensions to the other French pair, they had a carrying capacity of just over 555,000 deadweight tons. The *Pierre Guillaumat* was delivered in 1977, the *Prairial* in 1979.

As France turned towards nuclear power, the tanker section of the French merchant fleet began to decline. There was also a change from Middle East supplies to North Sea oil which affected the need for the large crude carrier. All four French-flag ULCCs were laid up in 1983–84. The huge *Prairial* was laid up at Brest on 19th January, 1983, then continued her lay-up at Vestnes, Norway, on 5th April. In June, 1985, she was sold out of the French register to the Nado Marine Company of Greece and renamed *Sea Brilliance*, but remained laid up. Early in 1986 she changed owners within Greece, was renamed *Hellas Fos* and later resumed trading.

The two Shell ships were also laid up at Vestnes, *Batillus* on 22nd August, 1983, and *Bellamya* on 26th January, 1984. The fourth, *Pierre Guillaumat*, arrived at Fujairah Anchorage on 5th February, 1983, and remained there until 13th September, 1983, when she was sold to Hyundai Corporation of South Korea. For her voyage to these Ulsan breakers she was renamed *Ulsan Master*. She was just six years old. The same South Korean company acquired the *Bellamya* for scrapping in October, 1985, and at the same date her sistership *Batillus* was sold to Taiwan shipbreakers.

One more ship in the 500,000 tdw class was the *Seawise Giant*, of Universal Petroleum Carriers Inc., of Hong Kong, but registered in Liberia. This vessel was launched as *Oppama*, for Greek owners, at Sumitomo Heavy Industries Ltd., Oppama Shipyard, Yokosuka, in 1975, but was never delivered. She then measured 189,200 gross tons on a length of 1,237 feet and breadth of 226 feet. Deadweight capacity was 418,610 tons. Sold in 1979, her leap in Ultra Large Crude Carrier status came in June, 1980, when she went to Nippon Kokan KK, Tsu, where a new centrebody was fitted and the ship

The lightening tanker *Esso Cardiff* is dwarfed by the 284,600 deadweight ton Danish tanker *Rosa Maersk*, from which she is taking part cargo for discharge at Whitegate on 2nd June, 1973.   *Esso*

completed. Her hull then measured 1,504 feet and her tonnages were increased to 238,558 gross and 564,739 tdw. She was, indeed, the largest ULCC and the largest ship ever. Since 16th May, 1983, she has been in the Caribbean, at Cayo Arcas Terminal, Mexico, in use as a storage vessel.

One problem to be overcome with the advent of the huge crude carriers was that when loaded they were too deep to enter some ports and waterways. This was solved by working some tankers as lightening ships which would transship crude oil from an anchored VL or ULCC alongside, protective fenders being carried by the lightening vessel and lowered between the two ships when working. At varying times the *Esso York*, *Esso Cardiff* and *Esso Forth* were used in this work. Loads of 50,000 to 90,000 tons were transferred, allowing the larger ship to move on to oil ports such as Fawley, Antifer and Europoort.

Very Large and Ultra Large (U) Crude Carriers of the Exxon Group, excluding those under the British Flag

Built for Esso Soc. Anon. Française (French flag)

	Built	Gross tons	tdw	
Esso Bretagne	1971	127,777	259,210	13.5.1982: Arrived Kaohsiung for scrapping.
Esso Provence	1971	127,777	259,210	17.3.1984: Arrived Inchon, Korea, for scrapping.
Esso Gascogne	1972	126,188	256,740	25.2.1985: Arrived Masan, South Korea, for scrapping.
Esso Languedoc	1973	126,186	256,999	June, 1986: Still in service.
Esso Normandie	1974	137,578	273,999	June, 1986: Still in service.
Esso Picardie	1976	137,578	279,467	June, 1986: Still in service.
Esso Flandre	1972	127,502	253,557	Ex *Esso Rotterdam* 1977. 28.5.1982: Arrived Masan, South Korea, for scrapping.

Built for Esso Tankschiff Reederei GmbH (German flag)

Esso Europa	1969	126,321	257,995	7.12.1982: Arrived Kaohsiung for scrapping.
Esso Bonn	1974	126,192	256,962	Launched as *Esso Bilbao*. 1985: *Esso Bahamas*. June, 1986: Still in service.
Esso Hamburg	1974	126,192	256,702	29.3.1985: Laid up Aalesund. 1986: *Esso Bermuda*; re-entered service 14.9.1986.
Esso Deutschland (U)	1976	203,869	421,681	16.3.1983: Laid up Aalesund. *7.1985: *Grand* (Loews Hotel and Leisure Group, New York).

Built for Esso Tankvaart Nederlandse Antillen NV (Netherlands Antilles flag)

Esso Europoort	1970	127,176	253,962	27.9.1982: Arrived Kaohsiung for scrapping.
Esso Nederland	1970	127,176	253,962	8.1982: Arrived Kaohsiung for scrapping.
Esso Bonaire	1973	127,502	255,027	10.7.1983: Arrived Kaohsiung for scrapping.
Esso Saba	1974	126,943	260,831	10.10.1983: Laid up Brunei Bay.

Esso Oceanic Inc. (Liberian flag).

Al Duriyah	1975	150,622	307,233	Ex *Esso Geneva* 1976. 1983: *Esso Al Duriyah*. 1984: *Esso Geneva*. 3.6.1985: Laid up Brunei Bay.

Built for Esso Tankers Inc. (Liberian flag)

Esso Copenhagen	1970	112,763	253,300	25.6.1982: Arrived Busan for scrapping.
Esso Skandia	1970	112,763	254,011	2.7.1983: Arrived Kaohsiung for scrapping.
Esso Wilhelmshaven	1970	113,752	253,873	17.7.1982: Arrived Kaohsiung for scrapping.
Esso Rotterdam	1972	127,502	253,557	1977: *Esso Flandre* (qv).
Esso Kagoshima	1973	114,797	261,158	3.4.1986: Arrived Kaohsiung for scrapping.
Esso Okinawa	1973	114,797	260,910	4.4.1986: Arrived Kaohsiung for scrapping.
Esso Osaka	1973	146,312	283,154	18.11.1985: Arrived Kaohsiung for scrapping.
Esso Singapore	1973	114,633	256,715	6.1984: Arrived Ulsan, South Korea, for scrapping.
Esso Honolulu	1974	146,309	283,397	2.10.1984: Anchored off Phuket, Thailand.
Esso Indonesia	1974	114,797	261,230	1.4.1986: Arrived Kaohsiung for scrapping.
Esso Kawasaki	1974	150,622	307,431	June 1986: Still in service.
Esso Africa	1975	137,166	274,467	June 1986: Still in service.
Esso Bilbao	1975	146,309	283,271	*1986: *Freedomship L* (Ceres Hellenic Shipping Enterprises (Piraeus, Greece)). 11.10.1986: Struck by Exocet missile 50 miles south of Kharg Island, Persian Gulf (Voyage: Kharg Island/Europe— crude oil), during Iraq–Iran dispute. Vessel immobilised; towed to Larak Island by Dutch tugs *Smit Rangoon* and *Smit Matsas 3*.
Esso Geneva	1975	150,622	307,233	1976: *Al Duriyah* (qv).
Esso Hawaii	1975	146,309	283,274	27.1.1984: Laid up Brunei Bay.
Esso Italia	1972	117,260	253,714	10.7.1983: Scrapped Kaohsiung.
Esso Japan (U)	1976	192,673	406,640	4.11.1982: Laid up Aalesund. *6.1986: Reported sold to Yemen Exploration & Produce Co., for storage purposes.
Esso Madrid (U)	1976	188,634	388,119	18.6.1983: Laid up Vestnes. *7.1985: *Capitol* (Loews Hotel & Leisure Group, New York).
Esso Tokyo (U)	1976	192,673	406,258	*1985: *Red Seagull* (Palgrave Ltd., Gibraltar). 11.9.1985: Arrived Aquaba for service as a storage vessel.
Esso Atlantic (U)	1977	259,532	516,893	4.5.1983: Laid up Aalesund.
Esso Caribbean (U)	1976	208,060	395,156	Ex *Andros Petros* 1977. 15.4.1983: Laid up Aalesund.
Esso Mediterranean (U)	1976	202,798	395,367	Ex *Homeric* 1977. 10.7.1983: Laid up Vestnes.
Esso Pacific (U)	1977	234,626	516,423	29.5.1983: Laid up Vestnes.
Esso Le Havre (U)	1977	173,086	387,936	8.3.1983: Laid up Brunei Bay. *6.1986: *Paramount* (Loews Hotel & Leisure Group, New York).

Why Exxon?

In late 1972 Standard Oil Company (New Jersey) changed its name to Exxon Corporation. One of the main reasons for the change was the long-standing confusion there had been between Standard Oil (New Jersey) and other competing companies in the United States which use the Standard Oil name, and the decision to change came after a Court ruling which made it clear that the Esso trademark could not be used nationwide.

Choosing a new name, registering it as a trademark and developing effective designs for its use entailed considerable research. Three stipulations regarding the choice were that it should be a word which could identify both the company and its products; as it might be used in overseas operations it should have no actual meaning and no adverse connotations in English or other languages; and since a short name is more easily read, has more impact and is more memorable than a long one, it should consist of no more than four or five letters.

Computer analysis of some 10,000 suggested names and then the old-fashioned method of public opinion was used to narrow the choice to six words. These were then subjected to research on a worldwide basis, with special studies conducted in areas of special marketing significance which included forty cities of the United States. From this mass of opinion, the word Exxon came out as top choice, being easily written, readily remembered, and with the double "x" creating not only a memorable word but offering opportunity for a distinctive design. It was also easy to pronounce in most languages and meant nothing vulgar or objectionable in any.

However, the change of title was initially intended for use as a primary trademark in the United States only and so only affected the existing names on 26,000 petrol stations and countless road tankers of the domestic Humble

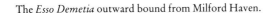

The *Esso Demetia* outward bound from Milford Haven.   *Esso*

Oil and Refining Company and the names of the ships of the Humble Transportation Company, Houston, Texas, which flew the flag of the United States and were registered at Wilmington, Delaware. The name of the Humble Transportation Company became Exxon Transportation Company, Houston, and from mid-1973 the ships were renamed with the prefix "Exxon" to their place-names.

The international affiliates were not involved in name changes as the name Esso offered no legal problems abroad. Nevertheless, the name Exxon was registered in virtually every country in the world where trademark registration is available in order to protect its possible future use worldwide.

In May, 1983, all ships of Exxon Transportation Company were transferred to Exxon Shipping Company, Houston.

Recession

The astounding growth of the world's tanker fleet capacity during the 1960s more than covered the 12% increase in actual ocean tanker carrying during that period. Even when the Arab embargo and the following explosion in the price of oil came in 1973, construction and fulfilment of some contracts continued so that when there eventually came a levelling out in oil demand, there was a surplus of some 100 million tons deadweight of

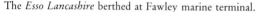

The *Esso Lancashire* berthed at Fawley marine terminal.

floating tankage. Indeed, if in the ensuing five to six years of the 1970s, construction had continued for an estimated 8% growth in oil production, the entire world tanker fleet would have been replaced, with a resultant over-tonnage. But this was not to be, for events in the Middle East beginning in 1967 were to completely alter the economy not only of Britain but of all the world's industrial nations. The effects flowed into international trading and the world moved into deep recession.

On 5th June, 1967, the Arab–Israeli six-day war broke out and within that time Israelis had occupied all Sinai to the banks of the Suez Canal, which was closed. It was to remain closed for another eight years. So began again the long-haul movement of oil from the Persian Gulf round Africa via the Cape of Good Hope.

The Suez Canal continued to remain a threatening troubled area, then in 1970 Egypt and Israel signed a peace plan which lasted until 6th October, 1973, when fighting began again, Egyptian attacks across the canal signalling the start of the Yom Kippur War, which lasted until the end of the month.

On 17th October the Organisation of Arab Petroleum Countries (OAPEC) began using their political bargaining weapon by increasing oil prices by 70% and cutting production 5% monthly until Israeli forces withdrew from occupied territory. Some countries were boycotted, some restricted; supplies to Britain—on which half her industry depended—were cut by 15%. And with this move came the realisation that higher prices of oil could be asked. With the reduction in supply added to the increased world demand at the time there began the possibility of an oil scarcity. Prices rocketed and in December an increase of 128% on oil prices was made by the oil exporters. The quadrupled price, in turn, reduced the call for imports; tankers began to be laid up; trading slumped and the recession began biting.

By the spring of 1975 tanker surplus was reckoned to be 35% of the world fleet, of which 10% was in lay-up and some 25% in slow steaming, awaiting cargoes or heading for the idling grounds of the Norwegian fjords. And when summer came the demand for tankers over the previous two years had fallen by 15%. Yet at this time, with hundreds of tankers inactive, new and virtually unwanted vessels were still being delivered from earlier contracts.

Between March and May, 1975, the Greek shipowner John S. Latsis acquired seven Esso tankers to augment his thirty-nine-ship fleet of "Petrola-(numbered)" vessels. The *Esso London* and *Esso Lancashire* were of British registry; *Esso Australia* and *Esso Colombia* were under the Panama flag; *Esso München* (German); *Esso Gothenburg* (Sweden) and *Esso Den Haag* (the Dutch flag, and in damaged condition). The ships were acquired at 20% above demolition value.

On 5th June, 1975, the Suez Canal was reopened to ships, but with a draught limitation. Yet although the voyage time for the Persian Gulf to Europe voyage could then be reduced by one third there was little interest, for an earlier arrival would mean finding an earlier charter in the over-tonnaged market. To the end of June twelve tankers sailed northbound through the Canal and nineteen sailed south. Indeed slow steaming of tankers was on the increase, ships running on one boiler at three-quarters speed and thus reducing tanker supply.

The first half of 1975 saw over twenty-three million deadweight tons of new tankers delivered, many of the ships to join the ranks of the huge unwanted fleet. Yet, in July, more new tankers totalling 450,000 tons were ordered, mostly from American yards. However, these orders were completely eclipsed by a rapid upsurge in confirmed cancellations and renegotiations of earlier contracts, which brought the total since August, 1974—a period of just eleven months—to more than forty-one million deadweight tons of cancelled orders. Among these July cancellations were three ULCCs from a Danish shipyard; the fact that each ship was intended to be of almost half a million tons capacity helps to put these massive tonnage figures into perspective. Among the re-negotiated contracts, vessels in the VLCC range, each of over 250,000 tons, were amended to non-tanker orders. Even so, at this time the world level of inactive tanker tonnage had increased to more than thirty-four million tons.

In the first nine months of 1975 no fewer than 203 tankers were sold for demolition, including the British-flag *Esso Yorkshire* (95,764 deadweight tons). Many more cancellations of orders took place in the September, including that of a 472,000-ton Norwegian vessel, the last of four ships of this size ordered from a German yard. In Japan cancellations included several in the 260,000–300,000 ton range and a block of five ships totalling 600,000 tons from one company alone. Three more VLCCs for American owners were cancelled from a Portuguese yard. The end of the month saw the total of inactive tonnage rise to nearly thirty-nine million tons. Thirty-six merchant ships were sent to the shipbreakers in October; twenty-three were tankers. Of the twenty-three, nine wore the British flag. In the following weeks more worldwide scrapping and withdrawals of ships to the inactive fleet brought the bleak year of 1975 to an end with some 500 tankers totalling almost forty-six million tons of carrying capacity laid up.

The year 1976 was no better. At the beginning several VLCCs were withdrawn and added to the laid-up lists, including four ships totalling one million deadweight tons of the Greek-owned Onassis fleet. However, the figure was tempered by the unfortunate loss of the new 275,000 deadweight tons *Olympic Bravery* which suffered engine failure and drifted aground on Ushant Island on 24th January while on her maiden voyage from Brest Roads to Farsund for lay-up—an indication of the tanker surplus. She later broke in two and was sold for scrap *in situ*. The *Olympic Bravery* had been launched at Chantiers de l'Atlantique, St Nazaire, only on 11th August, 1975.

By midsummer 1976, no fewer than 507 tankers totalling forty-seven and a half million deadweight tons were laid up. Twelve months later, partly due to scrapping sales, the number of tankers idle had reduced to 359, but in July, 1978, there was a deadweight tonnage of fifty-three million—436 tankers of over 25 million gross tons laid up.

Scrapping continued unabated. Fifty million tons had already gone to shipbreakers in the five years to mid-1979 and the newbuilding order book was virtually exhausted. Worldwide, oil consumption continued to fall. Many nations, particularly the highly industrialised countries, were using substitute forms of energy. Movement of oil by pipeline was ever increasing and there was conservation wherever possible. In some countries, as the possibility of an oil shortage disappeared, shore stocks were allowed to run down and in 1981 oil in some floating storage was transferred ashore, the empty ships then sailing to the Persian Gulf to join the armada of tankers waiting offshore for further cargoes. Too many ships were chasing too few cargoes and in early 1982 freight rates dropped below voyage costs. There was also war between Iran and Iraq and in May, 1982, insurances increased for tankers loading at Iran's oil terminals. All these factors combined to maintain the redundancy of tankers. Tanker owners pruned their fleets of unwanted tonnage, over sixty ships of VLCC-size going for demolition in 1982. Many more were put in lay-up and by the end of the year sixty-five million deadweight tons lay idle. And these laid-up figures did not include thirty or so semi-idle tankers which were lying in spot positions in the Persian Gulf, awaiting loading orders which failed to arrive.

The VLCCs scrapped early in 1982 included four Esso ships, the British-flag *Esso Northumbria*, two French-flag ships, *Esso Bretagne* and *Esso Flandre*, and the Liberian-registered *Esso Wilhelmshaven*. More summer sales were the Danish *Esso Copenhagen*, the British *Esso Caledonia, Esso Europoort* registered at Willemstad, and *Esso Nederland* registered at Aruba. The last Esso VLCC to be sold in 1982 was the *Esso Europa*, of German registry, which went to Taiwan in December. In addition to these large ships a number of smaller tankers were also sold out of the worldwide affiliated Esso fleets for further trading.

When the *Esso Northumbria* left the Tyne on 8th February, 1970, on her first voyage some 100,000 people watched her sail and the converging ten-mile traffic jams on the roads leading to the mouth of the river caused many more to miss the occasion. At the time she was the largest vessel ever to be built in Britain and was regarded as a precursor to a revival of the great shipbuilding era on Tyneside. The *Esso Northumbria* was just twelve years old when scrapped.

Following the nine giant tankers sold by the Exxon (Esso) group in 1982 for breaking up in the Far East, the British-flag ships *Esso Hibernia* and *Esso Ulidia*, both of just over 250,000 deadweight tons and only thirteen years old, were sold in early 1983 to the China Dismantled Vessels Trading Corporation, who acted as buyers for Taiwan shipbreakers. These sales brought to an end a twelve-month period during which eleven giant vessels left the company's fleet for demolition and only two were left under the British flag, the *Esso Dalriada* and *Esso Demetia*. During the seven years 1975–82 over six million deadweight tons of shipping had been scrapped by the Exxon group, plus another half-million in the first quarter of 1983. In fact, in the fifteen-month period to mid-1983, the number of VLCCs disposed of rose to fourteen.

There was still no sign of any coming demand for oil and the downward trend of transport of oil by sea continued. Some fifty VLCCs, owned by independent carriers, awaited cargoes in the Gulf. Then refineries began closing down. In Europe eighteen ceased production and in Britain British Petroleum closed its refineries on the Isle of Grain and at Belfast; Burmah Oil its Ellesmere Port function and Esso its refinery at Milford Haven. At this time over five million deadweight tons of Exxon (Esso) tanker tonnage was laid up and this included fourteen large crude carriers; six in Brunei Bay, the remainder in the Aalesund district of Norway. All fourteen were Liberian-flag ships, excepting *Esso Deutschland* (German) and *Esso Le Havre* (Panama flag), although some were later transferred to the flag of the Bahamas. The largest ships, *Esso Pacific* (516,423 tdw) and *Esso Atlantic* (516,893 tdw), were among those laid up. The world total of laid-up tankers rose to 515 ships of over 75 million deadweight tons.

There are about 250 sites around the world for the laying-up of ships, ranging from those with just enough water to drop anchor to places offering no size limitation, where ships can be placed in the hands of companies with skill and expertise to manage the services to a laid-up ship, and re-activation of the vessel when requested. Many sites are in Norway, where countless fjords offer shelter and deep water—Holmestrand, Bovagen, Fosenoy and Kaarstol in Haugesund District; Farsund, Onarheim and Askol in the Bergen area; and at Stavanger. Some lay-up sites offer shore connections of electricity and telephone; low humidity; ice-free conditions, watch-keeping and accessibility. Some sites can offer anchorages for ships only a few hundred feet from shore.

There are lay-up sites at many of the northern European ports, including Antwerp, Rotterdam, Emden and Lübeck, while in the United Kingdom lay-up grounds are available in the Fal, Clyde and Blackwater; at Liverpool, Southampton and London. Further afield, other sites available include Algeciras, Setubal and Lisbon, and in the Mediterranean at Toulon, Naples,

Venice, Genoa and La Spezia. There are many in the United States, while the largest of all is at Brunei Bay, in the Far East.

During 1983 tankers with a carrying capacity of twenty three million deadweight tons were broken up; yet in January, 1984, more than 350 tankers were still laid up—nearly sixty million deadweight tons. Of this figure nearly forty-eight million tons comprised 163 vessels of over 200,000 tons each. In addition to the total lay-up figure, seventy-three tankers were employed as floating storage and twenty-nine independently-owned large crude carriers waited for cargoes in the Persian Gulf, augmented by another twenty-one during the month which came to play the waiting game. In late summer 259 tankers with a carrying capacity of fifty-one million tons were laid up, one third under the flag of Liberia. There were also fifty in the Gulf.

One of the longest lay-ups recorded is that of the *Raila*, 109,500 gross tons, delivered to the Norwegian shipowner Hagb Waage of Oslo in 1971 from the Stord Verft A/S shipyard. For the first four years of the then buoyant oil market the VLCC carried cargoes of 222,375 deadweight tons from the Persian Gulf via the Cape of Good Hope to Europe. Then she was caught up in the collapsing market and on 15th February, 1975, arrived at Boken Fjord, in the Haugesund District of Norway, to lay up alongside her sistership *Ranja*, which had dropped anchor there fifteen days previously. The *Raila* was to remain for a decade, still and silent, and creating something of a record. In 1977 Sigval B. Sverdrup bought her, renamed her *Norbird* and placed her in K/S Nortank A/S, a company which had been formed to acquire the bulk of the assets of Hagb Waage. This new ownership lasted until June, 1982, when her new name became *Sinmar* of Finn Engelsen Holdings A/S, Bergen. The vessel then remained laid up until 9th May, 1985, when she left, in tow, bound for shipbreakers in Taiwan.

On 1st November, 1985, there were 310 tankers of just over forty-eight million tons carrying capacity laid up. This compared with 332 in the previous month and was the lowest figure since June, 1982.

Then in the spring of 1986 there came a dramatic fall in oil prices, and stock rebuilding by the major oil companies began. There also began a rising demand for petrol in the United States and the total world movement of oil in May alone was forty-seven million tons. This in turn caused a demand for tankers, with giant ships being reactivated, and in June the number in lay-up fell to a reported 155 vessels, totalling twenty-seven and a half million deadweight tons. Three months later the laid-up tanker tonnage around the world was reported to have declined to less than nineteen million tons, although the number of vessels idle was listed as 187. Included in this figure were forty-six ultra or very large crude carriers of just over fourteen million tons.

CHAPTER TWELVE

The 1980s

IN the 1980s distribution of Esso refinery products is made mainly by pipeline and by sea, each method contributing about 45% to the service with the remainder of the products moving by rail and road, including that from the Hythe marketing complex adjacent to Fawley.

In the national network 500 miles of pipeline and a fleet of coastal tankers distribute Esso products to eleven terminals, twenty-two bulk plants, seven major airport installations and more than eighty authorised distributor depots. Some sales are direct to industrial and commercial concerns, including the nationalised industries, government departments and public utilities but from storage plant to customer delivery is generally by road and rail, aided by a fleet of more than 1,500 rail tank wagons and over 700 road tankers. In this way products reach the motorist who uses the 4,000 service stations, one third of which are owned by Esso.

In 1981 petrol for the motorist accounted for 28% of home market sales; electricity generating stations took 18% of fuel oil sold, while industry took another 10%. Light oil for diesel engines, jet engines, tractors and central heating amounted to 37%, and chemical feedstocks, lubricants, liquid petroleum gases for the firing of furnaces and bitumen accounted for the remainder.

Distribution by sea involves a large quantity of products leaving Fawley in tankers and gas carriers. Esso owns and operates a large fleet of coastwise tankers, which is sometimes supplemented by modern foreign-flag vessels under charter or contract. In recent times, Esso has sold a number of uneconomic vessels due to substantially reduced oil demand, but at the same time, new ships have been added to the fleet. A new coastal tanker for the carriage of bitumen, *Esso Avon*, was added in 1981 and two larger vessels were acquired later from the parent company's foreign-flag fleet and became *Esso Tees* and *Esso Tyne*.

Under the ground

The pipeline system of distributing oil products was a late starter in Britain, although in the early 1950s there were one or two minor Esso pipelines in service carrying specialised products. These included a pipeline from Fawley which carried ethylene to a works on the bank of the River Severn and another which carried light products—petrol, paraffin, aviation and diesel fuels—to Esso's West London terminal. From there, through pipeline, naphtha was delivered to the North Thames Gas Board and aviation fuel to Heathrow airport. Additionally, liquid petroleum gases from Fawley were pumped into a Gas Board pipeline feeding installations at Southampton, Reading and Southall.

With the economic boom of the late 1950s and 1960s, there came a related demand for oil and its products and suddenly it became economic to lay more pipeline links in various parts of Britain. The need for the expansion of the system was met by parliamentary legislation in 1962 when the Pipelines Act was introduced, which laid down stringent conditions.

Work began and by the late 1960s and into the 1970s Esso had put several pipe-laying programmes in hand, including some to carry heavy fuel oil over long distances. Heavy fuel oil, with about as much capacity to flow as heavy glue, needed heat to become more fluid, but it was not feasible to heat the pipelines. Then in 1964, after various experiments, a prototype insulated pipeline was laid from Fawley to the electricity generating station eight miles away at Marchwood which proved successful and was soon supplying heavy fuel at the rate of 3.2 million litres day.

Esso followed this with the pipeline from Fawley to West London, completed in 1969. Over sixty miles in length, it was at the time the longest pipeline of its kind in the western world. The pipeline was insulated so that the five million litres of heavy oil carried per day could pass the entire length of the line without having to be reheated.

An even more ambitious project was completed in 1973 when the Mainline Pipeline System to supply the industrial markets of the Midlands and North-west came into operation. About 286 miles in length, it was a joint arrangement between Esso (75%), Texaco (20%) and Gulf Oil (5%), Amoco taking 10% from the Esso share three years later. Starting at Waterston, near Milford Haven, the single 400mm-diameter line finishes at Seisdon in the West Midlands, where the main control station is located. It then divides into two 300mm pipelines, one east through Birmingham and on to Nottingham; the other north to Manchester. By the 1980s Fawley refinery was further linked to West London with a heavy fuel line; a light products line was also laid to the Avonmouth terminal. A new major spur, from a junction of the West London line at Alton, Hants, led to Gatwick airport and then on to the Purfleet terminal on the north bank of the River Thames, in Essex, to serve the growing markets to the east of London. At the end of 1985 yet another link, between Fawley and Seisdon, was added to the system.

The greatest advantage of the Mainline Pipeline is that different products can be shipped through it without a barrier between them. In the early days of pipelines, products were separated by rubber spheres known as "pigs" but it was soon found that providing a steady rate of flow of about 4 mph was maintained very little mixing of different products occurred, enabling different products to be fed into the Mainline Pipeline without a barrier between them.

To identify the different products, which are often owned by different companies, the time is recorded when they enter the pipeline and also the pumping rate. These details form a basis for an estimate of arrival at the terminal but this, in itself, is not enough and greater accuracy is obtained from densitometers on the pipeline system. These detect changes in the density of the flowing material which are automatically relayed to the control room where, at a given moment, the two different products and the boundary between them, consisting of a mix of both and known as Interface, are routed to their separate storage tanks.

Before construction of the Mainline Pipeline System commenced consent had to be obtained, in principle and in compliance with the 1962

Esso's inland pipeline system, showing the Mainline Pipeline System from Milford Haven to Manchester and the various pipelines from Fawley. *Esso*

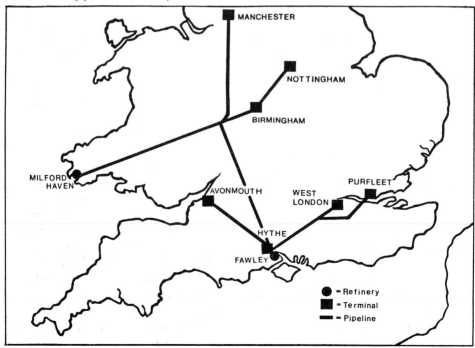

Pipelines Act, from the government's Department of Energy. The amount of planning was considerable. The route had to avoid built-up areas wherever possible and take account of areas of natural beauty and historic interest; agreements for compensation had to be made with more than a thousand landowners and, in addition, there were twenty-two rivers, seventeen canals, twenty-three railway tracks and ninety-three major roads to cross.

Flight

As the boom years of the 1960s followed on the heels of the application of the jet aero engine to commercial use, aircraft rapidly grew in size and the number of flights greatly increased. Almost overnight the skies filled with aeroplanes which could fly without propellers, for which aviation kerosene, Avtur, was developed.

Esso Avtur was produced both at the Fawley and Milford Haven refineries and distributed by road, rail and sea. But whatever the method of transport its prime and pure condition at the point of manufacture had to be maintained throughout the journey, with no effort spared to ensure that it arrived safely and without contamination.

Over the years Esso developed aircraft refuelling services at most of the airports throughout Britain, ranging from Benbecula in the north of Scotland to Jersey. By 1969 the company was already supplying 214 million gallons of aircraft fuel annually and in 1970 Esso fuel was in the tanks of the first "Jumbo" jet—Pan American's Boeing 747—to arrive in Britain.

Two major bases offering aircraft refuelling services are at London's Heathrow airport, the world's largest international airport, and at Gatwick, thirty miles to the south. Both are supplied by pipeline from Fawley, Heathrow's share being routed via Esso's West London terminal, situated at Stanwell, right by the airport boundary.

Nearly a dozen British suppliers are in the competitive business of refuelling aircraft, but the competition does not end there, for many of the airlines fly on international routes and their operators have an almost worldwide choice of the country in which they buy their fuel. Contracts are therefore logically placed to minimise costs and with consideration of reliability and efficiency of service.

At Heathrow, rapid refuelling was catered for by gigantic "bowsers" (tanker vehicles) which rolled out to the aircraft almost before it had stopped, but later a hydrant system was installed beneath the tarmac. Jointly owned by six oil companies, it links the individual storage tanks of the suppliers with many of the aircraft bays. The final connection between hydrant and aircraft is made by vehicles, their hoses forming the last link to the plane's fuel tanks.

Distributing ships of the 1970s–1980s

	Completed	Gross tons
Esso Tenby	11.1970	2,170
Esso Inverness	3.1971	2,178
Esso Penzance	6.1971	2,176

These three coasters, built by Appledore Shipbuilders Ltd., were sisterships, all with the same measurements of 299 feet (loa) and 42 feet breadth, yet each was designed to carry a different cargo. The *Esso Tenby* was for the transport of the heavier "black oils" to electricity generating stations, *Esso Penzance* was for kerosene, petrol and some lubricating oils and *Esso Inverness* for clean refined products.

The ships were fitted with bow and stern thrusters, at the time a recent development, which enabled them to leave a berth and manoeuvre without other assistance. They were planned to run from Fawley and Milford Haven with cargoes direct to one port and no offloading at wayports. Carrying capacity was 13,400 tdw and oil engines gave 13 knots.

Esso Mersey	7.1972	12,323
Esso Clyde	10.1972	12,317
Esso Severn	3.1975	12,317

These larger ships were built by Cammell Laird and Company Ltd. at Birkenhead. Length oa was 544 feet 9 inches, breadth 72 feet 6 inches and deadweight capacity 20,400 tons. Engines—oil. 15 knots.

The *Esso Penzance*, one of three sisterships built at Appledore in Devon in 1970–71, in the English Channel.   *Skyfotos*

The *Esso Mersey*, one of three ships built by Cammell Laird at Birkenhead, proceeding in ballast. *Skyfotos*

Esso Plymouth	9.1980	1,421	Built by Cochrane Shipbuilders Ltd., Selby. Measurements: 230 feet (loa) × 39 feet 7 inches breadth. Engines: Oil. 11½ knots. 2160 tdw.
Esso Avon	1981	1,599	Built by Nieuwe Nederlandsche Scheepswerven B.V., Groningen. Measurements: 298 feet 7 inches (loa) × 42 feet 8 inches breadth. Engines: Oil. An asphalt carrier, 3,266 tdw.
Esso Tyne	1968	13,228	Built for Esso Transport & Tanker Co. Inc., Panama as *Esso Kobe*. 1975: (Esso Tankers Inc. (Panama flag)). 1982: *Esso Tyne*. *1984: *Franca D'Alesio* (G. D'Alesio, Leghorn).
Esso Humber	1969	12,824	Built for Esso Transport Co. Inc., Panama, as *Esso Penang*. 1975: (Esso Tankers Inc. (Panama flag)). 1978: *Esso Humber*. *6.1986: *Marsud Seconda* (Marsud SpA, Bari, Italy).
Esso Tees	1970	13,154	Built for Esso Tankers Inc. (Liberian flag) as *Esso Bataan*. 1983: *Esso Tees*.

These three ships were part of a large Esso group order awarded to Ishikawajima-Harima Heavy Industries Company Ltd., Kure, in 1967 for fourteen products tankers. The ships were designed with twenty-seven cargo tanks to carry nine varieties of petroleum by-products at the same time. Their capacity is 21,000 tdw. Oil engines. 14½ knots. Measurements: 557 feet 9 inches (loa including bulbous bow) and 77 feet breadth.

The Dutch-built *Esso Avon* in the English Channel.

Skyfotos

North Sea treasure

The incident which led to the discovery of gas and then oil under the North Sea happened in 1959 at Groningen, Holland, when a vast reservoir of natural gas was found. The find was to add a new and exciting chapter to the story of Esso in Britain, for geologists in their continuing offshore searches in the North Sea itself in the early 1960s discovered huge quantities of gas and oil which were to transform Britain's source of energy.

Esso was involved in the exploration from the start, but it soon became apparent that the enormity of the project was one which could not be lightly faced alone. It was then decided that Esso and Shell would face the challenge together for the majority of their North Sea operations, pooling financial, technological and manpower resources in a joint venture.

In the mid-1960s a number of gas fields were discovered under the southern North Sea, off the coast of Norfolk, one of the earliest being the Esso/Shell Leman Bank find, where production began in 1968. This discovery, in conjunction with other finds, enabled Britain to turn almost completely from manufactured to natural gas during the following years.

In the later 1960s the search area spread to the deeper, turbulent waters to the north. In 1970 oil was discovered in British Petroleum's Forties Field, in the same latitude as Peterhead, Scotland. Others discovered by Esso/Shell in the same area included Auk in 1971 and Fulmar in 1975, one hundred miles east of the Firth of Forth and named, like all Esso/Shell discoveries at the time, after North Sea birds. North-east of the Shetland Islands there were also oil and gas finds in substantial quantities by the joint venture, in areas to become known as the Brent, Dunlin and South Cormorant fields.

Development of a field once it has been found and fully appraised takes time, and it was not until the mid-1970s that the first oil came ashore from the Auk and Brent discoveries. In the meantime exploration continued; in the central North Sea; to the west of Shetland; to the south of Ireland and even in the Western Approaches of the English Channel. But in some areas, even after successful finds had been made, development of their potential was retarded for economic reasons, the cost of production being considered to be greater than the value of the output. However, this changed after several sharp increases in the worldwide price of oil.

In the 1970s gas production came mainly from the major Esso/Shell fields in the southern North Sea, Indefatigable and Leman Bank, the world's largest producing offshore gas fields. In 1982 a "jacket" for a new production

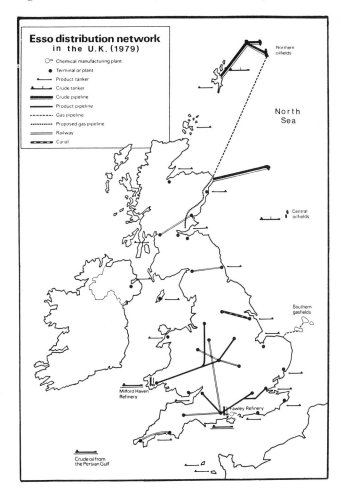

platform at Leman was installed beneath the North Sea to enable additional reserves to be tapped, beginning in 1983.

In 1978, an undersea pipeline some 280 miles long was completed to bring gas and gas liquids, produced in association with oil, ashore from the Brent field to St Fergus, north of Aberdeen. Natural gas and methane are separated, the methane content of about 80% being sold to British Gas and fed into the national grid system. The natural gas liquids, at first sold to Peterhead power station, were later sent 140 miles by onshore pipeline to two new plants at Mossmorran, Fife. One plant, a fractionator, separates ethane, propane, butane and natural gasoline, the last three products being shipped out via a terminal at nearby Braefoot Bay. The second plant was planned to use the ethane to produce 500,000 tons of ethylene a year.

Also completed in 1978 was a one hundred-mile-long pipeline to bring oil ashore to the Shetland Islands from Brent, one of the largest oil and associated gas fields in the British sector of the North Sea, and from Cormorant and Dunlin. An important development at Sullom Voe, where the pipeline comes ashore, was the construction of a collection terminal for pipeline systems bringing oil ashore from a number of prolific fields in the area. The plant became operational in 1978, when large crude oil tankers commenced loading at the island-based terminal for further distribution of North Sea oil. More production from the Cormorant area comes through an Underwater Manifold Centre, which was installed on the seabed during the summer of 1982.

In order that offshore oil and gas exploration and development rights are shared fairly between interested parties, the North Sea is divided into sectors or areas (British, Norwegian, Danish, German and Dutch) and blocks within each area are offered by the respective national governments to bidders for research in offshore licensing rounds. The seventh round in the British sector was completed in 1981, and in this Esso was awarded interests in twelve blocks, eight of these equally with Shell as part of the joint venture of which Shell is the operator. Esso are the operators of the other four, two north-west of the Shetland Isles and two off Bognor in the English Channel.

By 1980, oil production in the United Kingdom had equalled the nation's consumption and in 1981 it exceeded requirements, so that exports could earn valuable foreign currency. In 1982 Esso production accounted for about 10% of the total oil and 13% of the total gas produced from British offshore waters and at this time Esso had an interest in seven offshore oil-producing fields; 50% in Auk, Brent, North and South Cormorant and lesser interests in Dunlin, Fulmar and Forties.

To transport crude oil from Esso/Shell production platforms in the North Sea tankers have been specially converted to link up with the oilfields' loading and storage systems. The 85,000 tdw *Esso Warwickshire* was an ocean-going ship until 1976, when she was converted to lift Esso's share of oil from the Brent field. The oil is loaded from a specially-designed single bow mooring, floating "Spar" storage and loading buoy and is then carried to Fawley and to European ports. The "Spar" buoy has a storage capacity of about 50,000 tons of oil. It has a turntable top which rotates to allow the loading vessel to take up a position of least resistance to wind and waves and to operate in severe conditions. The *Esso Warwickshire* was specially

The *Esso Warwickshire* loading the first cargo of crude oil from the Brent oilfield during the weekend of 11th–12th December, 1976. She discharged the cargo at Fawley marine terminal on 18th December.

converted to take the loading hoses over the bow and to load oil and pump out ballast at the same time.

In 1985 Fawley refinery ranked as one of the world's largest and the biggest in Europe. A few years earlier its supplies of crude oil were all from the Middle East but in 1984 as much as 95% was brought in from the North Sea. Twenty-four million tons of crude and refined oils were handled at Fawley during that year and 3,300 ships used its marine terminal.

The largest ship of the British-flag Esso Petroleum Company Ltd. fleet in the mid-1980s was the *Esso Demetia*, which worked in a ten-day service between Sullom Voe, Le Havre and Fawley. Working continuously in coastal waters, she has bow and stern thrusters.

Over half of the refined products from Fawley are moved coastwise by

Fulmar "A" production platform in the Esso/Shell North Sea Fulmar field, February, 1982.

The *Esso Forth*, showing special lightening fenders on her port side.　　　*Skyfotos*

the products carriers, but increasing amounts flow through the pipelines stretching away from the refinery.

Fleet additions for North Sea work

	Completed	Gross tons
Esso Aberdeen	4.1967	59,267

Ex *Imperial Ottawa* 1978.
Built by Kawasaki Dockyard Co. Ltd., Kobe.
Measurements: 907 feet (loa including bulbous bow) × 136 feet breadth.
Engines: 2 steam turbines geared to a single screw to give 17 knots.

This ship was transferred from the Western Oil and Trading Company Ltd., Bermuda, in 1978 for work in the North Sea. She could load from Brent Spar Buoy, and modifications to fit her for North Sea work included alterations to turbines to enable her to run astern for long periods. She was the first addition to Esso Petroleum Company's fleet for five years when transferred in 1978. From 1982 to 1984 she was placed under Esso Exploration & Production (UK) Ltd., London.

Esso Forth	1967	40,675

Ex *Esso Antwerp* 1983.
Built by A/S Akers MV, Oslo.
Measurements: 807 feet (loa including bulbous bow) × 125 feet breadth.
Engines: Oil. 17 knots.
*1986: *Diamond* (Troodos Shipping & Trading Co. Ltd., London) (Cypriot flag).

The last ship of the Esso Belgium S.A. fleet, she was also the largest ever Belgian-flag Esso ship. Her work was in the North Sea, but she was used at times as a lightening ship.

Notes

1   *A German centner = 1 cwt, English centner = 100 lb.*

2   *W. A. Riedemann was a founder member of Deutsch-Amerikanische Petroleum-Gesellschaft and one of the pioneer German tanker owners. Using his initials, he formed the Waried Tankschiffahrt Reederei GmbH in 1928 which, controlled by Standard Oil of New Jersey, eventually became Esso Tankschiff Reederei GmbH.*

3   *Anglo-Persian Oil Company, formed in 1909, became Anglo-Iranian Oil Company Ltd. in 1935 and then British Petroleum Company Ltd. in December, 1954.*

4   *Tanks were so named because while they were still on the secret list they were described as "new water tanks".*

5   *All these tankers were disposed of in the later 1920s to other U.S.-flag oil companies: Cities Service Oil Company, New York, Tidewater Associated Oil Company, Gulf Oil Corporation, Socony-Vacuum Oil Company, The Texas Company, Richfield Oil Company, California, and Standard Oil Company of New Jersey.*
   The Agwilake was sold in 1929 and became Cities Service Denver. On 25th March, 1941, on a voyage from Port Arthur to Boston with oil, there was an explosion and fire on board when she was off Morehead City. The tanker was abandoned 80 miles off Beaufort, North Carolina, in position 33.16N 76.38W, and sank on 26th March.

6   *Standard Oil Company of New York and Vacuum Oil Company merged in 1931.*

7. *Bitumen: the residue from the distillation of crude oil, blended with further oils to produce a range of graded bitumens, mainly used for road-making.*

8. *Netherlands Antilles consists of six islands: the main one Curacao, the other large islands being Aruba and Bonaire. Small islands are Saba, St Eustatius and part of St Martin.*

ESSO PETROLEUM COMPANY LTD

Fleet December 1986

	Name	Built
s	*Esso Warwickshire*	1962
s	*Esso Aberdeen*	1967
m	*Esso Fawley*	1967
m	*Esso Milford Haven*	1967
m	*Esso Tenby*	1970
m	*Esso Tees*	1970
m	*Esso Penzance*	1971
m	*Esso Inverness*	1971
m	*Esso Mersey*	1972
m	*Esso Clyde*	1972
s	*Esso Demetia*	1973
m	*Esso Severn*	1975
m	*Esso Plymouth*	1980
m	*Esso Avon*	1981

British Mexican Petroleum Company Ltd.

FROM 1901 onwards there had been great expansion in Mexican oil production which, by 1921, reached twenty-nine million tons, about one fourth of the total world production of that year.

The largest developing area was in the state of Vera Cruz, the great oilfield of Poza Rica becoming the major producer in Latin America.

This was the peak of production and development then dropped, with some wells drying up. Legal difficulties between the Mexican and United States/United Kingdom governments also emerged and in 1938 some British and American companies were expropriated, with compensation being paid later.

The progenitor of the British Mexican Petroleum Company was E. L. Doheny, one of the most powerful personalities of the United States petroleum world in the early 1900s. It was he who, in 1900, purchased 400,000 acres of land in the Mexican states of San Luis Potosi and Vera Cruz and laid the foundations of the big Doheny interests in Mexico. It was also he who, in 1915, with Europe in the early battles of the Great War, put before the principal steamship companies a plan for the substitution of oil fuel for coal throughout the mercantile marine. Nothing could be done during the turmoil of war and some years were to go by before—without much publicity—there was registered at Somerset House, London, in 1919 a private company of considerable significance to the shipping industry. Its title was British Mexican Petroleum Company Ltd., its authorised capital of £2 million split equally in A and B shares.

The objects of the company were to enter into an agreement with Huasteca Petroleum Company (controlled by the Mexican Petroleum Company of which E. L. Doheny was President) to refine and deal in oils, petroleum, gas and minerals and their by-products and ingredients. The company was to build and operate storage bases in England, South America and other world centres and a fleet of tank steamers was to be constructed to distribute the oil to various ports. A contract was agreed whereby the Doheny group would supply British Mexican with its requirements of oil at fixed prices for a number of years. Half of the capital stock of British Mexican was purchased by the Pan-American Petroleum Company, which controlled the Mexican Petroleum Company; the other half by the shipping companies of Britain, practically all the larger companies taking shares. It was significant that British Mexican was launched at a time when the shipping industry was threatened by a coal famine.

Tank depots were to be constructed at the major ports of Britain for the bunkering of oil-driven ships and the intention was that refineries were to be erected in Britain, the crude oil being brought over in the company's ships.

Orders for bunkering barges were quickly forthcoming and eleven were ordered from Harland and Wolff Ltd., six to be built at Belfast, five at Govan.

At Liverpool, British Mexican established an oil fuel storage and bunkering depot at Dingle Bank. Four huge, cylindrical oil tanks capable of storing 32,000 tons were built with a 3,000-foot 10-inch feeder pipeline to the Herculaneum Dock. The oil was pumped by two of G. and J. Weir's largest pumps. This was in addition to the Mersey Docks and Harbour Board's facilities for bunkering oil-burning ships, also at Dingle Bank.

FUEL OIL

"R.M.S. "MAURETANIA " (30,696 tons gross), the express Cunarder running on BRITISH MEXICAN FUEL OIL supplied at Southampton."

RAPID BUNKERING

BY

THE BRITISH MEXICAN PETROLEUM CO., LTD.

FUEL OIL SUPPLIES AVAILABLE AT

GLASGOW, BELFAST, LIVERPOOL, AVONMOUTH, BRIXHAM, SOUTHAMPTON, LONDON, HULL, NEWCASTLE, and other United Kingdom and Continental Ports; also MEDITERRANEAN, FAR EAST, and all Important PORTS in NORTH and SOUTH AMERICA.

DIESEL OIL SUPPLIES AVAILABLE AT UNITED KINGDOM PORTS AND ALGIERS.

HEAD OFFICE :

WATERLOO HOUSE, 16, CHARLES ST., HAYMARKET,

LONDON, S.W. 1.

Telegrams :
" BRITMEXCO PICCY, LONDON."

Telephones :
REGENT 2134 (5 Lines).
REGENT 7901 (5 Lines).

An advertisement for British Mexican bunkering services.

Within a year or so, more fuel oil depots for bunkering ships had been sited at the main British ports, Southampton, London, Liverpool, Avonmouth, Belfast, Hull and Newcastle.

The first ocean tanker acquired was the *War Hagara*, a British war-built standard ship which was renamed *Inverarder*; the first distributing ship was named *Invercorrie* and was formerly the Admiralty oiler *Palmol*. Both of these were acquired in 1920. Another seven "N"-type standard ships were built up from war materials on hand when war ceased and by 1926 the fleet comprised twenty-three ships; eight ocean tankers, four distributing ships and eleven bunkering vessels. From the beginning the fleet was placed under the management of a major British shareholder, Andrew Weir & Company, the early ships carrying Weir's "Inver" style of nomenclature. An early success was in securing the contract to supply oil fuel to the big Cunarders, *Aquitania*, *Berengaria* and *Mauretania*, after their conversion to oil burning. At that time the *Mauretania* held the Blue Riband of the Atlantic, which she was to hold until 1929. The important Cunard contract was held for many years, the company supplying up to 30,000 tons of fuel oil weekly during the halcyon years of the North Atlantic giants.

In 1923 British Mexican Petroleum Company acquired the A.G.W.I. refinery at Fawley. Two years later, in 1925, the Pan-American Petroleum Company announced that it had sold its holdings in the British Mexican Petroleum Company to the Anglo-American Oil Company. However, the sale did not include British Mexican holdings in American properties, which included Lago Petroleum and Lago Oil and Transport Company, those interests being transferred to, and retained by, Pan-American Petroleum Company.

The assets of British Mexican acquired by Anglo-American included a large oil importing organisation, ten storage and bunkering plants, a large fleet of vehicles and the distributing business of "Redline" petrol, marketed by the British Mexican subsidiary, Redline Motor Spirit Company. There was also a fleet of ships. The deal included an interest in the A.G.W.I. Petroleum Corporation Ltd. (itself acquired by British Mexican in 1923) and was followed by complete control of A.G.W.I. in 1926. The most valuable A.G.W.I. asset was the refinery at Fawley, which was then processing some 350 tons of crude oil each day.

The Glico Petroleum Company was acquired in 1927. Like Anglo-American, it had been formed in 1888; in 1931 it was combined with the Redline Company to form Redline-Glico Ltd.

Management of the British Mexican Petroleum Company's fleet was transferred in 1930 from Andrew Weir and Company Ltd. to Anglo-American Oil Company Ltd.

During the 1930s there were some further ships placed under nominal British Mexican ownership. One was the *Francunion*, acquired from the Lago Shipping Company in 1933 and used for coastal and bunkering work, mainly at Southampton. The sisterships *Narragansett* and *Seminole* both built in 1936 were added, and the German-built *Victor Ross* was included shortly before war began. Also under the British Mexican heading was the *Beaconstreet*, the only tankship of the Beacon Transport Company of Canada Ltd. (operated by Colonial Beacon Oil Company Inc.) which was taken over by British Mexican in 1935.

A number of vessels were transferred to Anglo-American in 1938 and by mid-1939 only four remained listed under British Mexican management. Two were lost in the war and in 1944 the remaining pair were also transferred to Anglo-American.

Over the years British Mexican established its name as an international bunkering company, and at the end of war in 1945 new depots were planned for a number of strategic

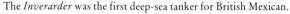

The *Inverarder* was the first deep-sea tanker for British Mexican.   *A. Duncan*

points on the world's shipping routes. The company was particularly associated with ports of the Atlantic Islands and in the Mediterranean where it acquired facilities at Port Said in 1948. In the same year installations were completed at Algiers where, until then, customers had been supplied from floating oil hulks and barges. The new facility, operated by the British Mexican agents, Cie Venture-Weir S.A., was situated on a small offshore island. A condition of the lease was that no equipment should protrude above the island skyline. As this was only some six feet or so above the water, undersea rock was blasted away and the entire installation, including the huge storage tanks, placed below sea level.

Fleet list

	Completed	Gross tons	
Inverarder	7.1919	5,578	Built by Sir James Laing & Sons Ltd., Sunderland, for the Shipping Controller as *War Hagara*. Measurements: 412 feet (oa)/400 feet length × 52 feet breadth. 8,400 tdw. Engines: T3cyl. 16.2.1920: Purchased by British Mexican Petroleum Co., renamed *Inverarder*. 20.6.1941: Bombed and damaged off Isle of Wight. Beached. 24.6.1941: Refloated, towed to Southampton. Repaired. 24.4.1942: Sunk by submarine (*U.558*) torpedo in North Atlantic, 44.34N 42.37W while on Admiralty service. Convoy ONS 67 (United Kingdom–Halifax, Nova Scotia).

The *Inverarder* was a "Z"-class standard ship of which forty were ordered by the Shipping Controller during the 1914–18 war. Only six had been completed at the time of Armistice.

The *Francunion* at Southampton in 1953. *G. A. Osbon*

The self-propelled bunkering ship *Inveritchen* was based at Southampton. *G. A. Osbon*

Invercorrie	5.1918	1,126	Built by Wm Gray & Co. Ltd., West Hartlepool, as *Palmol* for the Admiralty. Measurements: 210 feet length × 34.5 feet breadth. Engines: Oil. Twin screws. 2.1920: *Invercorrie* (British Mexican) 1923: Re-engined to T3cyl. 1925: (Lago Shipping Company Ltd.). 1931: (Lago Petroleum Corp., Maracaibo). 1938: Dismantled locally, hulk sunk.
Inverampton	11.1920	767	Built by Harland & Wolff Ltd., Glasgow. Measurements: 180 feet length × 40 feet breadth. Engines: C2cyl. (Compound). 1924: (Lago Shipping Company Ltd.). 21.4.1928: Wrecked at Maracaibo (voyage: Maracaibo/ Aruba—crude oil).
Invertyne	10.1920	259	Built by Henry Scarr Ltd., Hessle. Measurements: 127 feet (oa)/120 feet length × 23 feet breadth. 308 tdw. Engines: T3cyl (aft). 1938: (Anglo-American Oil Co.). 1960: Scrapped by Pollock, Brown & Co., Southampton.
Invertest	11.1920	259	Built by Henry Scarr Ltd., Hessle. Measurements: 127 feet (oa)/120 feet length × 23ft breadth. 308 tdw. Engines: T3cyl (aft). 1938: (Anglo-American Oil Co.). 25.1.1961: Sank at moorings at Dunglass (cargo—heavy fuel oil). 2.2.1961: Refloated. Constructive total loss. 30.10.1962: Arrived Glasgow for scrapping.

The *Inverpool* lasted nearly forty years before being broken up in Belgium in 1964.

Inveritchen	9.1920	708	Built by Harland & Wolff Ltd., Glasgow. Measurements: 180 feet length × 40 feet breadth. 750 tdw. Engines: C2cyl (Compound) (aft). Twin screws. For bunkering work at Southampton. 1938: (Anglo-American Oil Co.). 12.4.1968: Arrived Bruges for scrapping.
Francunion	4.1921	737	Built by Harland & Wolff Ltd., Glasgow, for Cie Venture-Weir S.A., Algiers (Andrew Weir & Company). Measurements: 180 feet length × 40 feet breadth. 975 tdw. Engines: C2cyl (Compound) (aft). Twin screws. 1925: (Lago Shipping Company Ltd.). 1933: (British Mexican). Coasting and bunkering work at Southampton and, during war years, at Liverpool. 1938: (Anglo-American). 25.6.1960: Arrived New Waterway, Holland, for scrapping.
Redline No. 1	11.1924	272	Built by Harland & Wolff Ltd., Glasgow. Measurements: 120 feet length × 23 feet breadth. Engines: T3cyl (aft). 21.1.1925: Foundered in heavy weather, fifteen miles W by S of Trevose Head, Cornwall. (voyage: Fawley/Gloucester—petrol).
Inverpool	5.1925	680	Built by Harland & Wolff Ltd., Govan. Measurements: 169 feet length × 31 feet breadth. 960 tdw. Engines: T3cyl (aft). 1938: (Anglo-American Oil Co.). 9.1964: Scrapped Bruges, Belgium.

Dalmuir	1904	928	Built by Wm Beardmore & Co. Ltd., Glasgow, as a sludge vessel for Glasgow Corporation. Measurements: 234 feet length × 38 feet breadth. 1220 tdw. Engines: T6cyl. Twin screws. 1922: (H. Davies). 1925: (A.G.W.I. Petroleum Corp. Ltd.). Converted to carry petroleum in bulk. 1926: (British Mexican). 1938: (Anglo-American Oil Co.). 1951: (Esso Petroleum Co.). 12.3.1960: Arrived Grays, Essex, for scrapping.
Beaconstreet	7.1927	7,467	Built by Palmers Shipbuilding & Iron Co. Ltd., Newcastle, for Beacon Transport Co. Measurements: 450 feet length × 60 feet breadth. 12,300 tdw. Engines: T3cyl. 1935: (British Mexican). 1944: (Anglo-American Oil Co.) (qv).

The *Beaconstreet* was the result of a joint financial venture between Sir Joseph Isherwood and the Palmers Company, who introduced his new bracketless type of tanker. The *Beaconstreet*, launched 31st May, 1927, was the first experimental ship of that type.

Narragansett	4.1936	10,389	Built by Fried. Krupp Germaniawerft, Kiel. Measurements: 490 feet length × 70 feet breadth. 14,800 tdw. Engines: Oil. 25.3.1942: Sunk by submarine (*U.105*) torpedo in North Atlantic, 34.46N 67.40W.
Seminole	4.1936	10,389	Built by Blohm u. Voss, Hamburg. Measurements: 490 feet length × 70 feet breadth. 14,800 tdw. Engines: Oil. 25.4.1940: Struck mine in Bristol Channel, 51.29N 04.07W. Beached, discharged, refloated and towed to Swansea for repairs. 27.2.1943: Damaged by submarine (*U.565*) torpedo in Mediterranean, 35.53N 02.33W. Towed to Gibraltar; then to River Tyne. Repaired. 1944: (Anglo-American) (qv).
Victor Ross	1.1933	11,188	Built by Bremer Vulkan, Vegesack, for Baltisch-Amerikanische Peteroleum-Import Gesellschaft. Measurements: 542 feet (oa)/521 feet length × 70 feet breadth. Engines: Oil. Twin screws. 1935: (Panama Transport Co.). 1939: (British Mexican). 2.12.1940: Sunk by submarine (*U.43*) torpedo in North Atlantic, 56.04N 18.30W.

After the two British Mexican vessels *Seminole* and *Beaconstreet* were transferred to Anglo-American Oil Company in 1944, no ships were listed under British Mexican ownership until 1951, when the *L. W. Haskell* was registered under the company name.

L. W. Haskell	1915	132	Built by Osbourne, Graham & Co. Ltd., Hylton, Sunderland.

Measurements: 105 feet length × 21 feet breadth.
Engines: Oil.
In 1933 owned by Southern Oil Co. Ltd., Hull.
1951: (British Mexican).
1954: (Esso Export Ltd.).
1961: (Esso Overseas Trading Ltd.).
4.7.1962: Aground, sank at Hvalfjord, Iceland (voyage: Reykjavik/Hvalfjord—fuel oil).

The "N"-type Ships

There were seven ships in this group which evolved from the "N"-(National) class of ship of the 1914–18 war. In this type there were all straight—no curved—frames, the idea being that the bridge-building companies and land engine works with little work in hand could concentrate on a mass-production scheme. The parts were to be assembled in two of the three National shipyards. But armistice came in November, 1918, and not one ship had been completed in a National yard. A number were completed by private builders, the first from the Tyne yard of Swan, Hunter, although the original plans had been drawn up by Harland and Wolff, Belfast.

There was a quantity of material left over from the programme when war ended which was acquired by shipyards and it was this material that was used to construct the seven "Inver" ships. The basic hull was the same as the "N"-type. Between the masts there was no sheer, the hull was almost rectangular in form with all frames above the chine line the same length. Outwardly the most important features were the "cheese-cut" transom stern, and a bunching of all the superstructure forward of the funnel and above a long trunk deck which extended from fo'c'sle to stern. Some had an open topgallant fo'c'sle, some just a short length of bulwarks forward.

The measurements were 428 feet length overall, 412 feet bp, 55 feet breadth and a depth of 34 feet with a corresponding gross tonnage of around 6,900. The deadweight capacity was just over 10,000 tons which was carried in cylindrical tanks in the holds. The speed was about 10½ knots.

They served the British Mexican Petroleum Company until the 1930s but with the world slump in trade were laid up for some time, *Invergordon* and *Invergarry* in the River Fal, *Inverleith* in the Gareloch and *Inveravon*, *Inverurie* and *Inverglass* in Sea Reach, off Southend. Three were then scrapped and the others sold for further trading as dry cargo ships.

Built by Harland and Wolff Ltd., Belfast

	Completed	
Inverleith	2.1921	*1936: Sold (A. Vlassov, Panama).
		1.1937: Tanks removed at Rotterdam, renamed *Sunstone* (Navigation & Coal Trade Ltd.).
		1938: *Castelverde* (SITMAR, Italy).
		14.12.1942: Sunk by submarine (H.M.S. *Unruffled*) off Cape Bon, Tunisia, on voyage from Naples to Tunis.
Inverurie	12.1921	1936: Sold for breaking up by Metal Industries Ltd.
		1937: Broken up at Rosyth.

220

Invergoil	11.1922	*1936: Sold, tanks removed and
		1937: Renamed *Nils Moller* (Mollers Ltd., Shanghai).
		1947: *Tien Loong* (Ta Chen Navigation Co., Shanghai).
		1950: *Atlantic Dragon* (C. Y. Tung, Hong Kong).
		5.2.1959: Arrived Osaka for breaking up.
Inveravon	3.1923	1936: Sold for breaking up by Metal Industries Ltd.
		1937: Broken up at Rosyth.
Invergarry	4.1924	*8.1936: Sold (Counties Ship Management Co.).
		1.1937: Tanks removed at Amsterdam, renamed *Mount Dirfys* (Kulukundis, Greece).
		1939: *Stad Maastricht* (Halcyon Lijn, Holland).
		23.9.1940: Torpedoed by German E-boat 559 (1st M.T.B. Flotilla) while in convoy FN 366, east of Lowestoft, 53.30N 02.00E (voyage: Southend/Newcastle).
		25.9.1940: Sank.

Built by John Brown and Company Ltd., Clydebank (as sub-contractor for Harland and Wolff Ltd.)

Invergordon	4.1923	*1936: Sold (Counties Ship Management Co.). Tanks removed, and
		1937: Renamed *Mount Helmos* (Kulukundis, Greece).
		24.11.1942: Sunk by submarine (*U.181*) torpedo and gunfire off East Africa, 26.38S 34.95E.

Built by Wm Denny and Brothers Ltd., Dumbarton (as sub-contractor for Harland and Wolff Ltd.)

Inverglass	11.1924	1936: Sold to T. W. Ward & Co. Ltd. and
		6.1936: Arrived Inverkeithing for breaking up.

Note: Sir Owen Philipp's group company rebuilding programme was so big that Harland and Wolff Ltd., the group shipyard, could not accept orders for the required delivery dates.

The *Inverleith*, one of the "N"-type ships.   *Harland & Wolff Ltd.*

Bunkering barges

The British Mexican bunkering barges were uniform in size and were all built by Harland and Wolff Ltd., six at Belfast and five at Govan. They were intended for port work and designed to carry 800 tons of fuel oil in three large tanks amidships. They were not self-propelled, but were equipped with a boiler and pumping machinery for the rapid discharge of the oil. There was a tall funnel aft. Of those built at Belfast, four were towed across the Irish Sea to Southampton for the fuelling of liners, which were then converting to oil-burning in increasing numbers.

Most of the vessels remained in service, in various locations, for more than forty years before being disposed of.

Details: 160 feet length overall (including rudder)/155 feet × 36 feet breadth × 11.5 feet depth. 475 gt. Single deck.

	Completed	
Britmex No. 1	12.1920, Belfast	Originally based at Belfast. 1938: (Anglo-American Oil Co.). 10.1966: Arrived Troon for breaking up.
Britmex No. 2	6.1920, Belfast	Originally based at Southampton. 1938: (Anglo-American Oil Co.). 6.1960: Scrapped Holland.
Britmex No. 3	6.1920, Belfast	Originally based at Southampton. 1938: (Anglo-American Oil Co.). *1956: Sold for use as a barge jetty at Woolston, Southampton.
Britmex No. 4	6.1920, Belfast	Originally based at Southampton. 1938: (Anglo-American Oil Co.). *1967: Sold to Dutch shipbreakers. Resold for use as a canal barge, renamed *Tanklichter 10*.
Britmex No. 5	6.1920, Belfast	Originally based at Southampton. 1938: (Anglo-American Oil Co.). 6.1960: Scrapped Holland.

Britmex No. 6	5.1920, Govan	Originally based on the Mersey. 1938: (Anglo-American Oil Co.). 3.1963: Scrapped Millom, Cumberland.
Britmex No. 7	6.1920, Govan	Originally based on the Mersey. 1938: (Anglo-American Oil Co.). 1960: Oil engine fitted. *1966: Sold for use as a grain store, renamed *Britten I* (T. Johannisson, Sweden). 1968: *Grandezza* (619 gt), (A/B Heimdal, Sweden). 1969: Converted to inshore sand and gravel carrier. 1971: (S. Lindberg, Sweden). 1973: (Lovstagrus H/B, Sweden). 1977: (Goteborgs Grus. & Sands, Sweden). 1980: Jehander 3 (Sand & Grus. A/B, Sweden).

Opposite: Britmex No 4, one of eleven dumb bunkering barges built in 1920.   *G. A. Osbon*
Below: Cunard Line's *Queen Elizabeth* being bunkered from the *Francunion* at Southampton in 1954.
Esso

Britmex No. 8	6.1920, Govan	Originally based at Southampton. *1928: *Francunion III* (Cia Venture Weir, Algiers (A. Weir & Co.)). 1942: Reduced to a hulk for harbour use only.
Britmex No. 9	12.1920, Belfast	Originally based at Belfast. *1932: *Francunion IV* (Cia Venture Weir, Algiers (A. Weir & Co.)). 1949: Reduced to storage hulk for harbour use only.
Britmex No. 10	3.1921, Govan	Originally based on the Clyde. 1938: (Anglo-American Oil Co.). *12.1966: Sold (J. Harker Ltd., Knottingley) and 1967: Deck-mounted Schottel outboard engine fitted, renamed *Springdale H*. Based on River Mersey. 1975: Sold.
Britmex No. 11	3.1921, Govan	Originally based on the Clyde. 1938: (Anglo-American Oil Co.). *1951: *Maroleo* (Maroleo Ltda, Lisbon). 1969: Reduced to a storage hulk.

The *Dalmuir* arriving in London River in March, 1960, on her way to the shipbreakers.   *Esso*

Irish American Oil Company Ltd., Dublin

(later Esso Petroleum Company (Ireland) Ltd)

THE formation of the Irish American Oil Company Ltd., registered in Dublin on 5th December, 1922, was the result of the creation of the Irish Free State on 15th January, 1922, the change in the national and economic status making it desirable that a separate organisation should handle, in that country, the business of the Anglo-American Oil Company Ltd. On 1st January, 1923, the new company officially acquired the business, in Eire, of Anglo-American.

Two notable facts in connection with the formation of the new company were that Anglo-American was among the first to recognise the changed status of the territory, and that Irish American was the first limited liability company under the new conditions to offer part of its capital to the Irish public for subscription.

Two seagoing ships were acquired by the company in 1924, both from the two-ship fleet of the Union Petroleum S.S. Company Inc., of New York, and they became the first ocean-going tankers owned in Eire.

By the time Irish American celebrated their 25th anniversary in 1948 all branches of the petroleum industry were covered and the company occupied the proud position of one of the largest trading organisations in Eire, with five seaboard installations and sixty inland depots. Its two main ocean terminals were at East Wall, Dublin, and at Foynes, on the river Shannon. Both were fully equipped so that the largest tankers of the day could be quickly and efficiently discharged. At the same time a thirty-acre site on the river front was acquired for further extension of the Foynes terminal, where additional storage tanks increased the total capacity to some 22,000 tons.

The immediate post-war development of air traffic between America and Ireland and the continent of Europe had made Shannon airport one of the most important air crossroads of the world and the proximity of Foynes enabled Irish American to provide an excellent aircraft refuelling service. Other depots for seaborne cargo were at Cork, Limerick and Sligo. Great interest at Sligo was aroused on 10th February, 1947, when the coastal tanker *Esso Dakotah*, (1942, 784 gt) arrived with a cargo of motor spirit and kerosene. This was the first cargo of petroleum products to arrive in the port since November, 1940.

Also at the end of the war, the company started to make good the demands accumulated during the war years, shortage of coal and oil having drastically curtailed railway services and motor transportation.

In 1951 Irish American became Esso Petroleum Company (Ireland) Ltd., a move to bring the company's title into complete association with the world-wide brand name. Subsequently in 1971 the company title was changed again, to Esso Teoranta, to emphasise its role in the development of Ireland's energy resources.

Currently, four seaboard installations are operated, these being at Dublin, New Ross, Cork and Shannon and there are also twenty inland depots. The Foynes terminal was closed some years ago and, instead, new facilities capable of taking coastal vessels were installed near Shannon airport, exclusively for aviation jet fuel.

Dublin continues to operate as Esso Teoranta's main installation, its berths capable of handling sea-going "coastal" tankers such as *Esso Fawley, Esso Mersey* and *Esso Milford Haven*. The other seaboard installations are serviced by smaller vessels, such as *Esso Penzance* and *Esso Inverness*, and by chartered vessels.

Limerick and Sligo, as sea-fed installations, have also been closed for some years, but they

continue to operate as land depots, the former now fed by road tanker and the latter by rail tank wagon.

Irish American ships

	Completed	Gross tons	
Queen Maeve	1.1903	4,634	Built by Greenock & Grangemouth Dockyard Co. as *Pennoil*.

Measurements: 365 feet length × 50 feet breadth.
Engines: T3cyl. 11 knots.
1914: *Gargoyle*.
1921: *Oswego*.
1924: (Irish American).
1931: *Petroil*.
1950: On fire, explosion. Sold to shipbreakers.

As *Pennoil*, the ship was ordered by the Pennsylvania Trading Company of Hamburg, and operated by the Pure Oil Company (U.S.A.), on the Atlantic trade.

A description of the vessel published soon after her building declared her to be "a most successful vessel" of the three-island type, carrying 6,775 tons of oil in twenty-two cargo tanks, loading and discharging being controlled by two pump rooms. Features of her outfitting included steam fans for the dispersal of volatile vapours and the fitting, throughout, of electric light. Her various bunkers had a giant capacity for 1,500 tons of coal and overhead trolleys conveyed the fuel to the stokehold.

Later, she served the Vacuum Oil Company as the *Gargoyle*, before passing to Union Petroleum as *Oswego*. In 1924 she changed her name when acquired by Irish American, and in the same year she was converted to oil fuel. Seven years later, in 1931, she was sold to John A. Galani & Company, of

Istanbul, and placed under the Greek flag as *Petroil*, becoming the only tanker in that nation's fleet. Two years later the ship went to Piraeus owners, S. A. Hellenique Maritime et Commerciale Transpetrol. She remained with these owners for the next seventeen years but hoisted the flag of Panama in 1947. Her end came in 1950 while she was at Sete, on the French Mediterranean coast. On June 5th an explosion on board set her afire and she was beached. The fire was extinguished after three days, but the ship was badly damaged and the wreck was sold for breaking up.

Queen Tailte   6.1914   5,088   Built by by J. Frerichs & Co., AG, Einswarden, as *Steaua Romana*.
Measurements: 388 feet length × 52 feet breadth.
Engines: T3cyl (aft).
1921: *Westwego*.
1924: (Irish American).
*1930: *Marangona* (5,257 gt).

As *Steaua Romana*, the *Queen Tailte* was built in Germany for Romanian owners. Then she, too, passed into Union Petroleum ownership, becoming *Westwego*, before being acquired by Irish American. Sold in 1930 to Guiseppe Calzavara, of Venice, she was renamed *Marangona*. Four years later she changed hands again, still within Venice, going to Cia. Industrie Marittima. On 10th December, 1940 the ship was lost in the Mediterranean, when she struck a mine and sank in position 36.13N 11.59E, off the island of Pantellaria, south of Sicily.

The *Queen Maeve*, built in 1903 as the *Pennoil*.   *A. Duncan*

Lago Shipping Company Ltd.

I N 1921 a Standard Oil affiliate, Standard Oil of Venezuela, was formed to carry on oil exploration in that country.

In 1924 the Lago Oil and Transport Company Ltd., (Lago is Spanish for lake) was registered in Canada and its ships, in the name of Lago Shipping Company Ltd., placed under the management of the British firm of shipowners and ship managers, Andrew Weir and Company Ltd. In the next year, after an extensive tour of the area by a management team, a decision was made that San Nicolas, some ten miles east of Oranjestad on the island of Aruba and eighteen miles off the Venezuelan coast, was to be their terminal for the transshipping of crude oil from Lake Maracaibo to ocean-going tankers. At that time, San Nicolas was merely a reefed bay with a narrow entrance, and the necessary widening of the entrance and dredging of the bay began at the end of 1925. In that year two small tank ships arrived from Britain to begin work, followed by a slightly larger third ship.

Meanwhile orders had been placed with Harland and Wolff Ltd., Belfast, for four specially designed ships for Maracaibo Lake work, and all were delivered between March and July of 1925. The Belfast yard immediately began constructing a larger group of similar ships and delivery of those began in May, 1926. However, in their naming, the "Inver" tag was dropped and the ships were given local Venezuelan names, although still registered at London.

In November, 1927, the company officially opened San Nicolas harbour for crude oil transshipment. The "Maracaibo" ships usually worked in convoys, their voyage timings being governed by high water at the Maracaibo bar so that loading time and discharge time had to be phased in with high water time to ensure the most economical voyage.

San Nicolas was now beginning to grow and storage tanks were mushrooming. Plans were drawn up in 1927 for a refinery there, and with it came the ancillary buildings, including those for the work force. The refinery came "on stream" in 1929 and was to become one of the world's largest and most important refineries. It was to play a large part in the Pacific war operations of 1942–45, with many U.S. Navy ships bunkering there on their way via the Panama Canal.

Slightly larger tankers were still being turned out by Harland and Wolff at Belfast, and dredging was increased, although tankers were not only employed on the run to Aruba but carried cargoes to Cuba and other West Indian ports of the Caribbean.

In 1928 Standard Oil Company (New Jersey) obtained a major interest in the Creole Petroleum Corporation, a company that had been organised in 1920 to operate in Venezuela. In another purchase in 1932, this time from Standard Oil Company (Indiana), Standard Oil of New Jersey acquired ownership of Lago Petroleum Corporation, not the British concern of similar name but a producing company with wide holdings in the Lake Maracaibo area. With it came ownership of their refinery at Aruba. In the same year Standard Oil of New Jersey also acquired the fleet of Lago Shipping Company Ltd., the British affiliated company, which then owned twenty-one tankers designed and built to carry crude oil from Lake Maracaibo to Aruba. Two of the larger ships, *Ule* and *Surinam*, were transferred to Standard Oil of Venezuela for service in the eastern part of the country, but the remainder continued to be managed by the Andrew Weir agency in Aruba, the same concern as had managed the fleet in the past. Also in 1932 Creole disposed of its Lake tankers in order that Lago Shipping might handle the transportation of all the crude oil of the two Standard Oil affiliates from Lake Maracaibo.

From 1931 until the beginning of World War Two, the affiliated foreign companies of Standard Oil of New Jersey encountered the same sort of tanker operating problems as did their American sister companies. In Europe, affiliates joined three agreements designed to provide for more efficient use of their tanker fleets. The first, in 1931, provided a pooling of tonnage, both owned and chartered, and a group consortium to which the vessels themselves were chartered; rates for hire and freight were fixed, each affiliate agreeing to share in the earnings or losses in proportion to the cargo carried for its account. The basis of these rates was changed five times in two years, but in general the rates were tied to the market rates for time or voyage charters. The second agreement, to run for five years from January, 1933, included Anglo-American itself. The third one, effective at the beginning of 1938, determined the freight rates to be used as the basis for the charges. In fact, this agreement provided the basis for arrangements by the British Government during the war. The scheduled freight rates for these European affiliates always fluctuated more widely than those paid by their American companies. In the main this difference was due to the American tankers being operationally more flexible, since they could be used in foreign trade, whereas foreign tankers could not be used for American transport.

During this time, Lago Shipping overcame a problem in the handling of its Lake tankers. The ships, each with a crew of twenty-eight, operated on voyages through Lake Maracaibo to Aruba, a trip which took fifteen hours, if all went well. But the trips were made hazardous by the shifting sand bar at the entrance to the Gulf of Venezuela. In 1938 continuous dredging by the ex-tanker *Invercaibo*, which had been converted to this use, was started. By 1939, the dredging, combined with the scouring action of the tankers, made it safe to use larger ships.

Previously, in 1937, the management of Lago Shipping had been transferred from Andrew Weir and Company to the direct control of the Anglo-American Oil Company, and further ships were added to the fleet over the following two years. By 1939 the Lago fleet included nine tankers each capable of carrying 30,000 barrels of oil per trip and fourteen each with a 20,000 barrel capacity.

The former Lake Maracaibo tanker *Esso Wandsworth* in the Thames in 1965 after she had been transferred to Esso for British coastal work. *G. A. Osbon*

Meanwhile, of the Standard Oil of New Jersey subsidiaries working in the Venezuela lake area, Compania de Petroleo Lago (formed in 1931 as the Lago Petroleum Corporation) utilised four small tankers for the transport of gasoline and other products to the Venezuelan market. Standard Oil of Venezuela, which used shallow-draught tankers and others with partial loads had, by 1939, turned to the more economic use of ocean-going tankers which could carry crude oil or its products from Caripito to other deepwater terminals.

In 1943, most of the Standard Oil's interests in Venezuela were consolidated into the Creole Petroleum Corporation, and a group of seven tankers for the Lake were built at Duluth and three more by the Bethlehem Shipbuilding Company at their Sparrows Point Shipyard. The ten were placed under Creole Petroleum ownership, with registration at Panama. After the war ended, four were transferred to Esso Petroleum Company Ltd., for British coastal work. Dredging of the channel to Lake Maracaibo led to redundancies in the shallow-draught tanker fleet and the ships were gradually sold. Sales included the *Icotea*, *Tamare*, *Ule* and *Surinam* which were towed, in tandem, from Venezuela to British Columbia in 1954. Three were converted to self-dumping log barges and one to a rail-wagon carrier.

Fleet list

Built by Harland and Wolff Ltd., Glasgow (two vessels)

	Completed	Gross tons	
Inverampton	11.1920	767	Built for British Mexican Petroleum Co. Ltd. (qv).
Francunion	4.1921	737	Built for Cia Venture-Weir S.A., Algiers (A. Weir & Co.). 1925: (Lago). 1933: (British Mexican) (qv).

Built by Wm Gray and Company Ltd., West Hartlepool

Invercorrie	5.1918	1,126	Built as *Palmol* for the Admiralty. 2.1920: *Invercorrie* (British Mexican) (qv).

Built by Harland and Wolff Ltd., Belfast (seventeen vessels)

Details: Length 315 feet (oa)/305.6 feet × 50.2 feet breadth × 11.7 feet draught. Two boilers fed steam to two sets of triple expansion engines. Twin screws. There was a long trunk deck on which the bridge-house was constructed.

Inverlago	3.1925	2,372	1947: (Esso Transportation Co.). *1949: (Trinidad Shipping Co. Ltd.). 1959: (Challenger Ltd., Bermuda). 2.3.1965: Arrived Santander in tow of tug *Jantar* (with *Inverruba*, see below) for breaking up. 6.1965: Scrapped Santander.
Inverrosa	4.1925	2,372	1947: (Esso Transportation Co.). *1949: (Trinidad Shipping Co. Ltd.). 1959: (Challenger Ltd., Bermuda). 1962: Converted to ore carrier, oil engines fitted (length 328 feet oa, 2,953 gt, 3,106 tdw). 1963: (Union Carbide Corp. (Ortran Ltd., British flag)). 8.5.1968: Damaged by stranding off Boca Ralon, Florida. 23.5.1968: Refloated, laid up at Jacksonville. 12.1971: Sold at public auction (Omega Manufactura S.A., Mexico). Towed to Tampico, and 1.1973: Scrapped Tampico.

Invercaibo	6.1925	2,372	1938: Converted to a suction hopper dredger for Lake Maracaibo service. 1947: (Esso Transportation Co.). 1952: (Panama Transport Co.). 4.1953: Scrapped Baltimore.
Inverruba	7.1925	2,372	1947: (Esso Transportation Co.). *1950: (Trinidad Shipping Co. Ltd.). 1960: (Challenger Ltd., Bermuda). 2.3.1965: Arrived Santander in tow of tug *Jantar* (with *Inverlago*, see above) for breaking up. 1965: Scrapped Santander.
San Nicolas	5.1926	2,391	16.2.1942: Sunk by submarine (*U.502*) torpedo 25 miles south west of Punta Macolla, Gulf of Maracaibo (voyage Lake Maracaibo/Aruba).
Ambrosio	7.1926	2,391	1947: (Esso Transportation Co.). *1950: (Trinidad Shipping Co. Ltd.). 1959: (Challenger Ltd., Bermuda). 1960: Converted to an ore carrier, oil engines fitted (length 328 feet oa, 2,959 gt, 3,149 tdw). 1963: (Union Carbide Corp., (Ortran Ltd., British flag)). 1968: (Government of Guyana). 1975: Out of service, laid up Essequibo River, Georgetown. Intended to be beached and converted to maritime training school, and 1976: Engine removed. Reported sold to local shipbreakers, but 10.1980: Wreck of vessel reported still lying in position 06.49N 58.11W.
Icotea	6.1927	2,395	1938: (Cia de Petroleo Lago, Venezuela). *1954: Sold, converted to a rail wagon carrying barge, renamed *Island Cedar* (Island Tug & Barge Co. Ltd., Vancouver, Canada).
Lagunilla	6.1927	2,395	1938: (Standard Oil Co. of Venezuela). 1943: (Cia de Petroleo Lago, Venezuela). 2.1953: Scrapped Boston, Massachusetts.
La Salina	6.1927	2,395	1938: (Cia de Petroleo Lago, Venezuela). 9.1953: Scrapped Mobile, Alabama.
San Carlos	7.1927	2,395	1947: (Esso Transportation Co.). 1952: (Panama Transport Co.). *1953: (Government of Dominica). 29.5.1965: Wrecked on breakwater at Rio Haina after breaking moorings in heavy weather.
Sabaneta	9.1927	2,395	1947: (Esso Transportation Co.). 1952: (Panama Transport Co.). 1953: *Esso Santa Fe* (Esso Transportadora de Petroleo S.A., Argentina). 1954: (Esso S.A. Petrolera, Argentina). 1963: (Petromar S.A. de Nav., Argentina). 1964: Reduced to a bunkering vessel for river service only. 1971: Reported scrapped Argentina.

Oranjestad	9.1927	2,395	16.2.1942: Sunk by submarine (*U.156*) torpedo while at anchor off San Nicolas, Aruba. (See also *Pedernales*, below).
Punta Benitez	3.1928	2,394	1937: *Criollo Fiel* (Cia Transportadora de Petroleo S.A., Argentina). 1938: *Esso Campana*. 1954: (Esso S.A. Petrolera, Argentina). 1963: (Petromar S.A. de Nav., Argentina). 1971: (Esso S.A. Petrolera, Argentina). 9.1978: Scrapped Campana, Argentina.
Tia Juana	4.1928	2,394	16.2.1942: Sunk by submarine (*U.502*) torpedo 25 miles south-west of Punta Macolla, Gulf of Maracaibo (voyage Lake Maracaibo/Aruba).
Hooiberg	4.1928	2,394	1947: (Esso Transportation Co.). 1952: (Panama Transport Co.). 1953: *Esso Entre Rios* (Esso Transportadora de Petroleo S.A., Argentina). 1954: (Esso S.A. Petrolera, Argentina). *1963: *Entre Rios* (Rio Lujan Nav., Argentina). 1981: Reported scrapped Argentina, but still listed in shipping registers.
Punta Gorda	5.1928	2,394	18.9.1944: Collision with tanker *Ampetco* (1926/8,718 gt), caught fire and sank off Cape San Roman, Curacao, (voyage Lake Maracaibo/Aruba—crude oil).
Yamanota	6.1928	2,394	1947: (Esso Transportation Co.). 1952: (Panama Transport Co.). 1953: *Esso Formosa* (Esso Transportadora de Petroleo S.A., Argentina). 1954: (Esso S.A. Petrolera, Argentina). 1963: (S.A. de Nav. Petromar, Argentina). 1966: Scrapped Buenos Aires.

Built by Harland and Wolff Ltd., Belfast (three vessels)

Details: Length 325 feet × 55.2 feet breadth.
Two sets of triple expansion engines.
Twin screws. Trunk deck.

Tamare	5.1929	3,046	1938: (Cia de Petroleo Lago, Venezuela). *1954: Sold, converted to a barge, renamed *Island Maple* (Island Tug & Barge Co. Ltd., Vancouver, Canada). 22.10.1963: Broke in two in high seas off Cape Flattery while in tow of tug *Sudbury*. Forepart sank, stern section capsized but remained afloat. Later scuttled in deep water (voyage Rayonier, British Columbia/Hoquiam, Washington—wood pulp liquid chemical).
Ule	5.1929	3,046	1932: (Standard Oil Co. of Venezuela). 1934: (Lago Shipping Co. Ltd.). 1935: (Standard Oil Co. of Venezuela). 1943: (Cia de Petroleo Lago, Venezuela). *1954: Sold, converted to a log-carrying barge, renamed *Island Balsam* (Island Tug & Barge Co. Ltd., Vancouver, Canada).

Surinam	5.1929	3,046	1933: (Standard Oil Co. of Venezuela).

1933: (Standard Oil Co. of Venezuela).
1943: (Cia de Petroleo Lago, Venezuela).
*1954: Sold, converted to a barge, renamed *Island Cypress* (Island Tug & Barge Co. Ltd., Vancouver, Canada).
14.10.1963: Broke in two and sank in gale off mouth of Quillayute River while in tow of tug *Sudbury II* (voyage to Hoquiam, Washington—wood pulp liquid chemical).

Built by Harland and Wolff Ltd., Belfast

Details: Length 360.6 feet × 60.2 feet breadth.
Two sets of triple expansion engines.
Twin screws.
Trunk deck.

Maracay	6.1931	3,794	1947: (Esso Transportation Co.).

1947: (Esso Transportation Co.).
1952: (Panama Transport Co.).
1953: (Creole Petroleum Corp., Panama).
1957: *Esso Maracay* (Cia de Petroleo Lago, Venezuela).
*1958: Sold, renamed *Waalhaven* (N.V. Simons Metalhaandel, Holland) for voyage to shipbreakers.
11.9.1959: Arrived Osaka in tow of tug *Barentsz Zee* for breaking up.

Built by Howaldtswerke A.G., Kiel

Details: Length 362 feet length × 64.2 feet breadth.
Two sets of triple expansion engines.
Twin screws.
Trunk deck.

Andino	9.1935	4,569	1947: (Esso Transportation Co.).

1947: (Esso Transportation Co.).
1952: (Panama Transportation Co.).
1953: (Creole Petroleum Corp., Panama).
10.1958: Scrapped Bordentown, New Jersey.

Built by Johnson Ironworks, New Orleans

Details: Length 100 feet × 24 feet breadth.
Engine: C2cyl.

Delaplaine (tug)	1920	182	Built for Mexican registry. Renamed *Pepe Morales* (Pan

Built for Mexican registry. Renamed *Pepe Morales* (Pan American Petroleum & Transport Co. Ltd., Tampico).
1931: *Delaplaine* (Lago Shipping Co., London).
1947: (Esso Transportation Co.).
1952: (Panama Transport Co.).
1952: (Lago Oil & Transport Co. Ltd., Toronto, (Panama flag)).
1952: (Lago Oil & Transport Co. Ltd., Aruba, (Panama flag)).
1955: (Esso Standard Oil S.A., Cuba, (Panama flag)).
*1965: *Cedros* (Trinidad Shipping Co. Ltd.), re-engined with oil engine.
6.1973: Scrapped Spain.

233

Built by Furness Shipbuilding Company Ltd., Haverton Hill-on-Tees

Details: Length 351 feet × 60 feet breadth.
Two sets of triple expansion engines.
Twin screws.

Cumarebo	6.1934	4,085	Built as *Creollo Fiel* for Cia Transportadora de Petroleo S.A., Argentina. 1937: *Cumarebo* (Lago Shipping Co.). 1947: (Esso Transportation Co.) (3,537 gt). 1952: (Panama Transport Co.). 1952: (Creole Petroleum Corp., Panama). 12.1958: Arrived Philadelphia for scrapping.

Built by Furness Shipbuilding Company Ltd., Haverton Hill-on-Tees (two vessels)

Details: Length 379.4 feet (oa)/371 feet × 64.2 feet breadth.
Two sets of triple expansion engines.
Twin screws.

Bachaquero	5.1937	4,193	1941: Requisitioned by Admiralty and converted to a Tank Landing Ship (*F.110*). 1945: Returned to owners. 1946: (Panama Transport Co.). 1952: *Esso Bachaquero* (Cia de Petroleo Lago, Venezuela). 25.4.1955: Grounded near La Salina; sustained heavy bottom damage. 26.4.1955: Refloated, towed to La Salina, laid up. Later sold and repaired. *1956: *Petro Lago* (Maritima Aragua S.A., Venezuela). 9.1960: Scrapped Cardiff.
Misoa	7.1937	4,193	1941: Requisitioned by Admiralty and converted to a Tank Landing Ship (*F.117*). 1945: Returned to owners. 1946: (Panama Transport Co.). 1952: (Creole Petroleum Corp., Panama). *1955: *Petro Mar* (Maritima Aragua S.A., Venezuela). 1957: *Stanvac Riau* (Lennox Corp., Liberia (Standard Vacuum Oil Co.)). 1962: Scrapped Hong Kong.

Built by Furness Shipbuilding Company Ltd., Haverton Hill-on-Tees (two vessels)

Details: Length 365.2 feet (oa)/356 feet × 60 feet breadth.
Two sets of triple expansion engines.
Twin screws.

Boscan	12.1937	3,953	1947: (Esso Transportation Co.). 1952: (Panama Transport Co.). 1952: (Creole Petroleum Corp., Panama). 1956: (Cia de Petroleo Lago, Venezuela). 1959: *Esso Boscan* (Maritima Aragua S.A., Venezuela). *1959: Sold to Terminales de Maracaibo (Signal Oil Co.); used as a storage ship. 1965: Scrapped Spain.

Tasajera	3.1938	3,952	1941: Requisitioned by Admiralty and converted to a Tank Landing Ship (*F.125*).
			1945: Returned to owners.
			1946: (Panama Transport Co.).
			1948: *Esso Avila* (Cia de Petroleo Lago, Venezuela).
			*1955: *Petro Avila* (Maritima Aragua S.A., Venezuela).
			2.1.1956: Broke in two about ten miles north-east of Maracaibo Bar entrance. Sank.

The three vessels *Bachaquero*, *Misoa* and *Tasajera* (above) were requisitioned by the Admiralty in 1941 and converted to become Tank Landing Ships, having been selected because of their shallow draught and the ease with which they could be put ashore on a beach. They were, in fact, the first LSTs (Landing Ships, Tank).

The landing of troops and equipment on beaches in "combined operations" has been performed throughout history using craft of all kinds, but not until 1924, when a Landing Craft Committee—a military inter-service body—was formed, was there any probability of specialised landing craft being constructed. This led to an experimental ship, forty feet long, of sixteen tons and with a winched bow ramp, being constructed by J. Samuel White and Company, of Cowes, Isle of Wight. It was capable of carrying one hundred troops and, itself, had to be carried on a troopship before being lowered to the water.

More experimental landing craft were built by J. I. Thornycroft and Company and after a good deal of attention Thornycroft's were asked to build an LCM (Mark 1)—Landing Craft, Mechanised—which completed trials in August, 1939, a few days before the outbreak of war. This craft was similar to the earlier experimental vessel but was fitted with petrol engines driving twin screws for 7½ knots, instead of the waterjet propulsion of the earlier craft.

After conversion the three ex-Maracaibo tankers were capable of carrying two LCMs (Mark 1). Alternatively, vehicle carrying capacity was either 22 × 25-ton or 18 × 30-ton tanks or 33 × 3-ton vehicles. There was also accommodation for 210 troops.

Apart from utilising merchant vessels such as these, Landing Ships (Tank) were later built in large numbers in the United States for the United States Navy; forty-five were built in the United Kingdom and thirty-seven in Canada.

Built by Cantieri Riuniti Dell' Adriatico, Monfalcone, Italy (two vessels)

Details: Length 365.2 feet length × 60.2 feet breadth.
Engine: T6 cyl. Twin screws.

Quiriquire	7.1938	3,945	1947: (Esso Transportation Co.).
			1952: (Panama Transport Co.).
			1952: (Creole Petroleum Corp., Panama).
			1958: *Esso Chaco* (Esso S.A. Petrolera, Argentina).
			1963: (S.A. de Nav. Petromar, Argentina).
			1971: (Esso S.A. Petrolera, Argentina).
			1979: Scrapped Argentina.
Pedernales	9.1938	3,945	1947: (Esso Transportation Co.).
			1952: (Panama Transport Co.).
			1952: (Creole Petroleum Corp., Panama).
			1957: *Esso Pedernales* (Cia de Petroleo Lago, Venezuela).
			*1959: Sold, renamed *Katendrecht* (N.V. Simons Metalhaandel, Holland) for voyage to shipbreakers.
			4.1960: Scrapped Holland.

The *Pedernales* and her companion ship *Oranjestad* (q.v.) were at anchor off San Nicolas, Aruba, on 16th February, 1942, when both were torpedoed by the German submarine *U.156*. The *Oranjestad* was sunk. The explosion on the *Pedernales* shattered and ruptured her mid-section, but it was possible to beach the ship, although in forty-eight feet of water. Examination showed that both the bow and stern sections were still in good condition and salvage was commenced.

The two ends were sealed and pumped out and the vessel was lifted and moved closer inshore. Then the damaged mid-section was carefully dynamited to separate it from the undamaged parts. These were then towed ashore and placed on a marine railway, where they were joined together. A wooden navigating bridge and pilot house were erected on board, the machinery overhauled and the shortened ship put to sea. The voyage from Aruba to Baltimore was made without mishap, and there permanent repairs were carried out. Again the ship was cut in two, a newly-built midbody was floated into her repair dock and the three sections joined together, forming a new ship. The *Pedernales* then returned to service.

Built by Palmers Shipbuilding and Iron Company Ltd., Newcastle

Details: Length 280 feet × 47 feet breadth.
Engine: T3cyl.

Esso Panama	1.1925	1,971	Completed as *Paraguana* for Venezuelan Gulf Oil Co., Maracaibo.
			1938: *Motatan* (Standard Oil Co. of Venezuela).
			1939: *Esso Panama* (Lago Shipping Co. Ltd., London).
			1947: (Esso Transportation Co.).
			8.1950: Scrapped Quebec.

Lake Maracaibo

Venezuela is rich in oil and there are three areas of oil production. By far the greatest is Lake Maracaibo, which yields some three-quarters of Venezuela's petroleum. Along its eastern shore is the great Bolivar field where drilling has been extended to the Lake itself and which bears a forest of derricks and wells drilled beneath its waters. There are more fields on the western side of the Lake and to its south-west. Eastwards in the Llanos—the lowland plains—there is oil north of the Orinoco and more fields in the Barinas–Apure basin in the central west Llanos. Long pipelines stretch to the Caribbean ports of Cabello and La Cruz.

Lake Maracaibo is 130 miles long and varies from fifty to seventy miles in width. And as the story goes, the Spanish navigator Alonso de Ojeda was sailing along the northern coast of South America in 1499 when he discovered the lake and was so reminded of Venice by the rough timber huts built on stilts in the shore waters of the lake, that he called the place Venezuela—Spanish for Little Venice.

From Lake Maracaibo, northwards, is a strait about thirty-four miles long, five to ten miles wide, and this leads to the Gulf of Maracaibo, about 150 miles wide and extending some seventy miles northwards from the strait.

Concessions for the development of oil were sold in 1907 to British and North American companies and in 1913, oil was discovered at Mena Grande, on the eastern shores of Lake Maracaibo. Early developers were Standard Oil Company of New Jersey, Shell and Gulf Oil.

The first discovery was developed into four pools, the additions being at Ambrosio and La Rosa and later, in 1926, at Lagunillas. The north-east coast belt of the Lake and the adjoining offshore area was named the Bolivar field.

At first, there was a problem, for the entrance to Lake Maracaibo was obstructed by a sand bar which prohibited the entry of ocean-going tankers. In fact, no ships over eleven feet draught could cross.

Then in 1915–16 the Royal Dutch Shell company constructed a refinery at Willemstad on Curacao,[8] an island some thirty miles off the Venezuelan coast, to crack the crude oil to be brought from the mainland. In 1917 the Curacaosche Scheepvaart Maatschappij began a tug/lighter weekly shuttle service across the bar at Maracaibo to San Lorenzo, then returning to Curacao with the oil. This was under the management of Curacaosche Petroleum Maatschappij who operated the tug *Samson*, 139 gt and built for the service by J. Constant, Kierits and Company, Dordrecht, Holland, in 1917. She was 95½ feet in length, 21 feet in breadth and had triple expansion engines.

From the end of the Great War in 1918 the development of the Maracaibo oilfields area became of great economic importance, for it was a natural source of crude supplies for the refineries of the North Atlantic seaboard of the United States. Maracaibo is, indeed, about 150 miles nearer New York than Tampico, Mexico, from where much oil was shipped during the 1914–18 war years and the 1920s. It is also seventy-five miles nearer to Standard Oil's refinery at Bayonne than the United States Gulf ports from where oil was shipped.

The arrangement of the tug/lighter service proved uneconomic and in 1920, in the aftermath of war, there came a reduction in British naval strength. In this period it was difficult to get shipbuilding orders executed. Many schemes were floated for making commercial use of

A forest of towers marks the expanse of the Bolivar coastal field on Lake Maracaibo. Electricity lines carry power to wells needing pumps to increase their pressure. *Esso*

surplus war materials, and Anglo-Saxon Petroleum Company (Shell) acquired six monitors from the Royal Navy in January 1920 and two more in May for conversion to oil-carrying vessels for Maracaibo Lake. The eight monitors acquired were part of a group of eighteen ordered from various yards in early 1915, mostly those which had not done any naval work at all. Some were single deck ships, some had two decks. With twin screws, some had oil engines and some were given triple expansion machinery; some had quadruple screws. They were 177 feet (oa) in length; breadth was 31 feet and as commercial craft, the tonnages were 490–500 gross.

Those acquired were *Tiga* (ex *M.16*), *Toedjoe* (*M.17*), and *Anam* (*M.18*), all from the yard of Wm Gray and Company Ltd., Hartlepool; *Ampat* (*M.32*) from Workman, Clark Ltd., Belfast; and *Delapan* (*M.19*), *Lima* (*M.20*), *Satoe* (*M.24*) and *Doewa* (*M.26*) all built by Sir R. Dixon and Company Ltd., Middlesbrough. The ships were purchased as a temporary measure pending the arrival of new ships and most of them had been sold by 1924.

Meanwhile, orders were placed in Britain for shallow draught tankers, able to work their way from the loading ports of the Lake, through the shifting sands of the Maracaibo bar to the ocean tanker anchorages of the deep water bays. Many shallow draught tankers were to be constructed over the next two decades.

Here a few figures are offered to illustrate the growth of the Venezuelan oil area. When the United States entered the war in April, 1917, the average daily production of oil was 618 barrels. From 1922 to 1926 Venezuelan production doubled each year and by 1927 had increased to 62,775,000 barrels from a total of 355 producing wells. This averaged 172,000 barrels a day of which 142,000 were shipped, the difference being oil run into storage and then put through local refineries and consumed as oil for drilling purposes. At the end of 1927 fifty-eight tankers, varying in size, were employed in the Maracaibo operations by three operating companies and by the end of 1928 the gross production approached one hundred million barrels.

In those days the depth of water on the outer Maracaibo bar was twelve to seventeen feet and on the inner bar at high water eleven to twelve feet, but in 1938 a shallow draught tanker, *Invercaibo*, was withdrawn from service and converted into a suction dredger for deepening the water at the bar.

The reality of war came to the Maracaibo area in the early morning of 16th February, 1942, when three U-boats, on "*Operation Neuland*", shelled oil installations at Aruba and sank several tankers in a four-hour attack. At San Nicolas, *U.156* sank Lago Shipping Co.'s *Oranjestad* and torpedoed the *Pedernales*, which had to be beached. The same submarine also damaged the United States-flag tanker *Arkansas* (1919, 6,452 gt) of The Texas Company, but all on board were saved. An hour later, *U.502* attacked three more ships, Lago Co.'s *Tia Juana* and *San Nicolas* both being torpedoed and sunk twenty-five miles west of Punta Macollo and the 1927-built, 2,650 gt *Monagas*, belonging to the Grande Oil Company of Venezuela, in the Gulf of Venezuela. The third submarine involved, *U.67*, cruising off Curacao, damaged the Curacaosche Scheepvaart Maatschappij tanker *Rafaela* (1938/3,177 gt) and shelled the refinery. But the lesson was learned, guns were fitted to the tankers and a convoy system introduced; and although U-boats cruised in the area and made spasmodic attacks, there were no further problems of this nature which affected the flow of oil.

A year or so after the war ended there was new thinking regarding the problem of the Maracaibo bar. Pipelines began to be laid carrying the crude oil from the Lake 160 miles north-eastwards to the deepwater bays of the Paraguana Peninsula, to Amuay Bay where Creole Petroleum Corporation have their large refinery, and to Punta Cardon.

A huge dredging programme was also begun, deepening the channel to the Lake, and by the early 1950s more dredging had increased the depth at the bar to twenty-five feet, enabling ocean-going ships to reach the city of Maracaibo on the western shore of the entrance. But all this work led to over-capacity in the shallow draught tanker tonnage using the lake and gradually ships were phased out of service for disposal.

By the later 1950s, Venezuela was producing 15% of the world's oil, accounting for over 90% of the country's export markets; 126 million tons was produced in 1956 by fourteen operating companies, mostly associates of American groups. Three quarters of this production was from the Maracaibo basin where the great Bolivar coastal field, the largest oilfield in South America with its 6,000–7,000 wells and forest of related derricks, stretches thirty-five miles along the north-east coast of Maracaibo Lake.

In 1960 came the first step towards nationalisation of the industry in Venezuela. As far back as 1907 concessions had been sold to British and North American interests by Venezuela which, over the years, received 50% of the profits of the ten or more operating companies. These companies produced the huge capital expenditure needed which, in those days, was far beyond the means of Venezuela. This arrangement was revived at the end of war in 1945 when a higher profit yield was sought and nationalisation of the industry was intimated. So in 1960 the Corporacion Venezolana de Petroleo (C.V.P.) was formed, a state company controlling some areas of production.

Nationalisation took place on 1st January, 1976, with all concessions and assets placed under Petroleos de Venezuela (Petroven) and with large sums of compensation paid to the foreign operators. The constituents of Petroven were then renamed: Exxon became Lagoven; Shell—Maraven; Gulf—Meneven and C.V.P., formed in 1960—Llanoven. Others followed—Deltaven, Palmaven, Boscanven . . .

On the Paraguana peninsula, Lagoven (Exxon) has a terminal at Amuay Bay, on the east side, for large ocean-going tankers: four finger-piers for eight ships, of which two are for 1,000 foot long vessels. There is also a Maraven (Shell) facility at Punta Cardon, four finger-piers providing twelve berths for up to 900 foot vessels.

The Lake ports are mostly on its eastern shores. Some are moorings adjacent to jetties, but at Bachaquero, Maraven have three berths and at La Salena Lagoven provide four berths for ships to 110,000 tons deadweight. Puerto Miranda, a newer Maraven facility, has ten berths to a maximum ship length of 910 feet and depth of water thirty-eight feet. Deltaven are at La Estacada, Palmaven at Punta del Palma del Sur and Boscanven, on the west side of the Lake, are at Bajo Grande. Maracaibo channel is dredged to forty-six feet and many of the ports of the Lake are dredged to that depth.

At the end of 1984 it was announced tht the Lago oil refinery at Aruba, Netherlands Antilles, owned by Standard Oil (Exxon) was to close down after some sixty years of operation. A suggested plan that Venezuela, as a major oil producer, might help keep the refinery in operation was turned down and it closed in April, 1985. It had been the island's largest employer.

And after operating at only half-capacity for some years and facing mounting losses, Shell transferred their refinery at Curacao, Netherlands Antilles, to the island authorities in October, 1985. The agreement marked the end of almost seventy years under Shell's ownership.

Tank Storage and
Carriage Company Ltd.

WHEN the Standard Oil Company (Ohio) was formed in 1870 the policy, at first, was to acquire refineries, and after a loose alliance with other major oil businesses in the mid-1870s, some 90% of the refineries of America were in their control at the end of the decade. Storage and marketing were the next priorities and not until 1886 was interest shown in the production of crude oil. In 1882 their combination of many firms had become the Standard Oil Trust, and at the same time the Standard Oil Company of New Jersey was established as the operating company. However the Trust, consisting of nine trustees and controlling interests in various States, and themselves subject to many differing laws, was not considered legally as a corporate body. In 1892 the Trust was found illegal by the Ohio Supreme Court and seven years later it was dissolved, its interests then being placed under the Standard Oil Company (New Jersey). This new title had been introduced in 1892 when changed from Standard Oil Company of New Jersey.

Again, in 1911, it was held by the United States Supreme Court that the Sherman Anti-Trust Law of 1880 was being violated, and in the dissolution and reorganisation of 1912 over thirty subsidiary organisations became independent.

In 1902, in Britain, shares in Tank Storage and Carriage Company had been acquired by Anglo-American on liquidation of the Kerosene Company, which had formerly owned the shares. Five years later Anglo-American acquired the whole of the assets of Tank Storage and Carriage Company.

It was to the Tank Storage and Carriage Company, whose offices were at 7, Gracechurch Street, London, that Anglo-American transferred their ships, the effective date of transfer of eleven steam tankers being 21st February, 1912, and one ship, *Impoco*, on 17th October, 1912. All these ships were renamed in 1913. Six sailing ships were also transferred and later, three more steam tankers. A number of ships on order by Anglo-American were delivered from their builders to Tank Storage and Carriage Company Ltd.

A year or so later the ships of the Tank Storage fleet were transferred to the Standard Transportation Company Ltd., Hong Kong, a subsidiary of the Standard Oil Company of New York (Socony). The effective date of this transfer was 18th August, 1916.

Ships transferred from Anglo-American Oil Company Ltd.

Steamships

	Built	Renamed		Built	Renamed
Tuscarora	1898	Powhatan	Saranac	1908	Satanta
Seneca	1901	Aspinet	Tamarac	1908	Sequoya
Winnebago	1901	Masconomo	Cadillac	1909	Samoset
Dakotah	1902	Kanakuk	Impoco	1910	Waneta
Cuyahoga	1902	Massasoit			
Kennebec	1902	Ponus	Tuscarora	1908	Tecumseh
Schuylkill	1903	Oneka	Tacoma	1909	—
Seminole	1903	Wabasha	Clio	1912	Wapello

Sailing ships

Daylight	Drumeltan
Hainaut	Brilliant
Calcutta	Comet

Ships intended for the Anglo-American Oil Company, but delivered direct from the builders to Tank Storage and Carriage Company Ltd.

Steamships

Uncas	6.1913	Tatarrax	1.1914
Winamac	8.1913	Tamaha	6.1914
Shabonee	10.1913	Tahchee	9.1914
Tascalusa	12.1913		

Details of these ships are under Anglo-American Oil Company listings.

The *Tamaha* in 1917 with defensive armament at the stern.   *Esso*

Ships managed by the Anglo-American Oil Company Ltd. for Ministry of War Transport 1939–1946

	Completed	Gross tons	
Leon Martin (tanker)	1936	1,951	Built by Ch & At de St Nazaire, Quevilly, France, for Standard Française des Pétroles, Paris (Standard Oil Co. of New Jersey). Measurements: 252 feet length × 46 feet breadth. Engines: Oil. 1940: Transferred from French flag and operated by Anglo-American for M.O.W.T. 13.11.1940: Mined and sunk near St Anthony Point, Falmouth.
Petrophalt (tanker)	10.1930	2,627	Built by Harland & Wolff, Belfast, as *Ebano* for Ebano Oil Co., Glasgow, for carrying asphalt or oil in portable tanks from Lake Maracaibo to the U.S.A. Measurements: 290 feet length × 47 feet breadth. Engines: T3cyl. 1933: (Soc. Aux. de Transports, Rouen). 1939: *Petrophalt* (Standard Française des Pétroles, Paris). 1940: Transferred from French flag and operated by Anglo-American for M.O.W.T. 1945: Reverted to French flag and owners. 1952: *Esso La Mailleraye* (Esso Standard Soc. Anon. Française, Paris). 1953: Scrapped Spain.
Christian Holm (tanker)	1927	9,119	Built by Burmeister & Wain, Copenhagen, as *Christian*. Measurements: 500 feet (oa)/488 feet length × 64 feet breadth. Engines: Oil. Twin screws. 1929: *Christian Holm* (Det Danske Petroleum A/S, Copenhagen (Standard Oil Co. (New Jersey)). 1941: Transferred from Danish flag and operated by Anglo-American for M.O.W.T. 1945: Reverted to Danish flag and owners. 1953: *Riza Kaptan* (Nazim Kalkavan, Istanbul). 1.1960: Scrapped Istanbul.
Empire Mica (tanker)	6.1941	8,032	Built by Furness Shipbuilding Co., Haverton, for M.O.W.T. Measurements: 479 feet (oa)/464 feet length × 61 feet breadth. Engines: T3cyl. 1941: Operated by Anglo-American for M.O.W.T. 29.6.1942: Sunk by submarine (*U.67*) torpedo in N. Atlantic, 29.25N 85.17W.

Empire Oil (tanker)	5.1941	8,029	Built by Furness Shipbuilding Co., Haverton, for M.O.W.T. Measurements: 479 feet (oa)/464 feet length × 61 feet breadth. Engines: T3cyl. 1941: Operated by Anglo-American for M.O.W.T. 10.9.1942: Sunk by submarine (*U.659*) torpedo in N. Atlantic, 51.23N 28.13W.
Empire Sapphire (tanker)	7.1941	8,031	Built by Furness Shipbuilding Co., Haverton, for M.O.W.T. Measurements: 479 feet (oa)/464 feet length × 61 feet breadth. Engines: T3cyl. 1941: Operated by Anglo-Iranian Oil Co. for M.O.W.T. 1942: Operated by Anglo-American for M.O.W.T. 1943: Operated by British Tanker Co. for M.O.W.T. 1946: *Esso Saranac* (qv)
Scandia (tanker)	12.1918	8,571	Built by Newport News Shipbuilding & Dry Dock Co. as *F. D. Asche*. Measurements: 464 feet length × 60 feet breadth. Engines: Quad. 1922: *Scandia* (Det Danske Petroleum A/S, Copenhagen (Standard Oil Co. of New Jersey)). 1941: Transferred from Danish flag, operated by Anglo-American for M.O.W.T. 1946: Reverted to Danish flag and owners. 1950: *Amada* (Cia. Mar. Iguana S.A., Panama). 2.1.1959: Arrived Savona for scrapping.
Bulkoil (tanker)	1.1942	8,071	Built by Welding Shipyards Inc., Norfolk, Va., for National Bulk Carriers Inc., New York. Measurements: 438 feet length × 59 feet breadth. Engines: 2 steam turbines. 1.1942: Transferred from American flag, operated by Anglo-American for M.O.W.T. 1943: (War Shipping Administration, U.S.A.). 1947: Returned to American owners. 1947: *Munger T. Ball* (Sabine Transportation Co., U.S.A.). 1958: *Transwestern* (Transwestern Shipping Corp., New York). 1961: (To U.S. Government under Ship Exchange Act). 21.8.1961: Arrived Burght, Belgium, for scrapping.
Empire Coleridge (tanker)	5.1942	9,813	Built by Sir James Laing & Sons Ltd., Sunderland, for M.O.W.T. Measurements: 504 feet length × 68 feet breadth. Engines: T3cyl. 1942: Operated by Anglo-American for M.O.W.T. 1945: *Esso Cheyenne* (qv).

Kentucky (tanker)	1942	9,308	Built by Sun Shipbuilding & Dry Dock Co., Chester, Pa., for The Texas Co., Wilmington, Delaware. Measurements: 488 feet length × 68 feet breadth. Engines: 2 steam turbines. 1942: Transferred from U.S. flag and operated by Anglo- American for M.O.W.T. 15.6.1942: Bombed and damaged in Mediterranean, sunk by naval escort in position 36.37N 12.10E while on charter to the Admiralty.
Empire Bronze (tanker)	11.1940	8,142	Built by Hawthorn, Leslie & Co. Ltd., Newcastle, for M.O.W.T. Measurements: 483 feet length × 59 feet breadth. Engines: Oil. 1943: Operated by Anglo-American for M.O.W.T. 1946: *Esso Cadillac* (qv).
Empire Dickens (tanker)	4.1942	9,819	Built by Furness Shipbuilding Co., Haverton, for M.O.W.T. Measurements: 504 feet length × 68 feet breadth. Engines: T3cyl. 1944: Operated by Anglo-American for M.O.W.T. 1946: *Esso Appalachee* (qv).
Empire Pike (tanker)	1905	1,854	Built by Government Yard, Sorel, Canada, as *W. S. Fielding*. Measurements: 248 feet (oa)/240 feet length × 43 feet breadth. Engines: T6cyl. Twin screws. 1914: *P.W.D. No. 1* (dredger) (Ministry of Public Works, Canada). 1943: *Riding Mountain Park* (converted to tanker by St John D.D. & S.B.Co., New Brunswick, for Canadian Government). 1945: *Empire Pike* (operated by Anglo-American for M.O.W.T.). 1947: *Basingford* (Bulk Storage Co. Ltd., London). 1949: Scrapped Dunston.
Empire Tagalam (tanker)	7.1936	10,401	Built by F. Schichau, Danzig, as *Paul Harneit* for Deutsch- Amerikanische Petroleum Ges., Hamburg. Measurements: 506 feet (oa)/488 feet length × 70 feet breadth. Engines: Oil 1945: *Empire Tagalam* (operated by Anglo-American for M.O.W.T.). 1946: Transferred to U.S. flag (U.S.M.C.). 1947: *Tagalam* (Marine Transport Lines, New York). 1955: *Cassian Sea* (Pioneer Shipping Corp., Liberia). 1960: Scrapped Split.
Empire Maldon (tanker)	1946	3,734	Built by Sir James Laing & Sons Ltd., Sunderland, for M.O.W.T. Measurements: 358 feet (oa)/344 feet length × 48 feet breadth. Engines: Oil. 1946: Operated by Anglo-American for M.O.W.T. 1946: *Imperial Halifax* (Imperial Oil Co., Toronto). 1970: *Congar* (Johnstone Shipping Ltd., Toronto). 1977: Sold for breaking up.

Twenty-four small tankers of the T1-M-A1 type, built in the United States during the war under the jurisdiction of the United States Maritime Commission, were loaned to Britain under Lease/Lend terms. They were operated under the Red Ensign on behalf of the Ministry of War Transport. Twelve of them were operated by the Anglo-American Oil Company during 1943 and thereafter management passed to a number of other British tanker shipping companies as fields of activity altered due to the demands of war.

By 1945 they were all being operated by the Anglo-Saxon Petroleum Company Ltd. (later to become Shell). After the war the eleven surviving vessels were returned to American ownership and in 1946 ten were sold to the China Merchants Steam Navigation Company and then, in 1947, transferred to the China Tanker Company, both of Shanghai. Following hostilities in China between Communist and Nationalist forces both the fleets were divided when taken over by the China People's Steam Navigation Company in 1949, although some vessels avoided confiscation by the Peking Government and escaped to follow the Nationalist cause, becoming registered in Formosa. In the May of that year the retreating Nationalist forces destroyed all the dockyards and workshops at Shanghai, on the eastern bank of the Whangpoo River. As the city fell into Communist hands and the last defending troops surrendered, all unwanted vessels on the river were scuttled. Among them were three T1-type tankers owned by the China Tanker Company (see below). Less than two months later it was reported that salvage teams working for the Communists had, in only twenty days, refloated thirty-one of the ships scuttled in the Whangpoo River.

All the twelve vessels were built by Barnes-Duluth Shipbuilding Co., Duluth, Minnesota, as their yard Nos 1–12.
Measurements: 210 feet length × 37 feet breadth.
Engines: Oil, 800 hp. 10 knots.
1,124–1,148 gt. 1,600 tdw.

Tarentum	5.1943	1943: Operated by Anglo-American for M.O.W.T. 1944: Operated by J. W. Cook & Co. for M.O.W.T. 1945: Operated by Anglo-Saxon Pet. Co. for M.O.W.T. 1946: Returned to U.S.A. 1946: *Yung Huai* (Oil No. 126) (China Merchants S.N. Co., Shanghai). 1947: (China Tanker Co., Shanghai). 24.5.1949: Scuttled in Whangpoo River during Chinese hostilities.
Mannington	5.1943	1943: Operated by Anglo-American for M.O.W.T. 1944: Operated by C. Rowbotham & Sons for M.O.W.T. 1945: Operated by Anglo-Saxon Pet. Co. for M.O.W.T. 1946: Returned to U.S.A. 1946: *Yung Siang* (Oil No. 127) (China Merchants S.N. Co., Shanghai). 1947: (China Tanker Co., Shanghai). 1949: (Government of China). 1984: Name still listed in some shipping registers but removed from others due to lack of information regarding vessel's whereabouts.

Titusville	6.1943	1943: Operated by Anglo-American for M.O.W.T. 1944: Operated by Immingham Agency Ltd. for M.O.W.T. 1945: Operated by Anglo-Saxon Pet. Co. for M.O.W.T. 1946: Returned to U.S.A. 1946: *Yung Han* (Oil No. 122) (China Merchants S.N. Co., Shanghai). 1947: (China Tanker Co., Shanghai). 24.5.1949: Scuttled in Whangpoo River during Chinese hostilities.
Glen Pool	6.1943	1943: Operated by Anglo-American for M.O.W.T. 1944: Operated by J. W. Cook & Co. for M.O.W.T. 1945: Operated by Anglo-Saxon Pet. Co. for M.O.W.T. 1946: Returned to U.S.A. 1946: *Yung Fei* (Oil No. 125) (China Merchants S.N. Co., Shanghai). 1947: (China Tanker Co., Shanghai). 1949: (China Tanker Co., Formosa). 11.1959: Scrapped Formosa.
Jennings	6.1943	1943: Operated by Anglo-American for M.O.W.T. 1944: Operated by F. T. Everard & Sons for M.O.W.T. 1945: Operated by Anglo-Saxon Pet. Co. for M.O.W.T. 1946: Returned to U.S.A. 1946: *Yung Loo* (Oil No. 130) (China Merchants S.N. Co., Shanghai). 1947: (China Tanker Co., Shanghai). 24.5.1949: Scuttled in Whangpoo River during Chinese hostilities.
Salt Creek	7.1943	1943: Operated by Anglo-American for M.O.W.T. 1944: Operated by C. Rowbotham & Sons for M.O.W.T. 1945: Operated by Anglo-Saxon Pet. Co. for M.O.W.T. 1946: Returned to U.S.A. 1947: *Punta Rasa* (Argentinian Navy). 1971: Deleted from Argentinian Navy list.
Tonkawa	8.1943	1943: Operated by Anglo-American for M.O.W.T. 1944: Operated by C. Rowbotham & Sons for M.O.W.T. 1945: Operated by Anglo-Saxon Pet. Co. for M.O.W.T. 1946: Returned to U.S.A. 1946: *Yung Luan* (Oil No. 124) (China Merchants S.N. Co., Shanghai). 1947: (China Tanker Co., Shanghai). 1949: (China Tanker Co., Formosa). 1965: Scrapped Formosa.
Benton Field	8.1943	1943: Operated by Anglo-American for M.O.W.T. 1944: Operated by J. W. Cook & Co. for M.O.W.T. 1945: Operated by Anglo-Saxon Pet. Co. for M.O.W.T. 1946: Returned to U.S.A. 1946: *Yung Lu* (Oil No. 123) (China Merchants S.N. Co., Shanghai). 1947: (China Tanker Co., Shanghai). 1949: (China Tanker Co., Formosa). 11.1959: Scrapped Formosa.

Cromwell	9.1943		1943: Operated by Anglo-American for M.O.W.T. 1944: Operated by Immingham Agency Ltd., for M.O.W.T. 1945: Operated by Anglo-Saxon Pet. Co. for M.O.W.T. 1946: Returned to U.S.A. 1946: *Yung Chang* (Oil No. 128) (China Merchants S.N. Co., Shanghai). 1947: (China Tanker Co., Shanghai). 1949: (China Tanker Co., Formosa). 1963: Scrapped Formosa.
Rio Bravo	9.1943		1943: Operated by Anglo-American for M.O.W.T. 1944: Operated by F. T. Everard & Sons for M.O.W.T. 2.11.1944: Torpedoed in engine room by German E-boat while at anchor in Ostend Roads, Belgium (voyage Ostend/River Thames—ballast). Vessel flooded aft and caught fire; accommodation destroyed. Ship capsized and last seen floating bottom up; presumed sunk.
Walnut Bend	10.1943		1943: Operated by Anglo-American for M.O.W.T. 1944: Operated by F. T. Everard & Sons for M.O.W.T. 1945: Operated by Anglo-Saxon Pet. Co. for M.O.W.T. 1946: Returned to U.S.A. 1946: *Yung Wei* (Oil No. 129) (China Merchants S.N. Co., Shanghai). 1947: (China Tanker Co., Shanghai). 1949: (Government of China). 1984: Name still listed in some shipping registers but removed from others due to lack of information regarding vessel's whereabouts.
Loma Novia	10.1943		1943: Operated by Anglo-American for M.O.W.T. 1944: Operated by C. Rowbotham & Sons for M.O.W.T. 1945: Operated by Anglo-Saxon Pet. Co. for M.O.W.T., in service with British Pacific Fleet. 1946: Returned to U.S.A. 1946: *Yung Fu* (Oil No. 121) (China Merchants S.N. Co., Shanghai). 1947: (China Tanker Co., Shanghai). 1949: (China Tanker Co., Formosa). 2.1962: Scrapped Formosa.

One vessel operated by Anglo-American Oil Company for Petroleum Shipping Company Ltd., Panama (Socony Vacuum Oil Company).

Algonquin	11.1920	7,229	Built by Bethlehem Shipbuilding Corp., Alameda, California, for Standard Transportation Co. Inc., New York (Socony Vacuum Oil Company). Measurements: 453 feet (oa)/435 feet length × 56 feet breadth. Engines: T3cyl. 1941: Transferred to British flag, operated by Anglo-American Oil Co. for owners. 1946: Reverted to owners. 1953: Scrapped Japan.

=AUTHORS'=
ACKNOWLEDGMENTS.

THE authors wish to record their grateful thanks to those who have helped in the preparation of this book; to the Esso Petroleum Company Ltd. in general, and in particular to Ian Glenday and Jenny McGregor of the Esso London office; Bernard Carter, formerly of the Purfleet terminal; Dr Frank Mayo, many years manager of Fawley refinery, and Len Belcher and Peter Gilmour, also of Fawley; to the Admiralty Library; to the Corporation of Lloyd's; to Lloyd's Register of Shipping, especially Jean Hood and John Freestone; and to Tom Rayner, Paul Dalton and Skyfotos Ltd. for photographic services.

References have also been made to magazines, journals, shipping guides and to a host of items from many sources, far too numerous to list. The following publications have been found particularly valuable.

Thirty Years of Oil Transport   (J. D. Henry).
Oil for the World   (Schackne and Drake).
Latin America   (H. Robinson).
South America   (A. Morris).
Outline of New Jersey History, 1882–1972.

Esso Magazine.
The Lamp (Standard Oil Company (New Jersey)).
Marine News (Journal of the World Ship Society).
Sea Breezes.

The Guinness Book of the Car.
Lloyd's Register of Shipping.
Pembrokeshire   (HMSO).
War at Sea   (Rohwer and Hummelchen).

And various publications of the Corporation of Lloyd's.

248

General Index

Illustrations in bold type.

Index

of British Petroleum, Anglo-American, and other subsidiary company vessels.
Also ships under their management.

Illustrations in bold type.